Empowerment in Action

Empowerment in Action
Self-Directed Groupwork

**Audrey Mullender, Dave Ward,
Jennie Fleming**

First published 2013 by
PALGRAVE MACMILLAN

Palgrave Macmillan in the UK is an imprint of Macmillan Publishers Limited,
registered in England, company number 785998, of Houndmills, Basingstoke,
Hampshire RG21 6XS.

Palgrave Macmillan in the US is a division of St Martin's Press LLC,
175 Fifth Avenue, New York, NY 10010.

Palgrave Macmillan is the global academic imprint of the above companies
and has companies and representatives throughout the world.

Palgrave® and Macmillan® are registered trademarks in the United States,
the United Kingdom, Europe and other countries

ISBN: 978–0–230–29817–0

This book is printed on paper suitable for recycling and made from fully
managed and sustained forest sources. Logging, pulping and manufacturing
processes are expected to conform to the environmental regulations of the
country of origin.

A catalogue record for this book is available from the British Library.

A catalog record for this book is available from the Library of Congress.

Printed in China

Audrey: To my mum and dad, who cared for me so lovingly and now it's my turn.

Dave: To St. Clement's Secondary School, Mansa, Zambia, where I learned the meaning of empowerment.

Jennie: To Martha and Joe who are my constant delight and inspiration.

Contents

List of Illustrations

Boxes

Figures

Tables

Acknowledgements

Thank you to all the people who have shared their experiences of group-work with us. They have given deep and rich insights into the reality of groupwork and most importantly have enriched our thinking and knowledge about self-directed groupwork and how it is being put into practice. Our conversations with them have helped connect and relate individual ideas, thoughts and groups to come together in creating a story reflecting the richness and complexity of what groupworkers and members told us.

Those Who Specifically Contributed Information for the Book

Action Autonomie, Canada: Sylvain and members of Le Collectif.

Advocacy in Action, UK: Julie Gosling.

Anti-Mosquito Device Campaign, UK: Harrison Carter.

Famijeunes, Canada: Kim Normandin and team members.

No Limits Dementia and Family Action Network, UK: Larry Gardiner.

SupportNet, UK: Carolyn Caldwell, Julianne Christou , Angela Hayes, Helen Jones.

University of Massachusetts, Boston, USA: Joan Arches, Elizabeth Boates, Archana Patel, Danielle Smith, Kelsey Warner.

Youth Dreamers, Baltimore, USA: Kristina Berdan, Dominique Davis, Miriam Harris, Aniya Hodges, Keyani Kenny and Chris Lawson.

Bill Badham, Thilo Boeck, Mathilde Buet, Ian Boulton, Andrea Clegg, Jo Dooher, Audrey-Anne Dumais-Michaud, Helen Price, Annie Pullen Sansfacon, Paddy McCullough, Marie-Joelle Robichaud, Fizz Shelton and Sebastien Simard.

Natalie Print for her help with the manuscript and Sarah Wilson for her help with referencing.

We must also acknowledge the contribution of all those who have worked at the Centre for Social Action, who have been part of self-directed or social action projects over the years or who have debated with us. All these people have made valuable contributions to the development of the theory and practice described in this book.

Introduction

What Is It All About?

The self-directed groupwork model arose from practice, not theory: a reflexive process of information-gathering, analysis, understanding, action and reflection that is mirrored in its practical application. The model emerged as result of in-depth enquiry and critical reflection with individuals, with teams and in networks where we discovered group-work was taking place. This formed the basis of Self-directed Groupwork: Users Take Action for Empowerment (1991), the original version of this book, and the process has been revisited and repeated in preparation for this new edition. Once more, we have asked people to describe what they are doing and to explain why, thus enabling us to build up a rich and deep description and analysis of their activity. Germane theory has been drawn upon to clarify and explain what, why and how, particularly why, practitioners have been doing what they were doing.

The term 'self-directed' emerged, in the first instance, as simply descriptive of the activity in groups we came across. This finding, that 'self-directed' portrayed what many practitioners were helping service users to be, led to our coining the term 'self-directed groupwork' as the name for a discrete, observable, explicable and recordable mode of groupwork practice. We found that we had moved from an informal, orally communicated practice tradition into a formally articulated one that became open and accessible to academic and practitioner scrutiny and critique.

Self-directed Groupwork

Our initial objective for this new edition was to find out how relevant people think the model is now and how widespread is its use or at least where there are people who are working in ways that relate to it. We have had contact with people in the UK, Ireland, France, the USA,

Canada and New Zealand and lengthy conversations with many. In the event, as the many examples in this book will reveal, we found a wealth of self-directed groupwork happening. We came across groups based in, and arising directly from, awareness of the model as well as people who, when we described the process and principles, immediately responded with 'That is a model I recognize' or 'That is just what we do'. Distinctively, all these groups, which have helped to develop our understanding of contemporary self-directed groupwork, incorporate a primary focus on addressing a shared structural issue rather than meeting the individual needs of the participants, although of course the latter may still happen.

One thing that we realized was that, in England at least (it is no longer possible to generalize for the UK), the substantial involvement of social workers and probation officers in such groupwork has evaporated since we first wrote. The focus of state social work has narrowed to the oversight and management of individuals and families; probation now sits within the National Offender Management Service as a 'community corrections' agency. Twenty years ago groupwork was a core element of training but now very few social work courses in England teach it (although this is not the case in other parts of the world). In compensation, however, we identified much self-directed groupwork in the voluntary sector and amongst many groups with no 'professional' involvement at all. There are many self-run, service user-led and egalitarian groups, facilitated by group members. In these groups roles are often fluid, with groupworker functions being recognized, agreed and shared amongst members.

In the course of our conversations, we also found self-directed groups in a far wider range of settings than was the case at the time of the first edition, most notably in schools and in a variety of independent movements outside the predominating contexts of health and social care. Thus, we found groups developing community support for older and disabled people and self-advocacy groups of people with dementia in the UK, groups of mental health service users in France and Canada, a range of groups supported by professional workers for family support in the UK, New Zealand and Canada. We spoke with people from Asian Pride, a self-directed group for lesbian, gay, bisexual and transgender Asians and Pacific Islanders in the USA, and with a university lecturer using self-directed groupwork as both method and subject in a service learning programme, with the students then taking forward self-directed groupwork with groups of young people in the community. There are young people in Baltimore, USA, who have worked hard over many years, facilitated by a high school teacher, to achieve their own community-based youth-run centre and, in the UK, young people used a self-directed groupwork approach to organize campaigns against 'mosquito' devices set up to keep them out of public spaces.

We located even more examples as a result of web-searching and reading books and articles: Rubyfruit Woman in Leicester, a group for all lesbian, bisexual and questioning women; Raging Grannies in Canada; groups of refugees and asylum seekers; the Extreme Group of young disabled people in Durham, working to improve access to leisure centres; and numerous patients and carers groups tackling health and social care issues. We discovered that some groups, such as Advocacy in Action, Turning Point and the Derbyshire Coalition of Disabled People (now Disability Derbyshire), that had contributed to the first volume, are still active as groups while, as will be seen later in this book, members of the Ainsley Teenage Action Group have carried forward their achievements into their adult lives. Self-directed campaigning by disabled activists and mental health survivors, which were somewhat novel when described in 1991, are now well established on the political landscape.

Furthermore, as will be illustrated in the final chapter, self-directed groupwork has crossed 'disciplinary' boundaries to be employed in education and training, in research and evaluation, in project and service development and in management and organizational practice on local, national and international levels. Selected examples from the rich and diverse array of groups that we uncovered are included in more detail as brief case studies at the end of the book.

Thus, we found that self-directed groupwork is widespread but, echoing findings at the time of the first edition, only rarely articulated as a dedicated approach or, with notable exceptions, named as such. Why might this be the case? To some extent, it is perhaps because the approach has been learnt through using it rather than through reading about it, so terminology becomes less important. There is also a tendency for those who facilitate in self-directed ways to identify themselves with identity politics and with social and political movements for radical and progressive structural change, rather than with particular ways of working. The method of working matures out of that identification and out of a clear value-base that we will discuss in detail in later chapters but its practitioners may not engage in a discourse of social intervention. Finally, the more radical practitioners often talk more about what they are not than what they are: not subscribing or working to prevailing, 'common-sense', neo-liberal understandings of social problems or responses to them; not implementing what is conventionally taught and promoted as social intervention because it is seen to replicate, in various guises, oppressive and devaluing top-down, expert-led models.

Compounded by these factors, self-directed groupwork poses a challenge to teach, assess and manage within conventional training or organizational structures. The reflexive nature of the process does not fit conventional, linear formats of assessment, planning or evaluation. Unlike other forms of groupwork the goals, methods and expected outcomes cannot be planned for, even speculatively, in advance. Furthermore, the methods and skills are to a significant extent represented in what the groupworker refrains from doing. The role is to allow the space for members' experience and understanding to emerge and to flower, by encouraging and nurturing, and to offer frameworks and structures for members' autonomous decision-making and action.

Self-directed groupworkers do draw upon orthodox group 'leadership' and other skills but these have to be adapted to a self-directed, member-led context. For example, groupworkers must be trustful of, and confident in, members' innate knowledge and abilities and able to contain their anxiety and consequent urge to intervene when faced with silence or 'messiness' – not taking control or prematurely structuring activity – in other words, they need to be able to trust the process and, in so doing, to live up to their statement of values.

The Structure of the Book

In this book, the structure represents and follows the stages of the self-directed groupwork process. Although framed within the same structure as the original 1991 edition, the text has been somewhat rewritten in the light of practice developments, new research, theoretical advances, political and economic changes and major world events. The first chapter introduces groupwork as the preferred and natural platform for the self-directed methodology, with Chapter 2 going on to outline the theoretical and policy context for user-led work. Chapter 3 establishes that a distinctive and critical phase for establishing competent practice of self-directed groupwork takes place largely before the group commences when the groupworkers take stock of themselves to establish a shared value position. On this foundation they can go on to prepare the ground for a group to meet (Chapter 4) and then replicate the exercise of taking stock in facilitating the group to prepare to take action (Chapter 5). During this process, the group will be becoming self-directed and the groupworkers supply non-directive support (Chapter 6). As the goals and action are those of group members, the groupworkers look to their agreed statement of values to reflect on and evaluate their own practice, with the group members by now very much in the driving seat (Chapter 7). The final chapter looks outwards, beyond the practice of groupwork, to other applications of the model in research, training, consultancy, and the like.

The text abounds with examples from practice. The majority are present-day but a few have been retained from the first edition where we feel they illustrate issues effectively and are not out of step with current policy and practice. Similarly, with references, original ones have been retained only if they still make valuable contribution to discussion and debate. Some we would consider to be 'classics' in the discourse of empowerment.

The biggest advance, however, is that self-directed groupwork is no longer a methodology simply grounded in the work of social workers, probation officers and youth workers in governmental and voluntary organizations. In 1991, we argued its potential to have much wider application. Since then, our own activities, backed up by the information gathered and support offered in preparing this new book, have shown the extent of the approach, its relevance and potential to make a difference in people's lives in many settings and in a global environment. Self-directed groupwork has come of age in these intervening years. It is now truly interdisciplinary, inter-professional and transnational; it encompasses governmental, independent and many kinds of egalitarian, citizen-led initiatives, projects and organizations. It straddles and frequently joins up the problems that citizens confront in health, social care, social security, education, criminal justice, planning, leisure and many other areas of their lives, and it offers an effective way to take action to challenge and change. We are none of us trapped – there is always a way forward.

1

Groupwork

The Most Empowering and Effective Approach

The Groupwork Heritage

Groupwork is immensely powerful. Groups are part and parcel of everyday life and have the capacity to control, pacify or empower, depending on the underlying philosophy and how they are organized. The self-directed groupwork model set out in this book has proved to be not only empowering but also widely applicable.

There is a close connection between groupwork in general and the values of equality and democracy (Ward 2009). Distinguishing features of groupwork have been its emphasis on commonalities within problems and collective commitment. In groups, personal troubles can be translated into common concerns. The experience of being with other people in the same boat can engender strength and new hope where apathy and disillusionment reigned beforehand; a sense of personal responsibility, internalized as self-blame, can find productive new outlets. Alternative explanations and new options for change and improvement can be opened up. The demoralizing isolation of private misfortune reinforced by public disinterest, or even worse, moral condemnation and day-to-day surveillance, can be replaced in the course of collective enterprise with a new sense of self-confidence, as well as tangible practical gains that individuals on their own could not contemplate (Munford and Walsh-Tapiata 2001). When affiliated to groupwork, anti-oppressive working becomes enormously powerful with, for example, an all-female group (Cohen and Mullender 2003) or a group consisting entirely of disabled people (Campbell and Oliver

1996). Groupwork, then, can be exceptionally effective if it is linked to a purpose that explicitly rejects the 'splintering' of the public and private, of person and society (Berman-Rossi and Kelly 2004). None of this will be at all surprising to those who have worked with groups before.

Categorization of Groups

In the 1960s, the American writers and groupworkers Papell and Rothman (1966) set out a categorization of social groupwork that encompassed three models. They distinguished the remedial, reciprocal and social goals models whose aims were, respectively: firstly (remedial), equating to individual treatment of health or social problems in a group; secondly (reciprocal), the creation of a mutual aid system for the solution of difficulties, which in Britain might be called a self-help group; and, thirdly (social goals), the use of the group as a vehicle for social action and social change. This book is about using groups to meet social goals.

The influence of Papell and Rothman's classification has been enormous. It underpinned all groupwork teaching in North America for decades and can be traced in writing on social groupwork from both the UK and the USA (for example, Brown 1992; Toseland and Rivas 2005; Preston-Shoot 2007). In turn, this influenced practice. The social goals model has been closest to community development and adult education approaches but its methodology was not developed in mainstream groupwork writing until 1991 when the first edition of this book appeared. Since then, self-directed groupwork has provided a clear framework for working towards social change through the medium of groupwork and many practitioners have adopted it for this purpose. The self-directed groupwork approach is characterized by a strong value base, an orientation towards external change and a refusal to label group members as sick or deficient in any way.

Of course, the very nature of what constitutes 'groupwork' (one word in the UK, two words in North America) can be debated and there is a danger that any classification will give the over-simplistic impression that models are competitive and mutually exclusive. A classification is only a way of trying to organize our thinking and will vary between authors. For example, Toseland and Rivas (2005) differ from Papell and Rothman (1966) in distinguishing two, rather than three, categories within which different types of groups can be found : 'treatment goups' (including therapy groups, support groups, education groups, socialization groups and growth groups) and 'task groups' (including social action groups, self-directed groups and multidisciplinary teams). The distinction they are making is primarily between internal and external change: that is, change in the members themselves or change in something outside of themselves. Self-directed groupwork clearly falls into the external change camp. Having said that, Cohen and Mullender (2000) have pointed out that members of self-directed groups may actually achieve a greater degree of individual change than members of deliberately therapeutic groups, simply because of the benefits of getting involved and of coming to believe in themselves through what they are doing. Certainly, self-directed groupwork is grounded in a great many generic skills, as identified in the *Standards for Social Work Practice with Groups* (Abels and Garvin 2010), and it is perhaps not surprising, therefore, to see progress on several fronts in well-run groups. Mullender and Ward (1985, 1991) have always seen the individual change achieved in self-directed groups as a 'secondary advantage' and it remains the external change goals that predominate.

Widely used among North American groupworkers (Pullen Sansfaçon *et al.* 2013) is a model explicitly defined as Mutual Aid (Schwartz 1971; Gitterman and Shulman 2005; Steinberg 2004). We have detected a tendency for self-directed groupwork to be seen as a variant of this model. However, while clearly there are commonalities and much that we have learnt and drawn from it, self-directed groupwork is different to the formal Mutual Aid model (Steinberg 2009). Mutual Aid group work sees the connection between environmental obstacles, stressful life conditions and interpersonal difficulties with group members sharing with and supporting other members in a similar position to themselves, whilst self-directed groupwork starts with the external and focuses there, celebrating the 'secondary advantage' of individual growth and change.

Does Groupwork Still Exist?

It is important to acknowledge that, at least in the UK, there has been a rapid decline in 'practising, teaching and writing about groupwork' by professionals (Cohen and Mullender 2003, p. 2). Others do take a more hopeful view (Doel 2006) and a recent special edition of the journal, *Groupwork*, featuring students' papers from Ireland and the United States, shows that groupwork is still a feature of social work programmes elsewhere. In contemporary social work, there is a good deal of evidence of a continuing interest in groups *per se* and, indeed, a considerable amount of work taking place *in* groups, but much of this is not recognizable as genuine groupwork (Ward 2009). It does not pay substantial attention either to the knowledge base of group dynamics or to the practice base in groupwork method and skills. Nor does it incorporate the democratic and collective values that are at the core of groupwork. The group as the *instrument* of change has become the group as the *context* for intervention; concern for the dynamics of the group encounter has been superseded by a top-down instructional orientation, while democratic and collective values have been replaced by authoritarian and individualistic ones (Ward 2000). These characteristics are particularly visible in the group-based cognitive behavioural programmes that have been largely imported from North America to work with offenders and others.

These changes can be contextualized within wider socio-economic changes. The introduction of market practices to the delivery of social services, new managerialism, a drive towards narrower specialisms in health and social care practice, new 'competency-led' approaches to professional education and training, have all made it unfashionable and difficult to own many of the values and purposes of genuine groupwork. These stress that the core process of groupwork is the interaction between a group of people based on mutuality as the means of achieving group purpose and that groupwork is naturally anti-oppressive in its context, purpose, method, group relationships and behaviour (Abels and Garvin 2010).

Genuine groupwork (as opposed to work-in-groups that does not use the group dynamic) may have become unfashionable amongst some precisely because it acknowledges that groups develop a life of their own over which the groupworker cannot ever have complete control and that the agenda can be holistic and the process democratic. Group members will want to raise what is important to them, no matter what rules and boundaries have been set. Also, workers need real skill to 'go with the flow' for productive ends (Blacklock 2003). Such free-flowing characteristics are out of kilter with a climate that emphasizes discipline and individual responsibility and, at an organizational level, pre-set objectives and audited outcomes. The reach of political control is deep and extends not only into government agencies but increasingly into the not-for-profit or voluntary sector, which has taken on more and more functions on behalf of government and has become reliant on the funding received for these (Sennett 2011). Pullen Sansfaçon (2011) has shown the influence and impact of what workers perceive as required behaviour by their organizations, in constraining critical thinking and practice and in setting the parameters of what is seen as possible. Unsurprisingly, genuine groupwork has become more difficult to set up in government social work agencies, in criminal justice settings and some voluntary organizations than we found twenty years ago – the available space has been squeezed.

However, there may be changes on the horizon. In the UK, the propensity for risk-averse, constricted approaches to practice is beginning to be seen to have unexpected, unintended and dangerous effects and outcomes. There has been a reassertion of the notion of professional judgement and recognition of the messiness and unpredictability of the situations in which social workers are involved (Munro 2011). This has been given official credence through the work of the Social Work Reform Board and the newly established College of Social Work in formulating a *Professional Capabilities Framework for Social Work* (The College of Social Work 2012). This sets out a map of the learning and capabilities required of social workers throughout their careers. Among the nine capabilities, which 'should be seen as interdependent, not separate' and which 'throughout their careers, social work students and practitioners need to demonstrate' (ibid., p. 1), are domains requiring the application and promotion of ethical principles and values; of anti-discriminatory and anti-oppressive principles; of human rights, social justice and economic well-being and the application of critical reflection to inform professional judgement, authority and decision making (ibid., pp. 1–3). If sustained, these developments would represent a climate more favourable to genuine groupwork. Furthermore, alongside a reduction in professionally facilitated groupwork – in the UK at least – has run a considerable increase in self-run, patient-led and service user-led groups, founded on the democratic and collective values that are the essence of groupwork.

There are signs that not simply genuine but critical groupwork is surviving and thriving in other environments. In the course of our own practice and whilst researching for this book, we have been working with or have discovered such activity in many places. In the UK, it is to be found within parts of the health services and of the voluntary sector and in some of the short-term community initiatives under the governmental programmes to combat community disadvantage. As explained in the Introduction, we have also found an ever-growing number of groups facilitated from within the group membership – without professional support – where people have come together to further their combined aims and to challenge the oppression they face. Moreover, inspiringly, we have discovered many examples in other countries and cultures, some of which we have had the privilege to be directly involved in. We will draw upon this broad span for the examples in this book.

The Emergence of Self-Directed Groupwork

Self-directed groupwork, as we shall go on to describe, has proved to be an effective and empowering vehicle for change, based on anti-oppressive values and capable of confronting entrenched mechanisms of power. Through resisting labels, raising awareness and then assisting people in setting their own agendas for change, it has led to the achievement of apparently unattainable goals by individuals previously written off as inadequate and beyond help, made subject to basic hand-outs and/or supervisory surveillance. Putting it another way, self-directed groupwork has opened up opportunities for people whose potential to take action on their own behalf has been stifled by externally based restrictions and by limiting self-beliefs and assumptions telling them that they do not have the abilities, rights or scope to act. These achievements will be demonstrated in many of the practice examples that will be used throughout the book. Self-directed groupwork is, then, grounded in the collective strength of people organizing together. Central to it is a synthesis of participant-led analysis and participant-led action.

Background to the model

Some considerable time before the term 'empowerment' became fashionable, our involvement in developing the self-directed groupwork model marked our striving towards an understanding of the relationship between oppression, power and change. The model was rooted in groups we went on to study but, initially, in our own practice: in the Nottingham 'Who Cares' Group, which ran a local campaign for children and young people in foster care and residential care, and with a group of young women who had children whilst still at school themselves, who were part of a campaign to improve the educational provision for students with children. The Ainsley Teenage Action Group, a neighbourhood-based group was another early example of the self-directed groupwork model that will be described in full in Chapter 6.

(See the Appendix 1 for a summary of the major past and current group examples that recur throughout this book.) Community-based group-work with young people in trouble with the law, of which the Ainsley Group was one example, was the context both of the first full-length practice accounts (Burley 1982; Ward 1982) and the earliest theoretical formulations (Ward 1979, 1982) of what later became self-directed groupwork.

The late 1970s had seen considerable moves in the sphere of youth work towards involving young people in developing and running their own services and towards a merging of the concepts of youth work (Department of Education and Science 1969) and community action (see, for example, Lees and Smith 1975). The theory of youth work up to that time had leant heavily on social 'education' (Davies and Gibson 1967), although in some quarters there were attempts to stretch the brief to encompass social change objectives (Davies 1979; Smith 1980; National Youth Bureau 1981). At that time there were also a number of linked initiatives, extending these ideas into work with young people in the social work and probation spheres (Ward 1979, 1982). These spheres of operation marked the work out as separate both from youth work and from community action, though it shared values with the radical end of the former and goals with the latter. The practitioners involved, in look-ing for an appropriate term to describe their work, lighted on 'social action' as moving away from the social education roots of youth work into the 'action' of community action.

In the 1970s and into the early 1980s, social work was sharply criti-cized for 'de-politicizing' social problems, falling to political inducement 'to see . . . new fields of practice as politically neutral – as part of the terri-tory of professionalism' (Jordan and Parton 1983, p. 1). Once the impos-sibility of neutrality is recognized, in that it colludes with oppression, we would argue that social action becomes inevitable.

In the course of our earliest investigations, from the mid-1980s, we came across individuals whose work we admired and whose values we shared. They were working to facilitate the users of social care and other services to confront oppression in its many forms and, in this way, were moving beyond analysis into action. We met and talked with group-workers and participants of these groups, read accounts in both standard and 'grey' literature (Mullender and Ward 1988) and found similar prac-tice principles to our own. Initially we were looking for groups located in mainstream services that aimed to achieve external change, based on goals set by their members and which attempted to work to anti-oppres-sive principles. We found many initiatives beyond those involving children and young people with which we were already familiar. Other exciting developments we read about, and found examples of, included the self-advocacy movement in the fields of learning difficulties (Williams and Shoultz 1982; Hadley 1987) and mental health (Barker and Peck 1987; Chamberlin 1988), the spread of organizations of disabled people that generated the social model of disability (Union of the Physically Impaired Against Segregation 1976; Finkelstein 1980; Nicholls *et al.* 1985; Derbyshire Coalition of Disabled People 1986a, 1986b; Oliver 1990) and more isolated initiatives with other user groups, for example, amongst older people (Flower 1983).

Many more examples and developments have emerged in the years since, across the globe, and as many as possible will be mentioned in later chapters. Simply to give a flavour of the range, these include some that will run throughout the book, notably: the self-advocacy groups, No Limits Dementia and Advocacy in Action; SupportNet, a group of residents and professionals in Nottingham, working together to develop community-based support services for older, disabled and isolated people within a local area; youth action groups such as Youth Dreamers in Baltimore and the service education groups of university students in Boston, USA; the RondsPoints parents' action group and the Action Autonomie centre for mental health survivors, both in Montreal, Canada. We have been inspired by the ideas of Nelson *et al.* (2001) in relation to the empowerment of mental health survivors, Taylor *et al.* (2007) in relation to people with learning difficulties, Bunting (2011) on the oppressions experienced by older people in general and in end-of-life circumstances in particular. The approach to achieving external change through service user-centred efforts has extended into and developed extensively in other areas such as health and education and in training and research, often under the banner of social action (Fleming 2009).

When we started out, those active in these different fields typically did not recognize what they had in common with one another. Consequently, they had no occasion to meet or compare notes. Since they were all working under extreme pressure, often as an oasis of empowerment in an organizational desert, they were left to draw largely on their own, rather narrowly categorized, links and networks for understanding and informed support. In practice terms, as a result, they tended to have to reinvent the wheel before driving the vehicle of change. As soon as we began to conceptualize a form of intervention that was clearly taking place across all these user groups and others, and particularly a set of principles, we found we had a framework for comparison and for shared learning (Mullender and Ward 1985). We began to see the possibility of enabling the best of the innovations to traverse what were previously impervious boundaries. A generalized methodology of empowerment that had, up to this point, been so sorely lacking began to take shape.

As we gathered the practice accounts for the original volume, we looked for the shape this methodology would take. We slowly began to discern in the accounts not only a shared belief in certain key values but also a number of other constant features that had not previously been recognized as such but which, taken together, could be assembled into a clear model for practice. We tested our emerging formulation through our own continuing work, our activities as consultants and trainers, and through practice exchanges. This work seemed clearly to demonstrate that self-directed groupwork, as we began to call it (Mullender and Ward 1985, 1991), was a newly-recorded approach in its own right and, furthermore, that it provided a way of moving beyond a 'common sense' approach to empowering forms of practice by setting down a model that could be learned, transferred, debated and refined in a constant interchange between direct practice and theory-building.

Transferability

This formulation eventually became the self-directed groupwork model, on which this book is based. It will be set out in summary in this chapter and explored, step by step, throughout the rest of the book. We will show how practice that is empowering has been, and can continue to be, pursued in a multiplicity of settings, with a range of participant groups, and by different professional disciplines and, not least, by volunteers, peers, patients, young people, carers and users of services themselves. In order to assist in the sharing and transfer of practice in all these different areas, we have not used the language of social work or health (terms such as 'assessment', 'diagnosis', 'treatment' or 'intervention', all of which relate to goals for individual, not external, change) but have developed a series of key phrases to summarize the basic steps in the model. These are intended to facilitate the transfer of skills and ideas between settings, disciplines and participant groups since they are not peculiar to any one profession or any particular context of practice.

This aim of transferability is appropriate because the genesis of the model bridged professional and theoretical disciplines. It was developed by social workers, community and faith group activists, volunteers, patients and users of services, students, community workers, youth workers, teachers, health visitors, paid and unpaid carers and others, drawing the best of each and from groupwork skills and concepts. They shared a grounding in certain practice principles that provided a common basis for the self-directed approach to grow. This value-base continues to allow the model to transcend the conventionally defined boundaries between the disciplines that practise groupwork. As subsequent usage has shown, it has much to offer teachers and adult educators, psychologists, psychiatrists and nurses, planners and architects, provided they have a 'social' or 'community' orientation to their work. If they can share the values and can envision and reach out beyond the conventionally defined boundaries of their disciplines, it is extremely effective in bringing about change. Furthermore, self-directed groupwork achieves change, not with carefully selected groupings of people who are thought to be the most articulate and able to respond but, potentially, with any group, whether they are users of the professional services or not. Everyone who can find a voice can make things happen.

The model can be adopted by groupworkers or by a group acting on its own behalf. The latter possibility should be borne in mind at all points where, for ease of expression, the model refers to the input or views of 'groupworkers' or facilitators. Among those who have acted as facilitators to self-directed groups have been community members, peers and fellow 'survivors', field and residential social workers, teachers, community workers, youth workers, volunteers, probation officers, and health professionals. They have all been able to play a part in the development of the self-directed groupwork model because they have held firm to the practice principles we shall explore in Chapter 3. The approach they have developed, embodying these values, is applicable not only with voluntary groups of 'ordinary' citizens but also with any marginalized and unfavourably labelled, often written-off, groups of people, including those for whom professionals have statutory and unavoidable responsibility.

Having the model available means that practitioners and natural groups have a 'ready-made' methodology of change to turn to, to help them refine their skills and techniques. An analogy is that of the novice swimmer. It is certainly possible to swim without learning technique. However, training is likely to make it possible to reach the end of the pool more quickly and efficiently. For self-directed groups, this should mean that they can move ahead further and faster in their achievements. Practitioners and activists would no longer have to trust to their instincts when, dissatisfied with the failure of conventional methods for empowerment in their particular field of practice, they depart from the tried and tested ways. We are, of course, full of praise for those who do take that leap of faith. The fact that the self-directed model grew, and continues to grow, directly out of such people's practice is the highest testament to their achievements, and represents a valuing of the crucial contribution that thinking practitioners and activists make to the development of more acceptable forms of practice (Mullender and Ward 1988). Left to themselves, people often fail to find time or encouragement to write about the best new ideas and, even where these are preserved, are typically not as rigorous in analysing, applying or extending them as we have tried to be (Beddoe and Harrington 2012), particularly through the continuing work of the Centre for Social Action (see Appendix 2).

The legacy of Paulo Freire

For the final part of the jigsaw – how to work face to face with people who participate in self-directed and social action groups and projects – we found particular inspiration in the ideas of Paulo Freire about a pedagogy of transformational education (Freire 1972). There are three key elements to Freire's approach: *dialogue*; *'problematization'*; and *'conscientisation'*.

Dialogue is a process that breaks down the traditional relationship between teacher and taught, groupworker and group member, replacing it with a partnership where roles interchange and they are co-investigators in creating knowledge through 'critical reasoning'. It takes place in groups, called in Freire's work 'cultural circles'.

Secondly, *problematization* is a process of drawing attention to situations that require action or change by posing questions. It helps to challenge commonly accepted ideas by posing more and more questions – digging beneath conventional or common-sense explanations of reality. It is problematization that gives Freire's work – and ours, in the form of asking the question 'why' – a distinctive critical edge. As we shall see more fully in Chapter 3, in professional practice, as in life, we too readily jump straight from 'what?' questions (what is wrong?, what is the problem?) to 'how?' questions (how can we change it?, how should we proceed?). In doing this, we unwittingly steer explanations, responsibilities and the scope of solutions to the private world around people and within their existing knowledge and experience. These have been fashioned by their position in society and the processes which keep this in place. In asking 'why?', people are encouraged to pursue an issue until the root causes have been identified and exposed. Asking 'why?' enables people to break out of the demoralizing and self-perpetuating narrowness of introspection and self-blame that are created by poverty, lack of opportunity and exclusion. With expanded horizons of what is possible, people conceive of new explanations in the wider social, political and economic context and consider how they can identify and engage with these. It turns the spotlight away from people as problems, to the problems they encounter, and enables them to see opportunities to develop a much wider range of options for action and change. Asking the question 'why?' is the key that unlocks this process.

The third component of Freire's model is *'conscientisation'*. This Freire describes as a permanent critical approach to reality in order to discover it and to unpack and expose the myths that deceive us and help to maintain oppressing dehumanizing structures. Conscientisation goes beyond merely raising awareness to the development of strategies for bringing about change. Encompassing both action and reflection, it is simultaneously the product and process of problem-posing dialogue.

The framework of the self-directed model

This understanding of the 'what?', 'why?' and 'how?' questions leads us neatly into setting out the self-directed groupwork model in skeleton form (Figure 1.1). There are five main stages, subdivided into twelve steps. These begin with the assembling of the groupworker team and the critical attention they must pay to empowering and anti-oppressive values, and take the group itself right through from starting up to action and evaluation.

Box 1.1: The Self-directed Groupwork Model

Taking Stock (See Chapter 3)
This stage is essentially a pre-planning stage undertaken before making contact with people to plan the group, or deciding to form a self-run group.

Step 1: Assembling a compatible co-worker team
Step 2: Establishing appropriate consultancy support
Step 3: Agreeing on empowering principles for the work

Continued

The Group Takes Off (See Chapter 4)

The groupworkers next engage with group members as partners to build a group, along 'open planning' lines. This initiates a style of work where group members will set the norms for the group, define and analyse the problems and set the goals.

Step 4: 'Open planning'

The Group Prepares to Take Action (See Chapter 5)

The group explores the questions 'WHAT?', 'WHY?' and 'HOW?'

Step 5: The groupworkers facilitate the group setting its own agenda of issues:
Asking the question – WHAT are the problems to be tackled?
Step 6: The groupworkers help the group to analyse the wider causes of these problems:
Asking the question – WHY do the problems exist?
Step 7: The groupworkers enable the group to decide what action needs to be taken, set priorities and allocate tasks:
Asking the question – HOW can we produce change?

The Group Takes Action (See Chapter 6)

The group members move from recognition to ACTION:

Step 8: The group members carry out the agreed actions
Steps 5 to 8 may recur, perhaps several times, before the group moves on. As members' confidence rises through experience, the process becomes self-reinforcing.

The Group Takes Over (See Chapter 7)

The group goes on to understand the connections between WHAT, WHY and HOW through a cyclical process of REFLECTION. By this means, a reflexive process of review and re-planning, members refine their campaigning and the functioning of their group. They extend their attention to broader issues and wider-scale struggles. Meanwhile, the groupworkers move increasingly into the background and may leave the group altogether. As well as 'taking over' the running of their group, group members are, by this stage, learning to take control of their own lives and of the way others perceive them. Their much improved self-confidence tells them that they have a right to do this.

Step 9: The group reviews what it has achieved.
Step 10: The group identifies new issues to be tackled – REFORMULATING WHAT?
Step 11: The group understands the links between different issues tackled – REFORMULATING WHY?
Step 12: The group decides what actions to take next – REFORMULATING HOW?
Steps 9 to 12 become a continuing process throughout the group's life.

Advantages and Disadvantages of Model-Building

One way of conceptualizing the above framework is as a grid (see Appendix 3), upon which can be placed all our ideas and actions in a piece of work, thus enabling us to see them in relation to one to another, rather than in a meandering linear progression. Or, like any model, we may think of ours as a kind of map, offering practitioners some landmarks and milestones that they may recognize along the way and use to get their bearings. There are many different paths to the goal which, to some extent, pass by these markers in varying orders – some of them many times.

We would not suggest that what actually happens in practice is as neatly tied and labelled as such an account may imply, nor that anyone should try to force reality to conform to the stages and steps of the model. Just as the model has been tested and modified since we first formulated it, it will need to continue being refined in the light of experience. It is neither perfected nor static, but must stand or fall on whether it is viable in practice with the capacity to encompass valid new practical and critical challenges as these present themselves. There are a few rules, however. We know from experience, for example, that groupworkers who do not carry out their pre-planning rigorously will find themselves floundering and lacking in direction. Also, there will inevitably need to be phases of reflection and re-planning during which they, together with group members, can stand back to review progress and think through the likely consequences of alternative courses of action.

Although not its main objective, self-directed groupwork leads to what we have always called the 'secondary advantage' (Mullender and Ward 1985, p. 156) of personal growth and change *within* the group members. This makes a lasting impact on, is recognized by, and is highly valued by group members (Boehm and Staples 2004; Fleming and Arches 2007). Indeed, as mentioned earlier, Cohen and Mullender (2000) have argued that individual change in self-directed groups, even though not the primary aim, is often marked and important. Members of groups have described how their life expectations, their life-styles and their behaviour, for example, as partners and parents and at work have been affected positively. In practical terms, participants have, among other achievements, met and presented their points of view to government ministers, and they have addressed the most senior policy-makers and officials, locally and nationally, as well as presented at conferences and made contributions on professional training courses; they have appeared on national television and radio during the course of their activities; they have joined the boards of a range of significant organizations. They have written blogs read by many, set up websites and made DVDs to draw together a larger community of like-minded people and create dialogue on issues of common concern as part of their action plan for change. In the process, group members have grown enormously in confidence, poise and the ability to express their own views on how they see the world and their place in it.

The Structure of the Book

In the next chapter we will explore the theoretical underpinnings of the self-directed model, starting by casting a critical spotlight on the concepts behind 'buzz words' such as participation, partnership and, in particular, empowerment. In Chapters 3 to 7, we will give a full exposition of the model, organized within the five-stage basic framework. The 'key phrases' from the model, which we have used to name and differentiate the stages and steps, will reappear as a framework for the ensuing chapters. Thus, in Chapter 3, we begin with the groupworkers 'Taking Stock', particularly of the value-base of the approach, as they come together to use the model. In Chapters 4 to 7, the group 'Takes Off', 'Prepares to Take Action' (through asking the questions 'what?', 'why?' and 'how?'), puts that action into effect in 'Taking Action' and, finally, increasingly 'Takes Over'. We will look in detail at the activities and major practice issues that are typical of each of these subsequent stages of the approach, illustrated throughout by a range of practice examples.

The importance of values in marking out the distinctive nature of each stage of the approach will be highlighted throughout. Informed by these, self-directed groupwork, together with the knowledge and experience people gain from carrying it out, forms an essential platform for a systematic, structurally grounded challenge to the degrading and stigmatizing conditions that are the practical manifestation of oppression. On this basis, group members and groupworkers can begin to chip away at all the forms of inequality that lie at the heart of current oppressive social arrangements.

2

Empowerment

What Does It Really Mean?

Self-directed groupwork aims fundamentally to empower group members. As such, it sits at the heart of a contemporary discourse that needs unpacking if we are to understand empowerment in its purest sense. The notion of citizen empowerment is a core feature of the policies of all mainstream political parties in the UK and has become established in government policy here and beyond. It can be seen, for example, in the 'personalization' agenda in adult social care, in 'patient choice' in the health services, in the extension of participation rights for young people in the education, children's and youth services, in 'active citizenship', in 'stakeholding' and in the notion of 'experts by experience'. This very ubiquity suggests that there is likely to have been dilution, co-optation, imitation and tokenism along the way, with relatively little real empowerment taking place.

Across the social, health and public services, internationally (Department of Health, Hong Kong 2008; Health Council of Canada 2011) and in the UK (see, for example, New Economics Foundation 2010), the terms 'user involvement', 'participation' and 'empowerment' are used widely and almost interchangeably. Yet such terms can reveal a disparity of underlying ideological positions and values (Beresford 2010). At one end lie neo-liberal values reflected in policies encouraging consumerism, the roll-back of universal provision and the creation of markets in health, welfare and public services generally; this position is now established consensually across erstwhile Right/Left divisions amongst conventional political parties, not just in Britain but in many parts of, at least, the developed world (Dominelli 2007). Here the terms often relate to forms of involvement and support focused on the individual patient or user of these services. At the other end of the ideological spectrum lie the collectivist and cooperative values and commitments to be found in advocacy and campaigning for universal rights, and for citizen voice and citizen control. These areas of action are to be found among groups, for example, of users of health, welfare and public services, in groups campaigning for minority rights, and in groups taking action on particular issues, for example, the environment or opposition to the austerity agenda. These groups may be supported by practitioners or self-run. Let us explore this further in relation to each of the above three terms in turn.

Involvement

User, carer and patient involvement stands as a leading principle, widely used in mainstream health and social services. In the UK, for instance, INVOLVE (www.involve.org.uk) is a national organization, funded by government, to promote public engagement in health and social care research. However, 'involvement' has come to be strongly associated with consumerism in the operational discourse of the public services, organized as they now are around market principles and around the concept of the user of those services as purchaser (Department of Health 1989, 2007, 2011). This is particularly the case under the 'personalization' agenda (Beresford *et al.* 2011), where consumerism is constrained by resource limitations and restrictive eligibility criteria. Here, service users employing their own carers may be open to physical, financial or other forms of abuse and may not be believed when they disclose because professionals identify more with the carers than with the service users (Thiara *et al.* 2012).

This is not to deny the progressive possibilities of 'personalization' in extending people's autonomy through control over what services they receive, but their influence can be minimized when comment and feedback are organized through single case complaints systems and mass-produced and anonymized questionnaires, devised and controlled by a service provider. These are concurrently the tools of new managerialism (O'Reilly 2011) and contribute to another side of market discipline: the need to adhere to the tenets of the 3 'Es' – effectiveness, economy and efficiency – in order to maximize private sector profit or, in public and health service parlance, ensure 'value for money'. These mechanisms provide an illusory promise of providing influence for service users.

Furthermore, in talking about services, we are not referring just to those provided directly by the state. One aspect of the trend towards consumerism and the market has been to change the role of the state from being a provider of public services to one that sets strategy and then 'enables' and purchases what is needed to meet its assessed goals. The effect has been to widen the range of organizations providing health, social welfare and, indeed, the whole gamut of 'public services' – schooling, housing, criminal justice, transport, and so on – to a diversity of 'providers'. These encompass organizations within what are variously termed the private or 'for profit' and the independent and voluntary or 'not for profit' sectors. The issues we will be addressing in this book apply to both of these contexts as much as to what are becoming increasingly residual state and local authority services.

Participation

Participation has stronger conceptual foundations than user and patient involvement (Brodie *et* 2009) .There are many examples of it having a real impact on people's lives. Examples abound of young people partici- pating in decisions that affect their lives in a variety of ways. The *What's Changed* stories (www.practicalparticipation.co.uk/whatschanged) give numerous examples of young people's participation in making improve- ments in health, housing, education, play, transport, the environment, and safety. One specific example is of young carers who identified they wanted more support during transition years and also on an individual basis. As a result, the Young Carers Project now has a system of named workers and reviews for all young people, that allows for more targeted support, keeping in touch with their caring role and the support they may need on an ongoing basis. A support group for older young carers has also been set up, making a significant difference to their lives. There are similar examples in adult social care, such as disabled people partic- ipating in the recruitment of staff and in strategic decision-making for support services (Beresford *et al.* 2011).

Yet participation is also a problematic concept in that the agenda is almost invariably someone else's. People are invited or sometimes even pushed into being involved. The idea or project concerned is derived from outside their own experience. Usually, one sees the more powerful inviting the less powerful to get involved, which can easily lead to tokenism. Thus , instead of gaining a voice, people feel controlled and unable to take any action that might threaten the professional identities of those who remain in charge (Hodge 2005). When people find them- selves marginalized and often blamed for problems that are not of their own making, invitational participation is not their first priority. It may even engender a reaction against professionals who are seen to impose agendas, whether in a participative way or not (Kunzru 2011; Moore 2011).

In sum, participation, while seductive as a descriptive term, has, as a form of practice, become co-opted to purposes predominantly geared to the maintenance of the status quo and has had its progressive potential largely squeezed out. This is not a one-off aberration but a recurring phenomenon. Throughout the past thirty years, following from the wide-ranging and varying challenges to traditional forms of authority in the 1960s, a number of participatory themes have come and gone: these include normalization, enfranchisement, active citizenship, stakehold-ing and, most recently, patient choice and the nomination of patients and service users as 'experts by experience'. There is no doubt that serv-ice users and patients certainly are experts by experience but the level to which they truly participate or merely lend credence to professional efforts can vary.

Empowerment

So what does 'to empower' or 'to be empowered' really mean? First of all, 'we cannot give power to individuals. They must claim it for themselves. Empowerment is the realization of that claim' (Mullaly 2010, p. 237). Otherwise, practice, for example assessment, will continue to work from pre-set agendas (Tew 2006), rather than really hearing what service users need and want. By itself, the term cannot provide an adequate founda-tion for practice. The language of empowerment trips too lightly off the tongue and is too easily used merely as a synonym for 'enabling' (Mitchell 1989), which tends to involve individual rather than collective change. Empowerment has even been adopted within neo-liberal initia-tives for example, by encouraging volunteer-run libraries and youth work facilities, competing for resources and managing with diminished public resources (Sennett 2011). So loose has the thinking become that, unless empowerment is accompanied by a commitment to challenge and combat injustice and oppression that shows itself in actions as well as words, there will be a tendency for practitioners simply to rewrite accounts of their practice, appropriating the terminology of empower-ment whilst retaining their status as experts with top-down power (Anderson 1996).

The way out of day-to-day, unchallenging work into a wider arena of change is to consider oppression as the key driver of empowerment. Oppression, unlike terms such as 'poverty', 'deprivation' and 'disadvantage', is not ambiguous as to the exploitative nature of economic and social relationships. Empowerment, if connected with a notion of oppression couched in these terms, can become a distinctive underpinning for practice, and one that does not become colonized or domesticated in the service of the status quo. However, oppression, if it is to be useful in providing substance to empowerment, must also have more precise definitions.

Defining Oppression

Oppression can be understood both as a state of affairs in which life chances are constructed, and as the process by which this state of affairs is created and maintained. We must look for working definitions of both. As a state of affairs, oppression is the presumption in favour of dominant social groups that skews all social relationships and is encoded in their very structure (Sisneros *et al.* 2008). It is not simply the sum of individual attitudes, though it is revealed at the micro level in the nature of personal relations and at the macro level by the existence of privilege and social hierarchies. It is to be found where power – a capacity or capability – is combined with privilege – a status – to exploit other human beings or to deny them their rights and opportunities. This denial can block many things, from access to resources and social or economic participation, through to developing personal identities and capabilities, expressing needs, thoughts and feelings, and renegotiating relationships (Tew 2006).

Oppression grossly impairs the lives of all who experience it and leaves them only the choice either of adopting the values of the oppressor or of fighting back. So pervasive and powerful is the oppression that, not infrequently, the former happens by default (Moreau 1990). Gaining awareness, and particularly collective awareness, then becomes crucial in awakening people to their entrapment and in freeing them to choose active struggle in its stead. We will see in more detail how this can work in later chapters.

Oppression is also the *process* that creates, maintains and emerges out of this state of affairs. Oppression is the process by which groups or individuals with power (the oppressors) unjustly limit the lives, experiences and opportunities of groups or individuals with less power (the oppressed). It is not necessarily a conscious decision on the part of individuals nor expressed with 'evil intent', nor should we assume a fixed identity between the two: people can be both, either oppressor or oppressed in different areas of their lives (Mullaly 2010). For example, a white straight woman may have to work harder at being anti-racist and not homophobic than she does at being anti-sexist. Nor does simply being a woman make her automatically a feminist or anti-sexist. This involves awareness-raising since, in taking on the values of their oppressors, women may end up policing their own oppression more fiercely than men, as did the nuns in the Magdalen laundries in Ireland, forcing labour out of young unmarried mothers, for example. Oppression is most often supported and perpetuated by society's institutions, such as family, faith institutions and state. Unless it is challenged and revealed, such institutionalized support does not need to show itself and is rarely seen as overt and direct repression although, in recent years – in such events as, for example, the G20 protests, Occupy Wall Street and the wider Occupy Movement in many countries, and in civil disobedience on environmental issues such as road and power-station building – even Western states have shown themselves increasingly inclined to respond to disorder and dissent with pure force. Even so, in a sophisticated society, oppression is more likely to take a variety of more subtle forms – moderating and containing conflict and defining what is to be seen as 'normal' and 'acceptable' through, for example, the workings of the law, the media and the educational system (Bourdieu 1998). In post-structural terms, the oppression does not have to be enforced through physical dominance but can be expressed through discourse alone: it becomes embedded in everyday language, as people are dismissed through the use of a single word, such as 'hooligan' or 'delinquent', in the case of young people in trouble with the law (see Chapter 6), or in a term like 'chavs' which, as Jones (2011) suggests in the subtitle of his book, has demonized the entire working class.

What is more, the various forms of oppression are entwined together. Mullaly (2010), drawing on the work of Sisneros *et al.* (2008), uses the metaphor of a 'web' for understanding the intersections of class, race, gender and other social characteristics. A person's position on one or more dimensions will either buffer or exacerbate their experience of oppression. Mullaly makes the crucial observation that multiple oppressions are not simply cumulative or additive. For example,

> a black woman will likely experience a more complicated and potent form of oppression emanating from sexism and patriarchy than will a white woman ... the interactive effects of multiple oppression

increase exponentially with addition of more forms of oppression. (Mullaly 2010, pp. 200–1)

The various forms of oppression must, therefore, be understood and confronted together (Dominelli 2008, p. 10). To do otherwise is to deny their interaction and severity. We cannot allow one oppressed group to be played off against another to create an invidious hierarchy that subverts into fruitless comparisons the energy that should be used in challenging the maintenance of injustice. The fight cannot purely be waged against racism or any other single '-ism'. It well suits the vested interests of those who benefit from oppression to see the effectiveness of those who would oppose it diluted and neutralized by competing claims to the position of 'most oppressed'. We must always be on our guard against suggestions that some are more deserving of help than others or that there is any kind of hierarchy of oppressions (Dorling 2010; de Castella 2012; NatCen Social Research 2012), for example, when only ethnicity and gender are considered and not other identities or social distinctions.

Power

The single most useful question an oppressed person can ask initially is 'Who holds the power?' This is important not only to determine where and how to fight back but also to avoid picking the wrong target. There was little point, for example, in disabled people pouring paint over benefits staff imposing tighter eligibility rules when a punitive government's policies lay behind these. According to Lukes (2005), power is the capacity not only to impose one's will, if necessary against the will of other parties, but also to set the terms of the argument, including at the national and international level. A good example of this has been the repackaging of public ills under the guise of private troubles (Wright Mills 1970; Harris 2012; McCarthy 2011) by Left, Right, Centre and Coalition governments. The austerity policies of the period from 2010 have been blamed on individual over-spending, to the point where people have willingly voted for the destruction of services they badly need, whereas governments have allowed corporate giants to pay little or no tax. This has left poorer families, older and disabled people to provide for themselves or to submit to aggressive re-assessment of their eligibility, or to beg for charity, as 'deserving cases'. Needless to say, the welfare of the poorest and weakest sections of the population has been attacked, both in hard financial terms and through cut-backs in the provision of both universal and selective services (Easton 2011; Wood 2012). This swingeing reconfiguration and diminishing of the welfare state can leave some people so preoccupied and demoralized by the suffering of their families and threats to themselves that they have neither the strength nor the motivation to band together in opposition. At the same time, however, it has spurred others, like the disabled people's movement and the trade union movement, into activist opposition.

If we put under the spotlight the extent and nature of competing and conflicting interests, not just in social and economic institutions but also in our daily lives, we can begin to understand what is going on in settings and relationships that are often taken for granted or assumed to be beyond our reach and our capacity to influence. Uncovering and analysing these conflicts and tensions may help to reveal more clearly what is really going on: a tussle over whether the privileged can hang onto the power with which they oppress others for their own advantage (Mullaly 2010; Huffington Post 2011) and a moving site of what must be continuing struggle.

The slippery and ambiguous nature of power is highlighted in the work of Foucault (1980), who argues against the notion of power as a fixed entity that some people have and others lack. Instead, he considers that people simultaneously express power and are affected by it. These exchanges are bounded by what people think appropriate and normal, with language playing a key role. To engage with the essence of power, Foucault argues, people have to participate in, influence and begin to engage with defining the facts, priorities and responsibilities we take for granted – in fact, to challenge the 'discourses' in which we are all enmeshed. Even those who appear to be most oppressed have the power to resist, and this 'bottom-up' power becomes critically important in all anti-oppressive practice. Consideration of Lukes and Foucault thus enables us to move outside 'zero sum' conceptions of power – power as no more than something dished out by one party and received by the other so that one person's empowerment must be another's oppression. Such 'zero sum' perceptions can also sustain a pessimistic view of empowerment, that it is just another confidence trick, serving establishment and professional interests if, in reality power cannot and will not be wrested away.

Though its effect is gross, then, the exercise of power may be hidden and subtle, not least in the way it is embedded in our expectations and perceptions (Munford and Walsh-Tapiata 2001). This more fluid understanding of power does begin to reveal, conversely, that it can also be deployed creatively to address and change the circumstances and factors that contribute to oppression (Mullaly 2010). This leads, in turn to a reversal of the internalization of negative labels (Munford and Walsh-Tapiata 2001) and to a new command over external situations, seen hitherto as unchallengeable (Sakamoto 2009). This is why we offer a model that enables people to empower themselves by enabling them to look behind the smoke-screens and to perceive power for what it is. (See Chapter 5, particularly, asking the question WHY?)

To Confront Oppression We Must First Confront Power: Empowerment in Practice

Thus, empowerment, as we will refer to it throughout this book, is committed in its politics. It recognizes that the response to what may appear personal has to be highly political (Hanisch [1969] 2006). This is unsurprising and inevitable, since, so long as society is differentiated along race, gender and other lines, small 'p' politics pervade all of social life – including health and social work and related forms of paid and unpaid intervention.

Empowering practice seeks change not only through *winning* power, so that those who have been oppressed exercise control over what happens to them, but through *transforming* it. Just as oppression is experienced through personal and everyday events so, equally, empowering practice can offer people the chance to try out and experience new ways of being involved in those events at the everyday level. This is the overall aim of our model of action: it looks to share power between group-workers and group members and to challenge them both to use it non-oppressively. Together, they can construct tentative models for more human forms of social relations that provide in microcosm, in both interpersonal relationships and in the groups or organizations that emerge, what is ultimately aspired to at the level of the total society.

In this way, even though we are raising the broad questions of power and oppression that so often limit practitioners because they see no way of tackling them at the level of day-to-day practice, we are also offering an approach that means these can begin to be tackled. This will emerge clearly from the practice examples we give, particularly in Chapters 5 and 6.

An understanding of oppression and power, then, is what draws empowerment away from the meaninglessness that otherwise afflicts and devalues the term. The focus provided by self-directed groupwork prevents all three of the terms 'involvement', 'participation' and 'empowerment' from disappearing into a terrifying breadth of scope. Practitioners can move from the inaction arising from a pessimism that nothing can be done into facilitating real change amongst groups of people with whom they work, without requiring superhuman skills or inexhaustible resources. While it is important to highlight the agenda for change (see, for example, Healy 2000; Dominelli 2002a, 2002b; Fook 2002; Adams 2008; Smith 2008; Mullaly 2010), it is also essential to indicate in sufficient detail how practitioners can engage with it. Self-directed groupwork is not only descriptive and analytical; it has an active element that gives both groupworkers and group members real indications of a way forward. This will be explored in detail in later chapters.

Postmodernism

There will always be those who cast doubt on such claims. Most importantly, perhaps, between the first and second editions of this book, postmodernism came and arguably went. Postmodernism made it hard to talk about 'oppression' or 'empowerment' because this was seen as symptomatic of 'grand theory' and therefore insufficiently subtle or diverse to reflect a more current understanding of power. In fact, diversity is strongly reflected even in the first edition of this book (Mullender and Ward 1991) and bottom-up power is what the whole book was about – we were ahead of our time in both respects – but we did believe then, and we continue to believe now, that diverse people can come together and make common cause against a shared oppression. True, this does not always happen – as, for example, when white working-class people blame local black, Asian and other minority ethnic communities for regional, national or even international trends in unemployment and lack of access to services like decent housing – but it can be helped to happen through processes of awareness-raising and collective endeavour. Thus, it is possible to retain, through groupwork, a hold on the importance of solidarity and interconnectedness as necessary features for action to bring about change.

Postmodernism does provide some insights that can be helpful to a progressive project. Postmodernists observe a society and its social life that are in a state of constant change and upheaval. The rapidity and extent of these changes exceed the capacity of any one universal theory to understand or direct action (Bauman 2000). We can also identify with observations that people may have multiple and diverse understandings and experiences of ostensibly similar situations. Although, ultimately, no version is better or truer than another, we are in accord with the view that some representations are more privileged and given more legitimacy than others, with the consequence that, while the social world might be open and 'free-wheeling', there are limitations on individual agency (Giddens 1986), that is, on the freedom to act as one would wish. Overall, this valuing of diversity of perspective and experience, recognition of the importance of context and its fluid and fast-changing nature, and understanding of the significance of small steps rather than grand schemes all resonate positively with self-directed groupwork. In fact, self-directed groupwork:

- engages with complexity and challenges reductionist methods and 'given' facts, explanations and 'truths';
- uses knowledge inclusively and does not privilege professional knowledge;
- enables 'silenced' voices to be heard;
- promotes open-ended dialogue and action;
- adopts a reflexive and transformative view of power:
  - valuing but not overestimating individual agency;
  - acknowledging that power can be fixed, real and oppressive; and
  - engaging with the oppressor in each of us;
  - recognizes and celebrates diversity and multiple subjectivities;
  - recognizes and allows for the complexities and interconnections of the social world;
  - starts with local, accessible and modest proposals for change.

Therefore, self-directed groupwork is not totally at odds with postmodernism, but we do strongly challenge any assumption that people lack sufficient commonality of identity and experience to link together for change.

Theoretical Insights and Groundings

Whereas postmodernism weakened the anti-oppressive agenda and hence the influence of empowering approaches like self-directed groupwork for upwards of two decades, through its attack on 'grand theory', a number of other theories have been emerging over the same period and more recently that can deepen confidence in the grounding of self-directed groupwork as a critical practice and can offer insights from related areas of exploration. Regrettably, there has not been a meeting of minds or a shared endeavour for change by these various theorists but there has been a coincidence of relevant insights derived from a similar *Zeitgeist* (mood of the moment). Concepts we will highlight and briefly address at this point are: discourse ethics (Habermas 1990, as applied by Houston 2009); social capital (Putnam 2002, as applied by Boeck *et al.* 2006); desistance, an application within criminal justice (Maruna and Farrall 2004, as applied by McNeill 2006); Sennett's position on the culture of new capitalism (2006); and Moreau's (1990) and Healy's (2000) 'structural' and 'post-structural' perspectives on social work practice. We shall briefly look at each of these in turn.

Discourse ethics

Houston identifies self-directed groupwork as a method that 'rests easily' (2009, p. 1287) with Habermas's formulation of 'discourse ethics'. Through discourse ethics, as a means of realizing the human potential for reason, Habermas posits the potential for transforming the world and arriving at a more humane, just and egalitarian society. Taking up the notion of 'moral discourse', Habermas sets out a number of complementary rules for communication and engagement that can contribute to this purpose (Houston 2009). These resonate clearly with the purposes and value-based methodology of self-directed groupwork and point towards micro-practices that can provide a means of embarking on the journey towards change (see Chapter 4).

Social capital

Next, there are the notions that have developed around social capital (Boeck *et al.* 2001; Boeck and Fleming 2005), that is, the connections and networks that people form based on principles of trust and reciprocity (Onyx and Bullen 2000). The development of social capital requires the active and willing engagement of citizens. It refers to people as creators not victims, to communities as *having* problems but not *being* problems and to communities as sites of skill and capability rather than apathy and dysfunction. Coleman (1994) had earlier observed how relations of trust and confidence among people acted as a kind of glue that enabled social groups to become successful in social, cultural and political terms. Putnam (2002) re-focused thinking on social institutions and social organizations and the ways and means by which people collaborate.

Some critics (for example, Erben *et al.* 2000) view social capital as inherently conservative and incompatible with a progressive empowerment discourse, arguing that it assumes that we all share the same objectives, while empowerment refers to change in societies characterized by conflicting interests and is realized by social action. By exploring the inter-relationships between bonding and bridging social capital (Putnam 2002), however, Boeck has developed the potentially radical notion of 'navigation', presenting social capital as a dynamic and malleable phenomenon that moves it outside and beyond the rather descriptive and conservative orientation of mainstream thinking on the topic (Boeck *et al.* 2006).

Desistance

A number of the examples of self-directed action that influenced our original writings were drawn from the work of probation officers. This might seem rather surprising to the contemporary observer as the probation service has, in the intervening period, become almost exclusively a corrections-focused agency geared towards delivering 'community punishments' and the 'management' of serious offenders in the community. Rather than supporting and staffing activities geared to the prevention of offending, such as self-directed groups, the work of probation officers has become increasingly ordered by pro forma assessments, structured individual supervision and pre-defined programmes of so-called 'groupwork'. However, the persistence of high levels of recidivism is, even within a punitive policy climate, bringing about a reconsideration of what might be more effective (Knight 2007; Rex 2010; Ministry of Justice 2011). An approach that has gained considerable traction, advocated in particular by Fergus McNeill from the Glasgow School of Social Work, is that based on a 'desistance paradigm' (Burnett and McNeill 2005; McNeill *et al.* 2005; McNeill 2006, 2007), which basically means stopping offending.

Desistance theory identifies a number of interacting features as influential in the achievement of desistance: an offender's self-assessment of it being worth staying out of crime and the development of the capacity to 'say no'; the role of a committed and helpful professional; and

improvements in the offender's community, social and personal circumstances.

Desistance involves not just the decision of an individual but also a
set of processes mediated by significant social institutions, such as
employment, education, the family, political engagement and peer
relations. It is essential to understand how these institutions operate
and how they might be harnessed to assist desistance (Farrall 2007).
Thus, self-directed groupwork shares with the desistance model recognition of the importance and nature of the practitioner–participant
relationship, in particular, in supporting people to establish their own
understandings of their problems and to make their own decisions on
pathways towards solving them. However, there is a difference in
emphasis, perhaps not surprising given the penal context of the paradigm, in that self-directed groupwork places more emphasis on change
in significant social institutions and on the inherent capacity of participants to engage in, and take a lead in, this change process (Ward
2008).

'A creditable Left'

Richard Sennett is renowned for his studies of social ties in cities and the
effects of urban living on individuals ([1970] 2008; 2006). He has built
upon a critique of what he calls the 'new capitalism' and, in parallel, of
the politics of the Left, to propose a new grounded politics to, as he puts
it, 'put the social back into socialism' (2011). Sennett distinguishes
between a 'political left' that focuses on elections and dealings with
government, and a 'social left' historically involved with mutual support
in, for example, settlement houses, credit unions and other voluntary
associations. He suggests that the former has proved self-destructive:
politicians on the Left have proved more adept at arguing and explaining themselves than at connecting to other people. These developments
provide a context for his observations about the ways in which the Right
has colonized and corrupted what, he calls 'civil society work', the natural terrain of the 'social left', as projects are forced to compete for scarce
funds and unpaid volunteers or interns are expected to replace professionals made redundant through the cuts.

To counter these forces, Eliasoph (2011), upon whom Sennett draws,
counsels organizations to set achievable, if modest, goals and to make all
participants expert in some way. The viable grassroots organization, she
argues, needs to bond people together, even if total achievement lies

beyond their grasp; it can do so by making the experience of coopera-tion an end in itself. Sennett also brings back to the table the work of 1960s community organizer Saul Alinsky (1971). Alinsky, he points out, believed that getting people to participate with others unlike themselves was an inherently radical project all its own. He did not practise identity politics of the sort that depended on racial, class or ethnic solidarity; he wanted diverse groups of people to connect and interact in a messy and informal politics that engaged with ambiguity, difference and incom-pleteness.

> I don't believe such engagement can be reduced to touchy-feely good will. Engaging well with others requires skill, whether the skill be that of listening well or cooperating with those who differ. (Sennett 2011)

This sentiment will be reflected throughout this book.

Structural and post-structural social work

Although the structural and post-structural approaches explored below have been conceptualized within the academic discipline of social work and developed particularly in Canada and Australia, they have much wider applicability.

The structural approach is associated for the most part with Canadian scholars, including notable contributions from French-speaking Canadians (Moreau 1979, 1990; Carniol 1992; Leboeuf 1994; Mullaly 1997, 2007). It is not surprising that this should emerge as a distinctive contribution from francophone Canada, given the Québecois allegiance to a strong public or (in literal form from the French) collective sector. This commitment is viewed as an important feature of Quebec's partic-ular identity, differentiating it culturally from other provinces in Canada and from the neighbouring USA.

Much of the early momentum for the structural approach was gener-ated by the late Maurice Moreau (1979), to whom later scholars have paid tribute:

> According to Moreau, professional practice is profoundly influenced by a society's economic and political forces. Western societies have gener-ated a fluctuating mix of unrest and apathy in response to the injustices caused by the intertwined systemic roots of patriarchal capitalism, heterosexism, racism, and other oppressions. (Carniol 1992, p. 2)

It is mainly the social structures that oppress by privileging dominant groups over subordinate groups ... [The structural approach] is concerned with moving from a society characterised by exploitation, inequality and oppression to one that is emancipatory and free from domination ... It recognises that fundamental social change cannot occur without fundamental personal change also occurring. (Mullaly 2010, pp. 16, 19, 21)

The key practice implication of a structural approach is a commitment to empowerment (Moreau 1990). The adult education approach of Paulo Freire (1972) is advanced as the method by which practitioners can help people to 'name' and discuss (rather than suppress) the more obvious oppressions affecting their living and working conditions. Through their words and actions in 'dialogue', practitioners come to show whose side they are on. Service users are welcomed as partners in the advocacy and social action that contribute to progressive personal and social change (Carniol 1992).

Another group of theorists, in this case based in Australia, have considered the importance of postmodernist ideas for social work practice (for example, Healy 2000; Fook 2002, Pease 2002). The one we find most helpful to our project is Karen Healy and her 'post-structural perspective' (Healy 2000). Healy outlines an agenda which is grounded in a critique of her own practice with a group of young women in an anti-violence against women project. She illustrates how imposing a consciousness-raising approach silenced those group members who did not adopt the expected structural understandings. Drawing upon Foucault's (1980) ideas about the privileging of particular discourses as a form of power that, in her group, drove away some non-compliant group members, Healy proposes an agenda that will allow for difference and complexity in empowerment practice. Drawing upon Payne's summary (2005), the key principles of Healy's approach are:

- an understanding of the complexity of how social and cultural factors interact to create discourses that effect how people behave;
- questioning and reworking taken-for-granted explanations of social conditions and human behaviour;
- focusing on social practices rather than social identities so that we do not assume and stereotype people's identities but search out the different factors that affect them;
- promoting provisional coalitions, celebrating modest successes,

rather than trying to create grand campaigns on the pretext of political solidarity;

- promoting open-ended dialogue without required outcomes.

Until now, however, the impact of all the above ideas and developments has been limited, as they have tended to be confined to fairly narrow areas, remaining on the edges of professional discourse. Even so, they can serve as signposts and points of reference. They can inspire and energize us and so lift the debate, not into an inaccessible intellectual stratosphere but, rather, out of the pedestrian and away from neo-liberal interests into directions that are critical, progressive, resistant and focused on change.

A Combined Way Forward

In summary, then, there is an urgent need to inject empowering theories into professional and self-directed practice, starting with the principles of anti-oppressive working (see Chapter 3). For instance, men as well as women must find a practice that supports the efforts of women for emancipation (Blacklock 2003; Pease 2003; Orme 2009), and white practitioners (Dominelli 2008), as well as black (Goldstein 2008), share a responsibility to make their work actively anti-racist. It is essential to have an approach that can readily be adopted by all those who share these aims for social justice and emancipation and who have a genuine desire to work in a way that supports activists' struggles.

Those who talk about empowerment must be clear about their responsibility and the skills they possess if they are to deliver support to those seeking their own empowerment (Munford and Walsh-Tapiata 2001). Nothing is more inexcusable than raising expectations and creating commitments that then flounder because practitioners do not know how to deliver their contribution. Self-directed groupwork can provide an answer because it is centred on people and because, at the same time, it is rooted in anti-oppressive values. As we shall go on to illustrate in Chapter 3, that the principles that underpin the new social movements (Todd and Taylor 2004) of disabled people, anti-racist, feminist, LGBT and related struggles are also embedded in self-directed work. Those who use the model are challenged to combine their own efforts with those of oppressed groups without colonizing them. This is achieved by placing the reins in people's own hands, organized together in groups, and by offering support to achieve their own goals, in place of the customary 'we know best' of traditional practice (Fleming 2012b). The detailed way this is done will be explored in Chapters 4 to 7, following an exploration of the critically important underpinning values and principles of practice in Chapter 3.

3

Taking Stock

The Centrality of Values

In Chapter 1, we presented the history and the outline framework of self-directed groupwork, stressing the crucial role within it, if practice is to be both empowering and effective, of clear and appropriate values aimed at anti-oppressive working. In this chapter, we will explore these underpinning values in greater detail, showing that they constitute most of the 'meat' of the first stage of the model, once the team has assembled and established its support mechanisms. We will then go on to illustrate in later chapters how the values lead naturally into the key features of the model, such as the open style of planning which fully involves participants (Chapter 4) and their full participation in setting the goals for, carrying out, and evaluating action aimed at achieving the changes they see as essential (Chapters 5 to 7). Overall, in this and the following four chapters, we shall offer a complete and value-based methodology for empowering practice.

Getting Our Own Act Together

To start with the values, then, we believe that we owe it to participants to clarify where we stand before making claims upon their time, their trust in us, or their flagging hope that the circumstances causing them distress and indignity may be susceptible to change.

Anti-authoritarian zeal and a loose commitment to tackling oppression alone are not strong enough starting points. It is essential to have cogent responses ready when people throw out remarks like: 'We've been written off now', 'Nobody listens to us', or 'What can the likes of us do?'

These issues need to be tackled in this first stage of the model as an essential precursor to asking people to engage in any process of work aimed at change. It is insulting and patronising to have no response to their perfectly realistic doubts, and yet to invite – or even expect – their co-operation. For the most vulnerable, who have known only repressive and institutionalizing services but who have at least found their own survival mechanisms within that deadening context, it is insulting to upset that stasis if we have only rhetoric to offer in its place. For the more hard-bitten, who have heard and seen it all before and who are tired of outsiders enquiring, interfering and, in the end, providing very little before retreating to the comfort of their own lives, it is patronising to expect a suspension of disbelief in your methods and abilities unless you offer positive proof by making the work participant-led right from the start. This is why we place such emphasis on involvement in basic planning, as will be seen in Chapter 4.

The First Stage of the Model: Pre-Planning

Even before meeting with potential participants, then, we have found it essential to go through a kind of 'pre-planning stage'. The tasks to be accomplished during this are, firstly, to come together as a facilitator team; secondly, if at all possible, to find the backing of a skilled consultant; and, thirdly, and most importantly, to agree on fundamental values, that is, the principles underlying the work to be undertaken together.

Assembling a compatible co-facilitator team

Deciding whether to work alone or with others and, if the latter, establishing an effective and skilled co-facilitating relationship is the first step in this pre-planning. Ideally, for reasons set out below, self-directed groups will have at least two facilitators who support each other in attempting to put their values into operation. However, we recognize that, in an increasingly resource-starved environment, this may not be practical and we certainly do not believe that the lack of a co-facilitator should *per se* veto engagement in the approach if the opportunity arises. Group members can sometimes be co-facilitators (Munford and Walsh-Tapiata 2001). Indeed, it must be the most rare of cases where a group-worker cannot find someone sufficiently on their wave-length to partner them, even if informally, through the activities of this pre-planning stage. They may be more in the role of 'consultant' than co-facilitator and we will say more about this below.

Nevertheless, the ability to co-work effectively, often across personal or professional boundaries, is a fundamental challenge in self-directed groupwork, requiring an informed and skilled response. Although beyond our brief to develop here, it touches upon the considerations of inter-disciplinary and inter-professional working, areas generating much concern and attention among the professions we are addressing (see, for instance, Littlechild and Smith 2012). Such collaboration requires, for example, a clear understanding of each other's values and goals, well-developed communication skills directed to the tasks in hand, full recording of planning and, later, of group process, adequate back-up from a consultant, and the ability to channel the lessons both from what is recorded and from support mechanisms back into the planning and into the groupwork itself.

Most of the advantages of co-facilitating are shared with other forms of groupwork (Stock Whitaker 2001; Doel 2006). Firstly, it doubles the attention that can be paid to what is happening in the group, so that Munford and Walsh-Tapiati (2001), in their work with Maori community groups, have found it useful to work with co-facilitators most particularly when discussions in the group are difficult and also when the group is large, as these situations can require intense concentration from the facilitators. Co-working also provides two or more role models, which can include diversity, based, for example, on age, ethnicity or gender. It models effective interaction between the groupworkers, provided they work hard on supporting one another. Co-workers can provide and receive mutual feedback and can cover for one another over the life of a long-term group. They can share the work arising from the group outside of meetings as well as during them, and they can help each other learn new skills. If a new worker joins the team during the life of the group, the new arrival can gain experience whilst also receiving good support.

A crucial further benefit of shared practice is that co-facilitators can assist one another in holding to anti-oppressive ways of working. Given that oppression as an issue lies at the core of empowerment, co-facilitating has an important part to play in assisting work to take due account of its impact on group participants, and in avoiding the replication of oppressive structures and relationships (see also below, on consultancy support). Published accounts of projects (e.g. Fleming and Wattley 1998) have stressed the importance of co-facilitators jointly developing coherent practice that incorporates an anti-oppressive perspective. Men United was a group for men with sole care of their children, who came together to support each other in what they perceived as the 'female-dominated world of parenting'. The group was facilitated by male groupworkers but, from the start, the need was identified for some female involvement, partly as a check against sexism, and also to allow for female input. This was provided by a female consultant to the groupworkers (Fleming and Luczynski 1999). The co-facilitators had to work hard to build on their commitment to, but different perspectives on, challenging oppression within the group in the context of a strong co-worker partnership.

Moving on to the decision whether to have more than two facilitators, assuming that this is an option (since a volunteer can always be included), this can also be beneficial (Doel 2006). Certainly, larger groups may need more than two facilitators, for example, with a group of forty or more members (see the section in Chapter 4 on group size). There is a need for facilitators in self-directed groups to be extremely attentive to group process, with a high level of concentration in order to ensure that the process remains empowering for all; too small a facilitation team would find it hard to maintain this in any group and particularly in a large one.

Self-directed groups often also invite people with particular skills into the group at appropriate times, for example, community artists, web-designers and lawyers, to share their expertise with the group. In these circumstances it may not be necessary for them to share the value base of the group, but they must understand that it is a self-directed group and be able to engage with the group appropriately.

Establishing appropriate consultancy support

In addition to deciding whether to work in conjunction with others, those initiating self-directed work have to decide whether to work with a consultant and, if so, who this should be. The isolated groupworkers from whose practice the self-directed model first developed, did not always have the advantage of consultancy support (or, arguably worse, were sometimes working with someone who did not understand their aims and principles) and yet, clearly, they made great strides in challenging accepted norms and pioneering a new approach. It would be precious of us, therefore, to suggest that work not underpinned by appropriate consultancy is more likely to fail. What we *would* say is that it may be more frustrating and more subject to dead-ends and false starts.

Self-directed groupworkers need support and survival strategies, not least in recognizing and dealing with the ways that they themselves are oppressed. They need to be enabled to protect themselves from hurt, to make demands on others and to consider ways of turning oppressive comments into useful discussions. Strategies are needed around opening up rather than shutting down debates and around protecting individual facilitator's privacy whilst also recognizing participants' needs to explore sensitive and challenging issues that may encompass, at various points, lifestyles, culture, sexuality, relationships, experiences of racism, sexism and other forms of oppression and discrimination.

Skilled supervision and/or consultancy, if this can possibly be managed, with adequate time before and between group meetings to use it, is the best means of resolving any possible problems. As will be shown in the next section, it is essential that, with or without a consultant present, this time be used in the early stages to establish an agreed value position. However, we would have additional reasons for stressing the advantages of supported feedback and planning at this early stage. We have discussed and developed these in more depth elsewhere (Mullender and Ward 1993) but they can be summarized as follows:

(a) a consultant can challenge the facilitators to formulate and clarify their agreed value position around anti-oppressive aims;

(b) a consultant can challenge the facilitators to hold to their value position when later planning or the work itself begins to deviate from the agreed principles under the pressure of day-to-day realities, or when different facilitators favour different solutions to a practical dilemma;

(c) if the model of intervention is a relatively new one in the context in question, where it may not yet have been fully absorbed into basic assumptions about practice, it can be useful to have someone continually drawing attention back to the fundamental principles that have been agreed on, such as throwing decisions back to group members, thus avoiding the tendency to slip back into old ways of working;

(d) both the skills and the techniques can feel new and unfamiliar so they may need discussing and rehearsing in privacy and safety, with an impartial observer, before being used in practice;

(e) the development of self-directed groups is far less predictable than many other forms of groups; someone experienced in using the model can provide reassurance and meeting them regularly offers the space in which to examine what is happening over time;

(f)   in order to be effective in a group, facilitators need to be very clear about their own respective roles and to establish an open style of communication between themselves; a consultant can help them to maintain this when the going gets rough;

(g)   a consultant can have an important role in avoiding the dangers of co-facilitating, notably disagreements about the group or about agendas brought in from outside it;

(h)   any new or unfamiliar form of practice is bound to lead to a certain amount of suspicion, or even opposition, from those outside the immediate team; a consultant can help them to be ready to answer their critics and to trust one another to respond appropriately at times when there is no chance to prepare a collective strategy or reply.

See also Figures 3.1 and 3.2 following (Bierley Youth Action Project, 1997).

Overall, then, the consultant can encourage the facilitators to plan for, and later to discuss group process and practice style based on empowering values. This helps them to be efficient enablers to the group and not to hinder it by slipping back into more conventional ways of planning or working, or by being unaware of the direction in which things are moving, or by failing to keep open communication amongst themselves or with group members.

The consultant's own style of operation should also, of course, be consistent with the values we will be discussing later in this chapter. They must hear and value what the facilitators bring to their role, enable them to 'own' the decisions they make about the group and push them to consider structural factors that underlie members' circumstances, for example. The person who plays this role ideally needs to have had personal experience of self-directed practice, although this is not essential and their position can be either more or less formal. We reiterate that it is compatible values that count first and foremost. Having a consultant with formal status might be helpful in securing groupwork time and permission to use the self-directed approach from employers. Experience of self-directed practice is valuable, not only in helping the consultant to follow and channel the flow of discussion but also because their interventions should set an appropriate tone for the resulting practice. Indeed, the consultant often directly models the facilitator role. This is done, for example, by facilitating rather than leading discussion and by using classic self-directed techniques like brainstorming and prioritizing exercises (see Chapter 5 for an outline of these), notably when the facilitators are planning for the group. Later, as well as

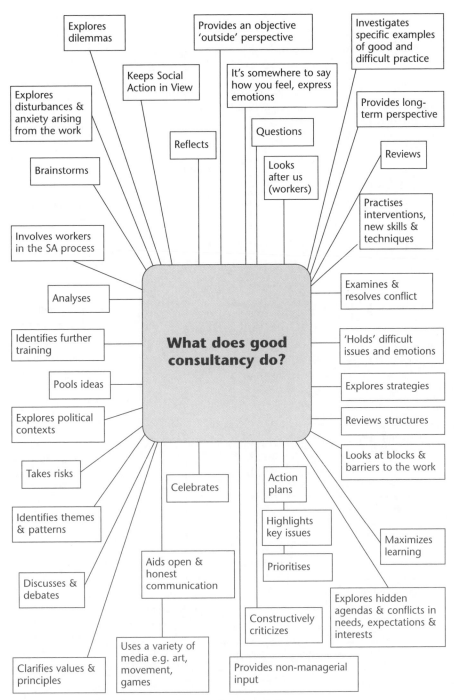

Figure 3.1 What does good consultancy do?

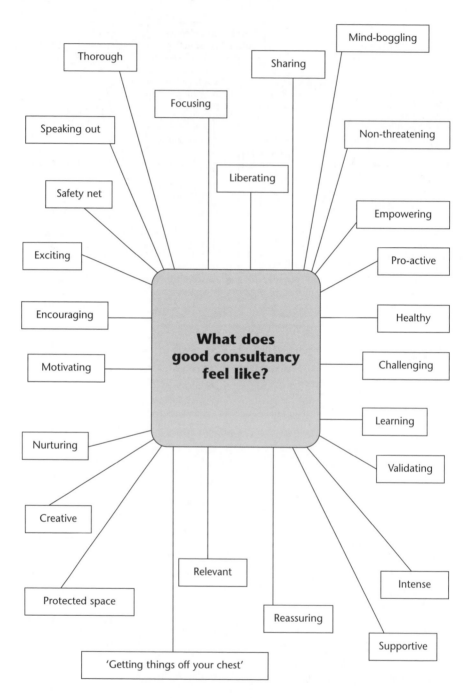

Figure 3.2 What does good consultancy feel like?

helping the practitioners to focus on key issues, the consultant may be able to use these techniques to draw any unacknowledged conflict out into the open before handing it back to the facilitators themselves to resolve, just as they will need to do in the group.

In the service learning model of self-directed groupwork used in the University of Massachusetts (UMass), Boston, USA (Arches 2012), the classroom became the consultancy with the lecturer and fellow students facilitating critical reflection on the group process and the facilitator's role within it. Weekly classroom sessions enabled them to reflect on the previous session and plan for the next one. In the Youth Dreamers project the group process merged into the consultancy even further. Over time they developed a team of young facilitators, the 'dream team', who alongside an adult member of staff facilitated the sessions with a wider group of young people. At the end of any session they had a meeting together to consider what had worked, what had not worked so well and why, and they then used this discussion as a basis to plan for the next session.

Agreeing on empowering principles for the work

As was established in earlier chapters, the self-directed model rests on an explicit statement of values that has clear implications for practice. Indeed, these values are firmly enmeshed in self-directed action; they cannot be verbally acknowledged but then ignored when it really counts – in the work itself. Conventional groupwork tends to be preoccupied with getting straight into the process of starting a group, with little thought of values or taking values for granted. The first stage of the self-directed model, on the other hand, involves agreeing a shared value position before engaging in what would more normally be the first stage: that of preparing to initiate a piece of practice. This can be a protracted and perhaps contentious process. At least one full meeting, and perhaps several, is likely to be required in order for each individual to state where they stand before similarities and differences of view become clear.

Only preliminary consensus about the sources from which ideology and understanding flow can assure the success of the resultant intervention. It may well be that agreement cannot, in fact, be reached and either the plans are aborted at this early stage or one person withdraws their involvement. This is vastly preferable, however, to ploughing on regardless. Submerged or unrecognized differences will always emerge at some later point, usually at a time of the utmost sensitivity, to haunt the practitioners and quite probably cause unnecessary distress to group members.

An example from practice illustrates what happens when a facilitator team leaves conflict unexpressed and hence fails to reach an agreed value position. A team of employed youth workers and a student volunteer started working with a group of young people who were hanging around on the streets and attracting attention from local residents and the police. The group were clear they wanted somewhere they could meet and plan or undertake activities on their own initiative. In contrast, the student wanted simply to provide those activities and would come to sessions with, for example, a football or another game and did not see the purpose of the group to be the young people themselves working to create something for themselves. He left the group after a few meetings, during which the facilitators had tended too often to be preoccupied with their own differences of opinion and sometimes distracted from drawing out the views and experiences of the young people. This happened, in large part, because the facilitators' differing views were not acknowledged or dealt with before the group commenced and there was no consultant to help draw them out. To have done this could have eased the path for the student volunteer to have opted out before the group started, rather than after.

A Statement of Values: Principles for Empowering Practice

Now we turn to the values themselves. We hold strongly to the view that there is no such thing as value-free or value-neutral work (Preston-Shoot 2007); there are only groupworkers who have not stopped to think what their values actually are. Unless groupworkers define and explore their own values before beginning groupwork, the group is less likely to succeed.

And, since thinking about values is often wishy-washy and based on vague concepts that apparently no one could disagree with, such as 'respect for persons' (see Banks 2006; Pullen Sansfaçon and Cowden 2012, for fuller discussions of the problematic nature of 'values'), it is safer to judge people by what they actually do than from what they claim are their values. A truly empowering approach is observable from its impact on the recipients of services.

Self-directed groupwork is underpinned by six practice principles that are used to guide all the work. The most current statement of these principles is as follows:

1. We are committed to social justice. We strive to challenge inequality and oppression in relation to race, gender, sexuality, age, religion, class, disability or any other form of social differentiation.
2. We believe all people have skills, experience and understanding that they can draw on to tackle the problems they face. We understand that people are experts in their own lives and we use this as a starting point for our work.
3. All people have rights, including the right to be heard, the right to define the issues facing them and the right to take action on their own behalf. People also have the right to define themselves and not have negative labels imposed upon them.
4. Injustice and oppression are complex issues rooted in social policy, the environment and the economy. We understand people may experience problems as individuals but these difficulties can be translated into common concerns.
5. We understand that people working collectively can be powerful. People who lack the power and influence to challenge injustice and oppression as individuals can gain it through working with other people in a similar position.
6. We are not leaders, but facilitators. Our job is to enable people to make decisions for themselves and take ownership of whatever outcome ensues. Everybody's contribution to this process is equally valued and it is vital that our job is not accorded privilege.

Each of these values will now be discussed in greater depth.

Commitment to social justice

> *We are committed to social justice. We strive to challenge inequality and oppression in relation to race, gender, sexuality, age, religion, class, disability or any other form of social differentiation.*

Self-directed groupwork is about fighting for fairness, equality and justice and this needs to be clearly stated. We recognize that injustice, discrimination and oppression exist and we take a stance against them, in all our work. We recognize that this requires continual efforts to confront prejudice in ourselves, as well as in others.

Mullaly (2010, p. 48) arrives at an understanding of social justice that may prove helpful. He starts from a standpoint on social injustice before moving on to social justice:

Social injustice ... entails not only an unfair distribution of goods and resources but includes any norm, social condition, social process or social practice that interferes with or constrains one from fully participating in society – that is from becoming a full citizen ... This concept of social justice is empowering because it goes beyond a concern with distribution to include the institutional conditions necessary for the development and exercise of individual capacities and collective communication and cooperation.

We have already stated that we see oppression not as something static but as fluid, dynamic, multi-dimensional and embedded in human relationships (Munford and Walsh-Tapiata 2001; Mullaly 2010). It seems clear to us that women and girls, lesbians, gay men, transgendered and bisexual people, black and minority ethnic people, young and older people, disabled people and those with learning difficulties and mental health problems, those who are homeless or in poverty, and those who do not meet other social norms experience oppression, at different times and in different combinations, across each of these boundaries and will continue to do so unless all forms of oppression are acknowledged and tackled. This will only happen if we listen to previously silenced voices and hear the collective demands of oppressed groups, seeking to understand the world from a BAME (black, Asian and minority ethnic) perspective (Graham 2007; Goldstein 2008), from a disabled people's perspective (Oliver and Barnes 2012) and so on, whilst also remembering that there is diversity within each of these identities.

The many dimensions of oppression must also be seen to interlink, each having the capacity to overarch several others at different times and in particular conditions; they need to be confronted with this interdependence always in view. Furthermore, we must not allow one oppressed group to be played off against another, to create a hierarchy of futile comparisons that distract from the task of challenging the maintenance of injustice.

For many people, of course, oppressions do not come singly. Black feminist writers such as bell hooks (1984) and Patricia Hill Collins (2000) encountered, recognized and revealed the multi-dimensional nature of oppression experienced by black women. Recognizing that white middle-class women did not serve as an accurate representation of the feminist movement as a whole, black feminists argued that the forms of oppression that white women experienced were different from those faced by black, poor, or disabled women. For example, while white, non-disabled women may be fighting for better access to birth control, learning disabled women and black women may simultaneously be facing coerced contraception or an over-hasty resort to hysterectomy. Thus it is essential to understand the ways in which gender, ethnicity, class, disability and other dimensions combine and intersect. Lewis and Guttierrez (2003, p. 135) had earlier applied these insights to their experience as groupworkers. They observed that

> frank and open discussions ... of how the intersectionality of sexual orientation, race and gender might influence the ability of [members] ... to work together ... helped the entire group to move consciously through the permutations of their relevant social group memberships ... [to develop] skills in conflict management and organisational/community change.

The point is not to deny that different forms of oppression may be distinct in some ways, but to see that they are also related:

> although there may be distinct categories of oppression, there is no oppression that creates a distinct group of people who are unaffected, one way or another, by other forms of oppression. Oppressed groups overlap each other – an important fact ... for seeking alliances and coalitions of oppressed groups. (Mullaly 2010, pp. 195–196)

Mullaly (2010) goes on, however, to caution against intersectionality obscuring the heterogeneity that exists within oppressed groups: we must acknowledge the incredible diversity inherent within people's various gender class race, age, sexuality and other social dimensions and not blur everyone together or see them as inevitable victims.

At the same time as we arrive at these more nuanced understandings of oppression, there is always a backlash, a dilution and a colonization going on, to protect entrenched interests and preserve the status quo. Whilst there have been improvements in the social and economic situation of disabled people for example, observes Morris (2011), further progress is limited by the fact that much of the language and ideas of the disability movement has been watered down and corrupted in their use by governments. She stresses that current theorization and practice are not radical enough because they are 'not accountable or democratic enough to bring about the fundamental changes that are required' so disabled people themselves must have the power to decide how support is delivered (ibid., p. 17). The wider point here is that we must remain vigilant in case, in the understanding and awareness of complexity, anti-discriminatory practice gets diffused and loses urgency and focus:

> Black people need to come together with others from their own back-ground, because mainstream user groups cannot comprehend racism and discrimination in the same way. Acting together, people from Black user groups can engage with mainstream providers from a posi-tion of strength. (Trivedi 2008, cited in Seebohm *et al.* 2010, p. 27)

Collective strength, then, is the way forward and groupwork is the means to harness it in practice.

An example of commitment to an intersectional approach within a social justice mission can clearly be seen in the work of CANA (Carrefour d'aide des nouveaux arrivants: http://www.cana-montreal.org), an inde-pendent body providing advocacy, information and educational services for immigrants, refugees and asylum seekers in Montreal, Canada. All the organization's stakeholders are committed to a more equal society and it adopts participative methods of working to help its members become active, well-informed, independent citizens. The team at CANA has noticed that many people come to its services because they experi-ence double marginalization. Besides the discrimination resulting from their official 'outsider' status in society and lack of integration, too, into existing immigrant communities, CANA's service users routinely encounter negative attitudes because they are black, Latino or from another minority ethnic community, young or older, disabled, female, poor and so on. The team at CANA has now decided to open up its facil-ity and format of working by offering a self-directed group, along the lines described in this book. It will be interesting to see how this devel-ops.

People are experts in their own lives

> *We believe all people have skills, experience and understanding that they can draw on to tackle the problems they face. We understand that people are experts in their own lives and we use this as a starting point for our work.*

Our job is to help uncover what is already there: to encourage people to use the insights and knowledge they possess to bring about changes in their own lives. The people we work with have capacities and valuable experience: they have strengths, skills, understanding, the ability to do things for themselves, and much to offer one another (Gitterman and Shulman 2005). This recognition is one of the key benefits reported by members of self-directed groups. Their qualities have frequently been underestimated, overlooked or disbelieved by professionals who have failed to look beyond the negative labels derived from previous contacts with the authorities (McCarthy 2011). Once people are accorded respect, however, they can begin to behave as very much more able than has ever been recognized by anyone, including themselves. The Youth Dreamers speak of working hard to counter the negative labels put upon young people and to realize and use the diverse strengths and skills of all group members.

This is the true revelation of empowering practice: just how strong, capable and aware people are, and what they can achieve for themselves, as the examples in this book testify. It is like going through the looking glass and finding that a world of quite different possibilities opens up on the other side.

While human beings are naturally powerful, the teachings we digest can be so invasive that powerlessness becomes accepted and people cannot see how life can be any different (Munford and Walsh-Tapiata 2001). Yet people can and do break out of the mould, either through their own efforts alone, or through encountering better practice and more empowering opportunities. If users of services are treated as the problem, they will sometimes live up to the perception, as a kind of self-fulfilling prophecy, in order to fit in with what is expected of them. If, on the other hand, they are asked to contribute their ideas, are really listened to, and are then encouraged to act on their own suggestions, these same people will present very differently. Young women with children attending a group run by health visitors and a social work student had initially assumed that they would be asked to discuss problems in coping with their babies; however, what the discussions in the group showed was that they already knew a great deal about caring for children but could not put it into effect because of lack of money, inadequate housing and the constant drain on energy and their own health posed by abusive partners. They brought out extremely perceptive views of male/female relationships and of the status of women in contemporary society and gave evidence of their own resilience as survivors in the face of sexual abuse, neglect and physical ill-treatment in their own childhood.

A commitment to 'strengths-based' and 'solution-focused' approaches has become *de rigueur* in the human services (Saleebey 2006). These are said to contrast with problem-based and other ecological and systems approaches, and to offer mainstream practitioners a method that explicitly takes into account the strengths and assets of people and their environments. However, it is necessary to question whether they really do mark a change of direction. Payne (2005) concludes that, like the theories they seek to contrast with, most strengths-based approaches remain grounded in assumptions that everything fits into a social order that establishes a pattern of consensually accepted relationships between people, groups and organizations. More sharply, Gray (2011, p. 11) sees in them a 'danger of running too close to contemporary neo-liberal notions of self-help and self-responsibility and glossing over the structural inequalities that hamper personal and social development'. Hence it is necessary to look at the underlying values as well as the superficial words.

People have the right to be heard and to define the issues facing them

All people have rights, including the right to be heard, the right to define the issues facing them and the right to take action on their own behalf. People also have the right to define themselves and not have negative labels imposed upon them.

Ordinary people's right to be involved in the changes that affect them, to have a voice and a stake in the society they live in, is fundamental to self-directed work. The right to name their world, to define themselves and the world around them, is something we insist on. Too often people have to contend with labels imposed upon them or the places they live in, for the ease of policy-makers and professionals.

When people's strengths and abilities are recognized, the practice that flows from this recognition has to accord people a far greater role in choosing what kinds of intervention they will accept in their lives and whether to get involved in directing their own process of change. They can only decide on the basis of full information about the alternatives. It is not tenable for practitioners to deprive participants of key information about the options on the assumption that they, as the professionals, 'know best'. People must be let into the professional 'secrets' about possible types of action and where the resources might come from to make them possible; they must be empowered to opt into or out of groups and campaigns, to define their own issues, and to set their own agenda for change.

Saying this in the context of self-directed groupwork, we might be accused of unfairly passing over official developments such as, for example, 'personalization' (Department of Health 2007) and the new nomination of patients and users of health and social care services as 'experts by experience' (Care Quality Commission 2011). In the previous chapter we questioned the progressive potential of such developments, given the neo-liberal agenda within which they are being promoted. Indeed, in relation to personalization, Wood (2011a) identifies some clear issues:

> Personal budgets are life-changing, no doubt, but they are a fundamentally individualistic tool ... individuals given a personal budget will be tasked with purchasing an individual package of care to meet their needs, bringing together traditional elements of care with other services such as transport, leisure or social activities.

This can also leave a service user open to abuse by a paid carer and potentially less likely than the pseudo-professional carer to be believed if they try and report any physical, financial or other maltreatment (Thiara *et al.* 2012), with no collective backing to develop safer employment practices or other safeguards. Referring specifically to care homes but with self-evident applicability to community-based services, Wood (2011b) argues:

> we must embrace alternative paths to personalisation ... Co-design of services, democratic structures, imaginative use of collective spaces to encourage greater independence ... are all viable ways of turning care ... from sites of collective disempowerment and passive service use into 'micro-communities', which, very much like housing co-operatives, are run by a powerful residents' association to ensure services are organised and meet the needs of the collective.

As ever, this call for collective strength leads us inevitably towards thinking about groupwork and social action.

The right to be heard

The first step in any programme of change is for groups of people to find their own voice. Typically, they have never been listened to before. This valuing of their views helps in finding words to express opinions and experiences that have hitherto remained keenly felt but unaired. For people who are new to this way of working, it can come as a shock to hear how trenchant and strongly felt are the results. The experience of

being part of collective efforts towards change makes those who participate in it more articulate, more confident, and more aware. We call this
the 'secondary advantage', that is, personal change within participants,
because it is not the primary purpose for which self-directed action is
undertaken. Cohen and Mullender (2000) have pointed out, though,
that this individual change can be as marked as that achieved in specifically therapeutic groups that target individual change alone. Arches and
Fleming (2007, p. 41) quote some examples in the words of former
members interviewed 20 years on from their involvement in a self-
directed group:

> When I was young I was treated like a baby, but now I treat young-
> sters like an adult ... when we started the club, I got a better under-
> standing.

> You're more sensitive to other people's needs, aren't you? You can see
> what they are going through.

> Yes, I think it has helped me in the job I'm doing now — I'm a super-
> visor — I listen to people at work now — if I hadn't had this experi-
> ence I would have thought I'm right and that's it. I listen — like when
> we first started, I didn't listen, we want this and we want that — there
> was no negotiation.

Group members learn a diverse range of skills through being involved in
self-directed groups, as one of the founder members of the Youth
Dreamers says:

> It's hard for me to explain how much the Youth Dreamers has posi-
> tively influenced my life – being surrounded by students who were
> dedicated to making change. During my whole journey with Youth
> Dreamers, I learnt information I would not have learnt in a regular
> classroom. I learnt how to balance a check [cheque] book, how to
> write a grant, how to start a non-profit organization and how to reno-
> vate a house. Being a Youth Dreamer allowed me to realize what was
> important in our neighborhoods and schools.

Once participants begin to find a voice, there are three separate areas on
which the facilitators need to encourage them to express their opinions:
that is, answering the questions 'what?', 'why?' and 'how?' The ways in
which this can be done will be looked at in more detail in Chapter 5.

Challenging negative labels

The people we work cannot be defined or encapsulated by depersonalizing terms such as 'NEET' (not in education, employment or training), '*the* disabled', '*the* elderly', 'inadequate parents' and so on. One of the greatest dangers with such labels is that one dismissive characteristic, or one incident of behaviour accounted as unacceptable, can be enough to suck an individual into a system of intervention, oversight, containment or punishment, after which their whole functioning may be called into question and opportunities to control their own lives removed (McCarthy 2011). Even in the twenty-first century, we are never far from Victorian concepts of the undeserving poor.

To use a phrase adopted in the field of learning difficulties, we have to re-learn to see users of services as 'people first'. That is, they are ordinary people who are facing challenges and oppressively difficult circumstances in their lives that would leave anyone who is less than superhuman struggling to cope. The current rapid increase in the population of older people is generating some wider awareness of this. More and more people are entering into the remit of health and social care services, many of whom have never before in their lives had such contact, and they are not liking what they are finding: insufficient or poor quality provision, adverse attitudes and prejudice towards them. This is attracting media publicity for issues that oppressed groups have always faced, in myriad ways, but been expected to put up with.

Injustice and oppression are rooted in social policy

> *Injustice and oppression are complex issues rooted in social policy, the environment and the economy. Self-directed groupworkers understand that people may experience problems as individuals but these difficulties can be translated into common concerns.*

We recognize that there are many different problems in individuals' lives. They may feel overwhelmed and daunted by these, they may even feel blamed for them. Self-directed groupwork gives people the opportunity to break free from this negative view, to understand their individual problems in a wider, political context and to do something about organizing to overcome them.

Once people's negative labels begin to be challenged, and once their own views on the circumstances they face begin to be sought, a far more complex range of factors can be taken into account. Typically, practitioners are daunted by this kind of analysis because they do not see how they can incorporate it into their own everyday practice. Self-directed action empowers practitioners to bridge this gap, just as much as it empowers service users and group members.

The view that macro social problems can begin to be resolved through campaigning at a micro, that is a localized or personal, level opens up many doors. Whilst priorities set by central government are obviously crucial, our work has shown the importance and potential of action that begins at a local level and its capacity to move beyond parochial issues into campaigning for, and achieving change at, a national level. This process can be seen at work wherever the establishment of a small, local group has led to the burgeoning of other such groups elsewhere or to the creation of a national body that can take up the campaigning on a wider scale or where a local campaign has moved onto a national canvas. An example is provided by a local campaign by young people – against high-pitched sound 'mosquito' devices that were used in UK cities to exclude them from certain public places (because young people can hear higher frequencies than adults); this then developed into a national campaign (BBC 2011). Other examples are the Family Advocacy Network, a local group that joined together with other similar groups under the umbrella of Children's Rights Information Network and, of course, developments within the disability field which we consider in some detail in Chapter 7. Such developments resonate with aspects of the campaigning by 'new social movements' (Thompson 2002; Todd and Taylor 2004).

Collective power

> *We understand that people working collectively can be powerful. People who lack the power and influence to challenge injustice and oppression as individuals can gain it through working with other people in a similar position.*

As we saw extensively in the last chapter, oppression is maintained through isolation and division, though it is experienced by the majority. Our job is to bring people together so that they can share their experiences and pool their resources and skills to fight injustice. Finding common cause may give individuals the will and power to tackle more complex issues than they might have dared on their own.

What happens in self-directed groupwork, then, is that people come together into groups where they tackle problems external to themselves, normally on a localized basis at first, but often broadening out to attain national dimensions when tackled in conjunction with others. Through these, often, the wider communities of interest they represent are also empowered. We have already explained the importance and potential of groups in working for change and empowerment and will not repeat this here.

This process means that groupwork in self-directed groups is explicitly concerned with helping people who are relatively powerless to become more powerful. For this to be possible, it is necessary for the practitioner to be willing really to *hear* when people say that structurally based problems are uppermost in their lives and, *crucially,* to make the leap of faith to see these as approachable through the medium of self-directed action.

Non-elitist ways of working

> *Practise what you preach: methods of working must reflect non-elitist principles. We are not leaders, but facilitators. Our job is to enable people to make decisions for themselves and take ownership of whatever outcome ensues. Everybody's contribution to this process is equally valued and it is vital that our job is not accorded privilege.*

We value all skills and knowledge equally, making no distinction between experience and formal qualifications. Our job is to work alongside the group, resisting the temptation either to become a group member or a group leader. Self-directed groupwork does not abrogate practitioner knowledge, responsibility or skill but is grounded in partnership rather than control. The expertise of the groupworker lies in the skilled and sensitive implementation of the self-directed groupwork process, whilst group members define the content and outcomes. Thus, though special skills and knowledge are employed, these do not accord status and are not solely the province of the groupworkers.

Group facilitation

Self-directed groupworkers must want to work with people and not to direct intervention 'to' or 'at' them (Ward and Mullender 1991; Fleming and Ward forthcoming). The groupworker must consequently regard his or her most effective contribution as being facilitation rather than leadership in the traditional sense, which has quite different *power* connotations. It is always essential to question to what ends the groupworker's control is directed, and over which areas of the group's functioning it is exercised and to watch out for retreats into old-style leadership assumptions. A professional worker may betray a misplaced sense of 'ownership' of the group, through the use of terminology such as 'my group', for example. Power (see Chapter 2) is never value-free or value-neutral but, by definition, value-laden (Lukes 2005). Facilitation can never be simply a technical exercise in management; it necessarily stems from explicit or implicit intentions and purposes. Empowerment relies on asking who determines those intentions and purposes and handing back the power over decision-making to group participants.

This role, and this handing over of decisions, will require careful elucidation with group participants because it will be an unfamiliar one to many people. More common experiences in groups, from school onwards, tend to be of being instructed what to do. It needs to be clear from the start, therefore, that self-directed groupworkers will be placing full responsibility on members to decide what action to take.

Group members as facilitators

A number of the groups in this book have no professional or practitioner involvement. This is a deliberate choice on their behalf. Members of No Limits Dementia say that professionals can be gatekeepers to services and are often one of the problems in people's lives and not necessarily seen as potential allies. Group members take considerable care to create a safe atmosphere where people can share experiences and emotions. Their experience is that this is more difficult when professionals are in the group as there can be issues of power and control. They prefer to organize themselves and then offer their own support and invite professionals to the group if they think it would be useful.

In Advocacy in Action, which has no 'professional' involvement, facilitators can be anyone at any time; people take different facilitating roles within the group. They recognize there are tasks that need to be performed for the group to function and to be able to act on things but they do not see these as the province of one or two people; everybody makes their contribution to this. No one at Advocacy in Action has been on a course in groupwork; rather, they develop and share the skills by doing things within the group. Munford and Walsh-Tapiata (2001), in their work with Maori communities in New Zealand, have found it useful to share the facilitator role between group members, but consider it important that 'at the beginning of the group process the group identifies the key aspects of the facilitator's role and monitors this throughout the process' (p. 67). This is similar to how No Limits Dementia works, where roles are informal and skills are shared and capacities built. The roles are flexible and often arise when people see a need and fulfill that role. They acknowledge facilitation might be smoother and more practised if there was professional involvement but prefer to be facilitated by peers with common experience. This approach is reinforced by Munn-Giddings and McVicar (2007) who found that peer self-organizing groups, run by and for their members, can provide space where they gain empathy, emotional and experiential knowledge as well as information based on reciprocity, which can be harder to access in groups supported by professionals. Whilst Youth Dreamers does have on-going support from a teacher, aspects of their meetings are always facilitated by young people who decide for themselves who will take which roles in each meeting.

Special skills and knowledge

When groupworkers come from outside the group, they can assist with finding means to achieve the group's desired ends, but should never dictate what those ends should be. They may well make suggestions and offer alternative scenarios for consideration by group members but their chief involvement will be in easing and highlighting group process, not in influencing the direction of the work undertaken by the group or its outcome.

This style of working is essential if the earlier principles are to be observed. Opening themselves up to hearing what people are saying, empowering them to set their own goals, and taking collective action, imply supporting group members to contribute their knowledge and experience and to determine where they want the group to go, rather than the groupworker imposing their own agenda. Groupworkers can, however, have a hard job explaining and maintaining this in the group. If groupworkers are also professional health and social care workers, members will be more used to professionals as authority figures and as providers or withholders of resources and access to services. Consequently, they may expect to be told what to do and how to do it and to have everything the group needs to make it function procured for them. For example, teachers working with Youth Dreamers in America had to work with their students in setting aside the notion that 'teachers make classrooms *for* their students' to students and teachers working together to construct working classrooms. It takes frequent direct explanation and practical demonstrations for group members to recognize that they can look to the facilitators for help but not for instruction: facilitators have to be directive about being non-directive!

Often, groupworkers who are unfamiliar with the role of facilitation fall into the trap of going too far the other way and becoming totally non-interventive. This is not what is implied by facilitation. It does not mean falling over backwards to keep one's self and one's own views invisible and unheard. It means playing an active role - for example, in challenging the fatalism that members may bring to a new group: 'But there's nothing we can do about it' – yet being sensitive to the differences between keeping issues in play and not dominating.

In view of the subtle judgements that are involved, there is certainly no less skill involved in this kind of work than in groupwork that is led from the centre. There are specific methods and techniques that help in the empowerment of group members and these can be studied, learned, practised and evaluated. This will be apparent in the chapters that follow, when we explore what self-directed groupworkers actually do. Groups can require facilitation at any or all stages of the process: in coming together to share their experiences, in finding the means to form views and set goals, and in generating the knowledge and skills needed to carry out tasks.

All of this means that empowerment practice is a skilled discipline. We would argue that in *all* groups, whether or not they have paid groupworkers or are self-run, the role of facilitator needs to be played and that groups could sometimes make better progress by acknowledging this need within their own internal organization. Group members taking responsibility for facilitation and group processes can often play the role very well but may appreciate the same consultancy and other support as any other groupworker and may otherwise miss opportunities to involve all members equally and to keep the group moving forward effectively. We would suggest that this book could be as useful to them as to professional groupworkers or practitioners, though no doubt they already hold clear value positions. Where, in contrast, practitioners are paid to perform the facilitator's role, they must be prepared to demonstrate their responsibility for themselves and to the group. It is not sufficient merely to claim goodwill, commitment or a set of ideals. Group members have a right to expect skilled and effective support.

The groupworkers' bottom line

Not only are self-directed groupworkers active and skilful, but they also have rights of their own within the group. Sometimes, new facilitators get hold of the idea that, because groupworkers in self-directed groups do not impose agendas on the members, they therefore must express no views and set no boundaries of their own. In fact, since involvement is constructed as a partnership of facilitators and group members, it would be dishonest for facilitators not to share the things they feel strongly about. It would also be misleading because, if left unspoken, expectations and assumptions will be taken for granted as being in agreement with the group. Racism and sexism, for example, and other discriminatory attitudes, will always be challenged.

It is essential to be honest with members about your 'bottom line', about what you can and cannot accept. It is perfectly appropriate, for example, for the groupworkers to say at the outset that they retain a veto on their continued involvement with the group. This can be used if the members decide, after full consideration, to pursue an objective with which the facilitators refuse to be identified, such as trying to stop immigrants having access to social housing on the estate where they live. If attempts at challenging this and opening up further discussion all fail, and it would not be acceptable to stay involved under these circumstances, the facilitators would have to say that they could not go along with the proposed actions and leave the group.

Group maintenance

Facilitation functions are not the special province of the groupworkers, whether they are peers or paid or voluntary practitioners. Group maintenance, for example, is shared as far as possible with all group members, and increasingly so over time. The group itself needs to learn the skills of resolving disagreements but also to recognize that such expressions of hostility, as of self-blame, can represent a misdirecting of anger that could more fruitfully be focused on the actual source of their oppression and hence channelled into energy to achieve external change. Where a facilitator does exercise such functions, it is important to remember that this is done, not through any special privilege or superior understanding, but on behalf of the group.

Group maintenance functions are now part of the 'common sense' of groupwork and presented accessibly by many authors (see, for example, Kindred and Kindred 2011). In self-directed groupwork, they need to be adapted to the value framework of empowerment and exercised in a style that is compatible with its overall principles. This requires that the facilitator should merely state what he or she is experiencing, not attempt to interpret it. Where a facilitator does try to pick up and voice the prevailing mood or feelings in the group (which can assist participants' voices to be heard, in line with the practice principle *'People have the right to be heard and define the issues facing them'*), members must at all times feel perfectly free to disagree with what the facilitator has sensed to be the case; there should be no hierarchy of control over this, just as there is not over any other aspect of the group's functioning.

Though we adapt them, we do not undervalue group maintenance functions. It is often the case that a facilitator will require the skills to deal with people who have had little or no experience of working collectively and who may need a good deal of individual support within the group early on: through mediating conflict, and attempting to mend relationships where trust has broken down. This is as important as the harder-edged issues of campaigns and action. If we are serious about the *'non-elitist ways of working'* principle, we have to rethink the meta-language which we use when talking about 'taking action' as much as the action itself, since the two are heavily intertwined.

Conclusion

Through its explicit stating of essential principles, the self-directed groupwork approach provides a common basis for practice and hence transcends the conventionally defined boundaries between disciplines such as social work, community work, youth work, teaching, adult education, community-based nursing, health visiting, health promotion and others. Practitioners in any of these settings can work in an empowering way if they fashion their practice according to an appropriate value-base, formulated within an understanding of wider political perspectives, and if they then translate its implications into their work. We have expressed our values as 'practice principles' that can be used by all those who are committed to empowering groupwork: whether they are paid or unpaid, volunteers or professionals; group facilitators or members; survivors, carers or concerned citizens moved by the need for progressive social change. While these principles may represent, at the end of the day, little more than a statement of intent, if that intent is given proper recognition as the core of practice, a clear statement of values can help transpose well-intentioned, committed, but undisciplined work into a dynamic and refined approach which can, firstly, withstand evaluation and scrutiny and, secondly, sustain a clear commitment to social change and social justice.

In the next chapter, we shall begin our detailed exploration of the difference these practice principles make to actual practice, following through, chapter by chapter, the stages of the self-directed model.

4

The Group Takes Off

In Chapter 3, we outlined the process of the groupworkers preparing themselves to conduct self-directed groupwork. In this chapter, the potential members come on the scene and we explore what happens when they come together with the facilitators to carry out the detailed planning for a group.

The key question throughout the next four chapters is: what difference do the values we outlined in Chapter 3 make to practice? The answer, as far as this chapter is concerned, is that whereas, in most forms of traditional groupwork, the initial planning is done *on behalf of* group members, in self-directed groupwork, the groupworkers engage with them as partners to build a group along open and member-led, rather than closed and worker-led, lines. This initiates an empowering style of work where people make key decisions such as whether to join the group, where and when to meet, and what arrangements will feel least oppressive. A new style of 'open planning', as we have called it (Mullender and Ward 1989), has to be developed in order for member-led action to ensue.

Making Planning *Em*-powering: A Detailed Examination of Open Planning

We have worked with many groupwork practitioners now, unpaid as well as paid, in different disciplines and, indeed, in different countries, on unlearning and rethinking ideas on planning. We use exercises which can also be used by facilitators with their consultants to thrash out their values prior to starting work, in order to ensure that they have a clear agreement about the model of planning they will adopt and about its compatibility with the self-directed approach. In fact, by engaging in the processes of pre-planning (Taking Stock – see Chapter 3) and open planning (Taking Off – covered in this chapter), the facilitators are moving through and experiencing for themselves all of the stages of the self-directed groupwork process. They are asking themselves the same key questions – WHAT? WHY? (in Taking Stock) and HOW? (in Taking Off)-- before Taking Action (see Chapter 6) as facilitators and Taking Over (see Chapter 7) responsibility for their own practice. These questions will lie at the heart of their role as group facilitators and also will guide their continuing reflection on and evaluation of their own practice and the progress of the group.

An effective technique to get open planning going is to invite group-workers to adopt a completely polarized approach: to think about the extremes on a continuum of open and of closed – or, we might say, of empowering and disempowering – planning. They are firstly invited to consider how many of the items on conventional planning lists could, in fact, be postponed until potential group members can be involved. In other words, what is the bottom line in advance planning? Of course, the facilitator or groupworker team has already had to decide on an interest in groupwork and will have thoroughly carried out its own pre-planning (Taking Stock), as mentioned in the last chapter. Other than this, the only work that absolutely needs to be done in advance of convening potential group members is to discuss with potentially inter-ested participants:

1. whether there is sufficient reason to call a meeting and what a possi-ble group might do (potential *goals*);
2. who is interested enough to attend once and give the group a try (potential *membership*);
3. a place for a first meeting (*venue*);
4. a time for a first meeting (issues of *timing*).

Thought also needs to be given to how to let people know about the first meeting and how to handle that first occasion when people need to be put at their ease, for example, with refreshments. They will need to have a relaxed opportunity to talk about themselves and their lives, but will also want to leave feeling a sense of purpose and the viability of change. Arrangements for any further meetings (such as venue, timing and activ-ities) need not be fixed in advance; it is more empowering if they are jointly discussed and agreed by all the emerging group members when they first come together.

As far as possible, even the decisions listed above are best made through a process of discussion with the people who might wish to attend. Thus, the idea for the group should have arisen from contact with potential members. There needs to be a shared feeling that something needs changing, held by a core of people who are willing to attend a first meeting. This view can then be floated with others to see if they agree, and whether they are prepared to come along and add their strengths to the combined effort for change. General views can also be sought on a good time and place to hold the meeting, how best to publicize it: who needs to be told and what means might be used. This can include social media such as Facebook and Twitter, if appropriate, but without forgetting the more traditional posters, leaflets and word of mouth. Other details about the arrangements, such as childcare, access for disabled people and the availability of hearing loops will need to be considered (see Glynn *et al.* 2011). It is important to check that people will not be kept away at this early stage by not having heard about the meeting, by domestic commitments, by access or communication issues, by feeling uncomfortable or out of place in the suggested venue (it should be 'a safe place with good atmosphere', as one group member put it) or by not being able to manage the proposed time.

As well as giving their own explanations of why the meeting has been called, facilitators may well be able to involve participants in addressing the meeting to outline what concerns they have and why they decided to attend. Members of existing groups with similar concerns and successes already under their belt can also be effective speakers. The Nottingham Who Cares Group had a speaker from the National Association of Young People in Care (NAYPIC) at its inaugural meeting, who outlined the tremendous strides that organization had made. The only drawback was that his involvement in NAYPIC had made him such a poised and self-confident 17-year-old that those young people attending the meeting thought he was a social worker! At a first meeting, members will begin to decide whether they accept the initiators as facilitators and themselves as capable of self-direction. At the same time, the facilitators will encourage and support members' early testing of their own and the facilitators' attitudes and members' first efforts to articulate their views and feelings.

The following exercise can be a useful one in preparing facilitators for this first phase of a self-directed group. First, ask those present to consider how one could set up a group in the most *dis*empowering way imaginable. Once the 'disempowering' lists are assembled and written up, down the left-hand side of a flip chart, or on a smart board, go back down the list and work out what the opposite of each item would be:

i.e. how to initiate a group or project in the most empowering way possible.

Naturally, the lists that have resulted from these fairly light-hearted sessions are exaggerated – caricatures, even – and it is not our intention to suggest that anyone would deliberately set out to work in an overtly disempowering way. To their surprise, however, the participants conclude that there is more than a grain of resemblance between the left-hand, 'disempowering' list they have drawn up and conventional practice, including their own. They find it liberating to consider afresh just how much of traditional, worker-led planning (see, for example, Northen and Kurland 2001; Phillips 2001; Doel 2006) can be replaced by shared deliberations with intending members about the style and shape they would like their new group to take.

What follows is a compilation of some responses on empowering and disempowering planning and an exploration in greater depth of the ideas on what can make planning empowering (the right-hand column in each case) (Table 4.1). This allows consideration in greater detail of the effect of keeping the process as open, uncommitted and participative as possible, rather than pre-ordained and heavily worker-led.

Table 4.1   Reason to hold a group: potential goals

Disempowering approach	*Empowering approach*
The boss thinks it's a good idea **or** I think it's a good idea	Facilitators acknowledge and contract to work with a pre-existing group on members' own issues
	or, alternatively,
Practitioner's pet project	Idea arises from one or more members and is checked out by the facilitators with others who might like to join
Student on placement is required to run a group as determined by agency	Student holds to own value position and follows one of the above routes into groupwork
Goals pre-set by practitioners/ imposed on group	Goals set by group

Pre-existing groups

Much self-directed action takes place in 'natural' or 'peer' groups, that is in groups that are not brought together by professionals. Groups of people with interests in common, such as groups of work colleagues, friendship groups and, as we will see in many examples in this book, groups that gravitate around an almost infinite variety of interests, activities and causes are a feature of everyday life. However, the professional practice of groupwork has tended to be biased in favour of groups that are artificially constructed to meet professionally defined purposes.

An example of where this 'top-down' tendency was avoided was in relation to the Ainsley Teenage Action Group (see Chapter 6). Here, a probation officer who received a number of individual referrals to prepare court reports on young people accused of offences that had all been committed on a particular housing estate (public housing scheme), recognized that these young people already constituted a natural friendship group that could be a source of mutual support and strength. He determined to work with the group of young people as a group instead of splitting them up and seeing them individually. A number of the groups we have drawn on for this edition have no 'professional' involvement. As mentioned in the last chapter, this may be a deliberate choice. No Limits Dementia, for example, say that professionals can be gatekeepers to services and are often one of the problems in people's lives and not seen as potential allies. They prefer to organize themselves and invite professionals to the group only when they think it would be useful.

Idea arising from members

Even where a group does not already exist, the idea may arise in the normal course of discussion with local people in a neighbourhood, young people in a class or users of services. Perhaps a problem appears to be particularly widespread in one district or with particular provision or, less specifically, a significant number of people have all mentioned the same worry or discontent. The practitioner's attention, or any other individual's attention, is drawn to the issue and they raise it with other people, seen during the normal course of professional practice or daily life. Gradually a picture emerges of an issue that is causing undue concern and that sufficient people feel motivated to tackle, to make it worthwhile to call a preliminary meeting. Potential members of a group put out feelers to others to gauge the level of interest in doing something about it. The facilitation task is to assist and participate in this process, to ease communication, perhaps to help in suggesting or providing a meeting place, and so on. It is not to determine the focus of intervention as an expert on other people's problems. Many self-run groups have started in this way, such as the UK Youth Climate Coalition (http://ukycc.org), Asian Pride, the Family Advocacy Network and No Limits Dementia.

Giving groups the space to come together

Some groups, particularly those associated with education (Berdan *et al.* 2006; Arches 2012), come about in a slightly different way. Groups of young people are already in a 'group' (e.g. a class or after-school provision) and teachers, students or volunteers present them with the opportunity to take part in a self-directed group and identify an issue if they choose to. The work of the University of Massachusetts (UMass) students with a group of high school students would fit into this model, where young people attending after-school provision were invited to identify issues of concern to them and address them using the self-directed groupwork process and principles (Arches 2012).

Student involvement in groupwork

While the place of groupwork on social work courses in the UK has weakened (Ward 2009), in other countries it is not uncommon for students to want, or to be required, to undertake some groupwork in a practice placement, as the above example shows (see also Johnson and Wilson 2011). Our expectation of students would be akin to our expectation of anyone else: that they should develop a clear value-base before launching into practice and that their work should flow from this. Joan Arches, of UMass, organizes an exciting and innovatory scheme whereby students undertaking service-learning classes participate in an outreach partnership with community organizations in a disadvantaged area of Boston, in which the students follow parallel processes in the classroom and in the community, applying theories of self-directed groupwork and wider social action (Arches 2012).

Goal-setting by the group

Leaving aside the question of the need to set goals, which any group needs to do, the issue of *who* sets the goals for the group forms one facet of the *People have the right to be heard and define the issues facing them* principle in the value-base set out in Chapter 3: that people must have control over their own agenda of action. It also brings us to the heart of open planning. Goals constitute the most crucial area of deliberation that must be undertaken by the participants themselves, with facilitation, as opposed to being pre-determined by group 'leaders' and imposed on members. Most groupworkers are accustomed to deciding the goals for a group in advance. Teachers and health professionals would also typically work in this way. Many practitioners are so used to setting goals in advance that they come to see this as inevitable and as necessary for the functioning of the group, otherwise why would anyone want to attend?

In fact, the experience of self-directed groupworkers has been that a shared area of oppression or of concern, and the wish to discuss it and see if any action is possible, are enough to bring potential members together. The facilitators obviously have an overarching purpose in involving themselves in supporting this to happen but this is the general one of supporting people to seek their own solutions to wider social problems. To go beyond this, into dictating detailed goals to the group, would take away the ownership of the group and its efforts from group members. Only the members have had the life experiences that legitimate their establishment of aims and priorities within the group. Our role is to facilitate them in this.

Not only must members formulate their own goals but the facilitators must actively accept these goals as their own and not merely appear to do so while in fact clinging to hidden agendas. Goals can take a good few meetings to emerge and hence take us beyond the proper content of this chapter, which concerns itself with planning for the work. There will, of course, be a process of discussion and negotiation within the group, once it is launched, in which the facilitators can participate to support the process but not to guide the outcome.

Non-selected membership with wide publicity

Open planning does not involve setting criteria for membership or taking referrals (Table 4.2). Potential members are simply invited along

Table 4.2   Membership

Disempowering	Empowering
Membership is restricted by referral and selection	Group is widely advertised and invitations are also dispersed by word of mouth; there is no selection
Members are deterred from joining because diversity, difference and equality issues are ignored	All potential members, whatever social differentiation they are subject to, are given clear signals that their experience in the group will not be oppressive
Members are limited by selection process	Numbers fluctuate, with no minimum group size
Closed membership imposed by practitioner	Open-ended membership
Compulsory membership	Voluntary membership, members can join or leave at any time

on the basis of a shared problem, or they see the group or project advertised, or someone tells them about it and they decide to go along and give it a try. There may be a two-stage process involved, in that a practitioner or other key individual may spread the idea of a potential group partly to see if there is likely to be any take-up for it. In responding positively, potential participants are indicating both their own interest and the viability and validity of the project itself. In this way, a new idea may be 'seeded' to see if it takes root.

Although members may have heard about the group initially through a professional – their social worker or health visitor or teacher, maybe – who has a significant involvement in their lives, they cannot be 'referred' as such; the group is merely suggested to them for their own consideration as a potentially useful or interesting idea. Whilst pre-meetings are not associated with any process of selection for a self-directed group, many self-directed groupworkers do, nevertheless, meet potential members individually before the group starts. What will be explored is that this will be *their* group or project in which they will meet others, or be with others they already know, who are facing similar problems to their own and that the groupworkers will only be there to help them discuss what form the problems take, which of them are experienced as the most severe, why these problems exist and how, as a group, they might choose to tackle them.

Ensuring open access: diversity of membership

As discussed in Chapter 2, oppression takes many forms and manifestations of which self-directed groupworkers need to be aware. We have long known what is needed to make a group inclusive: issues highlighted by Muston and Weinstein (1988) for ensuring open access and participation include composition of facilitator teams, external support to facilitators (consultancy), group content, early acknowledgement in the group of the mix of people in the group and the possibility of discriminatory behaviour (including inadvertent), challenging denial of prejudice by the members, working with distrust and negative feelings, and not using members with particular lived experiences as cultural experts. People will often be far readier to join a group in which they know they will find a perspective congruent to and in tune with their experiences and circumstances. Unless these intentions are flagged in advance, potential members are justified in having little confidence that the experience that they will have in the group will not be oppressive and may well see no point in subjecting themselves to attending. Other changes must include appropriate methods of outreach and publicity. These will include the use of locally-spoken languages, social media and alternative press and other forms of media developed by, or used by, the groupings we have mentioned, as well as community and faith-based groups to publicize meetings. This means, in other words, engaging with far wider sets of networks from those habitually used.

Open membership is not really 'open' if groups of people stay away. In order, for instance, to attract black, Asian and minority ethnic (BAME) members to a mixed group, not only will the facilitators need to think about the overall ethnic balance and avoid a tokenistic presence in ones or twos; they will also need to make it publicly clear that they have thought about and are prepared to act on issues of racism.

Potential women members may well have had bad experiences of social work and social care organizations that, for example, exploit them as unpaid carers or accuse and blame them for failing to maintain officially sanctioned standards as mothers. They may require proof that their experiences will be listened to and understood before they trust the group to meet their needs. The latter will always be far easier in an all-female environment, as many of the contributors to Cohen and Mullender's book show (Cohen and Mullender 2003). Pease's (2003) paper on pro-feminist practice also offers pointers that could be of great help, particularly coming from a male author, both in challenging male group members not to silence women and to facilitators in mixed groups not to let this happen.

The best form of proof that any group intends to provide an appropriate service is practical provision: access, mobility and communication aids, child-minding facilities, cover for responsibilities for dependants and so on.

Fluctuating group size

It is obviously not empowering to deny someone access to a group or project that is relevant to their life experience and that they are interested in joining. Yet, since encouraging their attendance means leaving membership unselected and open, the facilitators will later be faced with complete uncertainty about attendance at any particular meeting. The number of participants will inevitably fluctuate over time and there may be stages when it is very large. This can lead groupworkers into unfamiliar territory; their previous practice, or assumption if they are coming in anew, is likely to have given precedence to a narrow band of group membership ranging from three, or ideally from six, to 12 members (Northen and Kurland 2001; Zastrow 2009), a prescription that predominates in the literature on groupwork. Nevertheless, youth workers, community workers, and most people who operate in health, social care and educational settings will be used to dealing with larger numbers but not necessarily to involving them all in a process of change. Also practitioners may feel tempted to edge the group towards a size that feels safer and more familiar or to work with subgroups of the whole in the belief that this is the only workable option. Some writers see the tendency to sub-grouping in a larger group as positive: it can be used to sub-divide various tasks and activities (Brown 1992) and, according to Douglas (2000, p. 43), subgroups are where 'most of the new ideas and inspirations tend to come'.

Larger groups are treated with suspicion by many groupwork writers. For instance, Northen and Kurland (2001, pp. 136–137) write:

As the size of the group increases, each member has a large number of relationships to maintain. Each member not only has more other members to interact with but also responds to the dyadic and triadic relationships that have developed. There is less pressure to speak or perform and more opportunity to withdraw occasionally from active participation for silent reflection. Beyond the number of approximately 8 to 10, formality in leadership emerges and so do subgroups within the larger group. As groups increase in size, more communication tends to be directed towards the groupworker rather than towards members and to the group rather than to specific members. The larger the group, the greater the anonymity of the members and the greater the difficulty in achieving consensus in decision making. A larger group tends to have greater tolerance of domination by a leader, and the more active members tend to take over the discussion.

This statement serves to set in context some of the differences between conventional and self-directed groupwork. The picture presented here of group processes and of relationships with members is clearly not congruent with the values and principles of self-directed groupwork. We would regard the more extensive and complex relationships described to be rich opportunities rather than problems. Issues of individual member participation, member/member and member/facilitator interaction are the very stuff of skilled and sensitive facilitation: challenges that we intend that self-directed groupwork facilitators should be equipped to address successfully.

Preston-Shoot (2007) considers that members themselves may also find size problematic, fearing that in big groups freedom of expression can be threatened, reluctant members can hide and others remain uninvolved or under-involved in the group's task. On the other hand, there will be more experience and creative energy available. The latter reflects Brown's (1992) acknowledgement of the positives of higher numbers. For problem-solving, activity and 'open' groups, he says, larger groups provide more resources and can work well.

In self-directed contexts, no upper limit is set on attendance. It is not uncommon to find numbers in excess of 20, and 40 is not unheard of. The facilitators of large groups have to involve everyone in discussion and planning without resorting to formal committee structures that would be quite inappropriate. Youth Dreamers and Family Advocacy both speak of fluctuating attendance at group meetings, with some being easily in excess of 20 members attending but also sometimes just having three or four.

There is little assistance on groups of this dimension in the existing literature, which tends to be out of harmony with self-directed values and the orientation towards social action. Most is set in the discourse of the management, in particular the restructuring, of large organizations (see, for example, Bunker and Altan 2006, or psychotherapy in large institutions (Kreeger 1975 is the 'classic' on the topic) or the dynamics of crowds (see, for example, Schnapp and Tiews 2006). However, we would contend that there are particular techniques that can draw well-attended groups into discussions, which deliberately and safely involve everyone, thus allowing the group to benefit from the larger numbers present. These ways of working do not pander to the loudest voices but allow for differing views to be heard and result in the group's work being efficiently carried out. Family Advocacy often has well-attended meetings where people have much to contribute. The group has developed quite formal ways of starting its discussions to allow for this: each member can speak but they can only make a second contribution to the discussion when everyone else has had the opportunity to make their first contribution. The group has developed this rule and all members are responsible for ensuring they keep to it. In addition, there are exercises designed to raise a wide range of issues, such as brainstorming, and others aimed at sifting and prioritizing the resulting ideas and setting tasks arising from them, with games designed to help the group look at its own process. (Examples of all these may be found in the following chapters.)

At other times in self-directed contexts, when only a few members are present, it is important not to retreat into feeling that they represent a more 'authentic' small group and to treat them as if they were the whole group by letting them take fresh decisions in contravention of all the work done thus far. One way of holding on to what the large group has set as its priorities is to display its work to date recorded on flip charts, or on the 'smart boards' that are now found in many educational settings, or to use a laptop to record points and discussions that can be projected on to a wall for all to see at every meeting. However it is made, this record of the groupwork to date is kept to the forefront as representing the direction in which the group is aiming to move. The contribution and views of all are thus acknowledged and built on, even when not everyone attends.

Self-directed groups may go through periods of feeling that numbers have shrunk too far and may decide to re-publicize the group to attract more members. This can be done by members informally through their own networks when, for example, they bring their friends or neighbours along to the next meeting. Alternatively, a group may consider more formal advertising such as putting posters up in its usual meeting place, using its website or Facebook page to advertise activities and meetings, as did the Mosquito campaign, or it may advertise in the press.

Open membership

It is appropriate that members should opt in and out of self-directed groups as they feel able to make the commitment of their time or when they experience the issues at stake as touching on their own current concerns. This can be very positive for the group since success is closely tied to motivation. Someone whose attention is preoccupied with debts or domestic problems or who has simply moved on to other things, will not feel inclined to stay and give their best to the group, whereas others with a key contribution to make may respond to renewed publicity or be encouraged to join by remaining members.

Although Galinsky and Schopler (1985) long ago showed that, in practice, open groups are not uncommon, the majority of mainstream theorists on groupwork appear biased in favour of closed groups, in that a closed group seems to promote cohesion and trust and to provide security for members who initially are apprehensive or lacking in confidence. Yet Henry (1988) marshalled evidence that open groups do not become stuck because of the constant arrivals but pass progress on from generation to generation while retaining a central 'essence' of goals, norms and shared history. A core of the membership often remains involved over a long period, and new members, seeing that change is possible in the example of others who are at more advanced stages of action, recognize that change is possible because of what the *group* has achieved. More recently, Preston-Shoot (2007), drawing upon both Henry (1988) and Margot Breton (1991), has cited a range of other potential benefits for participants in open membership. Those that can be applied to self-directed groups include: people entering and leaving at their own pace; 'marginalized' populations gaining influence, respect and security; space being provided for people to learn and grow in different ways; and members keeping control over what and how they learn.

All these features are very typical of self-directed groupwork and so will be explored elsewhere in this book. If it is clearly built in from the beginning, we would maintain that a turn-over of membership can be well handled, by ensuring full discussion of the changes in the group and sharing responsibility between facilitators and members for handling the welcoming and leaving process. As regards the advent of new members, most open groups take this in their stride and welcome the potentially valuable contribution that new members may make to their collective efforts. An appropriate way of involving them can be through making a clear presentation of group goals and work achieved to date, with the proviso that new folk can certainly have a role in further shaping these.

It is true that a difficulty can arise if a group becomes rather 'cliquey' after a period when membership has remained unchanged and the facilitators will need to help the group look at this and maybe undertake some work with members on refreshing both aims and membership. Since members know why they themselves chose to join and why they have found the group useful, discussion will usually swiftly re-awaken the conviction that others facing similar difficulties should also have the option to join. The Youth Dreamers, for example, have been running for many years now and have a formal system for pairing 'seasoned' Youth Dreamers with 'fresh' Dreamers to support their induction into the group. There is a component of peer-teaching in pairs, as well as a sharing of skills, knowledge and experiences. However, they do find that more recent members who come to the Dream House, now it is set up and established, do not necessarily have the same level of ownership as those who worked so hard to get it.

In an open-ended model, departures will not be unexpected and the facilitators can enable full discussion of the feelings they evoke. If members have become important to one another, they can continue to meet outside the group. Only if anyone opts out of the group with bad feeling is the group likely to need to discuss their departure at length. Since we believe that members should not just 'disappear' under these circumstances and since their going can sometimes be a clear indication of barely submerged rumblings amongst members, here again, facilitators should encourage full discussion of what has happened.

Involuntary membership

No doubt members who are obliged to attend a group can, on occasions, find the experience empowering once they have made their own decision to opt into what the group is doing. The fact of compulsion itself, however, is normally profoundly disempowering and, if one is wishing to practise empowerment, it is necessary to seriously question the reason for it before creating such an initial stumbling-block.

Self-directed practice has been shown to be workable alongside mandatory involvement, however. Membership of a self-directed group is not precluded for those on orders made by the courts or those subject to compulsory monitoring or investigation provided that there is no actual or implied requirement that they will join *this* group. Groups have taken place successfully in schools (Berdan *et al.* 2006) and even in prisons (Badham 1989). The question of compulsion is of crucial importance in self-directed groupwork since the right to decide whether or not to participate is an essential feature of the practice principle: *People have the right to be heard and define the issues facing them* (Chapter 3).

So how can mandatory controls and voluntary membership be reconciled? There has been a long-standing debate in work with offenders, from Bottoms and McWilliams (1979) differentiating between constraint and coercion in their progressive 'paradigm' for probation practice, to the desistance model developed by McNeill (2006, see Chapter 2). Coercion, it is argued is unacceptable, whereas constraints exist in all situations in which people interact and real choice remains possible within them. A similar discussion in social work revolves around the notion of 'contract' and stretches from a classic paper by Maluccio and Marlow (1975) to contemporary work including that of Preston-Shoot (1989, 2007). Here again, even where legislation or statute limits people's rights and the freedom of welfare workers, argues Preston-Shoot, it is still possible to identify a degree of freedom to make choices including, in a groupwork context, 'to participate actively in devising and running a group, and to make an informed choice about membership' (1989, p. 44).

A court order or formal requirement provides a framework but, beyond this, the person who is subject to the order remains free to choose what arrangements to enter into, which may include receiving individual help or joining a group. In the Ainsley Teenage Action Group, for example, the probation officer who set up the group gave members the option of fulfilling the reporting requirement of their orders by attending the group. He made it clear that, should they withdraw from the group, their primary contract – the statutory order – would not be broken provided that they worked out an alternative arrangement for contact. Since subsequent withdrawal from attendance at the action group would not prejudice the conditions of the court order (which would remain in force), the existence of the order itself did not prevent potential group members from exercising a real choice.

Access

In the UK, equalities legislation in relation to disability (now incorporated into the Equality Act 2010) sets out clear requirements in relation to access in public places but, because there is much catching up to do and only finite resources are allocated at any one time, inadequate access continues to be an issue (Table 4.3). A recent report highlighted inadequate access to many government buildings, including:

> poor provision of disabled bays in the car park, difficulty gaining access through the front entrance, little (or no) disabled signage or even guidance to the organisation's offices and disabled toilets used for storage. (Benefits and Work 2008)

As this shows, the attempt by non-disabled people to anticipate the needs of disabled people can be very misleading and only a true process of consultation with disabled people themselves is genuinely reliable and empowering. It is not only those who try to attend the group or take part in the project or conference who are liable to be disempowered. Even more serious perhaps is the issue of those who never even try to attend because they assume their needs will not be met. It is one thing to seek a sign-language interpreter, a portable hearing loop or a scanner to transfer text into large print or Braille *after* the lack of suitable communication techniques has become glaringly obvious. It is quite

Table 4.3 Venue and access

Disempowering	Empowering
Stairs-only access	Lifts and accessible venue
No provision for childcare	Dependants' care for children and others
Communication obstacles	Induction loops, BSL interpreters
Office of formal agency	On groups' own territory or in an appropriate setting on neutral ground in members' own community
Members are transported in agency vehicles	Members make their own way or transport is unmarked

another to take appropriate advice beforehand and advertise the group as genuinely able to welcome everyone. It is necessary to announce publicly that this group is different from all the tired old disempowering practice.

The recognition of caring responsibilities

In just the same way, people with responsibilities for caring for dependants may automatically rule themselves out of meetings if no provision is made to meet their caring commitments. If their presence is excluded by practical obstacles, they may assume from this that they themselves are not wanted or are considered to have nothing to offer. Once again, the only truly empowering course is to consult potential members themselves as to their actual needs and to work with them to ensure their support needs are met. It should be recognized that childcare provision to enable a parent to attend is a collective responsibility, rather than an individual challenge to overcome, and that carers may be looking after vulnerable adults as well as children. Although there have been vast improvements in recent years, where care services are lacking, the self-directed group may first have to campaign to get appropriate support services provided, as opposed to simply finding out what exists and putting potential members in touch. This was indeed the focus of the SupportNet project in Nottingham, which worked with groups in the community to develop and campaign for local community-based services.

On the group's own territory ...

In so far as open planning means involving members in deciding what they want their group to be like, this can also be extended to choosing the most appropriate location for group meetings. They may, in fact, be indicating this through the places where they tend to congregate naturally, such as the members of a group of Asian students from a further education college who spent a lot of time in the library because their parents approved of it but they could still see their friends there. It can be patronising to assume without asking, however, that they are where they ideally want to be, as opposed to where they feel forced to be through lack of any alternative.

Young people, for example, are often out the streets or in a public open space of some kind and this can be the best place to make contact with them. We often give the example of a detached youth worker who was very skilled in self-directed groupwork techniques doing precisely this when he met a group of young people 'hanging around' on a housing estate. Wanting to encourage them to voice their own experiences of living on the estate, he proceeded to pull a piece of chalk out of his jacket pocket and to hold a 'brainstorming' session with them there and then, by writing on the paving stones. This led to the group negotiating for somewhere to meet. They had previously felt alienated from all the obvious possible meeting places, mostly commercial, once the local youth club had been shut down but it became a matter of considerable pride to book a room entirely for their own use in a community centre or, as others have done, in their own college or school.

Existing locations such as residential, day care and ward settings can be used to start a self-directed group. The use of self-directed groupwork in penal settings (Badham 1989) should remind us, however, that a group's everyday setting is not necessarily one in which people feel perfectly at ease. One way round this is to 'customize' the surroundings and make them feel more like the group's own territory. This can either be done just for group meetings if the prevailing climate is an unchangeably hostile or authoritarian one – by putting up the group's flip charts, for example, and re-arranging the furniture – or it may be a permanent adaptation, such as pressing for members to be allowed to choose the decoration in a centre.

… or on neutral territory in members' own community

When individuals are being brought together for the express purpose of starting a self-directed group and there is a completely open choice of venue, the initial one or two meetings should normally be held on 'neutral' territory, such as a community centre, away from professionals' normal workplaces if they are acting as facilitators. The preferred location of future meetings can be discussed with those members who come along at this initial stage. The setting must be appropriate for the type of group and they have to feel happy in it. A large, bare room may look uninviting to middle-class professionals but may feel ideal to a group of boisterous young people who do not want to be accused of damaging anything. Once again, we are emphasizing that no aspect of planning should unnecessarily be taken out of group members' hands. Ultimately some groups, such as the Ainsley group and the Youth Dreamers, are successful in creating their own space for meeting. According to the facilitator of Youth Dreamers, such 'youth created space is huge plus for ownership' (Berdan 2011).

Transport

It is not normally appropriate for transport to be provided to a self-directed group because it influences people to attend when they may not want to make the commitment or may have other priorities. It is questionable as to how far attendance remains truly voluntary when transport arrives without fail every week; it is easier to attend by default than to send the driver away. There would have to be some special reason to provide transport, for example, if members require accessible transport that is not publicly available. Even then, they may well be able to find their own community transport and book a place on it only when they choose to. The issue of stigmatizing labels on 'official' vehicles is an international one. State Wards (young people being looked after by the state) in New Zealand won their battle for the removal of identification words emblazoned down the side of Department of Social Welfare cars. The logos were replaced with small windscreen stickers for insurance purposes only.

Timing of meetings: who decides and for whose benefit?

Similar principles relate to the timing of meetings as to every other issue over which groupworkers have traditionally taken charge but in relation to which the self-directed approach advocates member involvement. The classic literature (Brown 1992) naturally regards discussing meeting times with members as desirable within many approaches to groupwork; we would not claim this as specific to our work. It is of particular

Table 4.4   Timing, frequency and overall number of meetings

Disempowering	Empowering
All fixed by the groupworker	All decided by agreement
Inconvenient, not taking into account other commitments and responsibilities	Mutually convenient

importance here, however, because it relates to the practice principle, *People have the right to be heard and define the issues facing them*, and to members choosing for themselves the kind of intervention they find acceptable and being in control of it.

Frequency of meetings

Once again, the frequency of meetings constitutes a feature that is not fixed in advance in self-directed groupwork. There is a tendency, in adult-led long-term groups, to assume that meetings will take place once a month, whilst fixed-term groups may well meet weekly. 'Weekly meetings dominate the groupwork scene' (Preston-Shoot, 2007, p. 89). In self-directed groups there is a far greater element of the members determining what feels right for them and what will best enable them to meet the group goals they have set.

RondsPoints is a self-directed group that takes place in a family centre, Famijeunes, in a disadvantaged district of Montreal, Canada. Here, the group, which has both open membership and open-ended length, holds scheduled meetings *every* weekday morning except Fridays and on some evenings, together with not infrequent extra events, for example, to watch the fixtures of the Montreal Canadians ice-hockey team on the TV. A playroom is provided for any children members may bring along and the parents organize themselves to help the authorized childcare worker. The schedule for meetings evolved on the demand of group members. Its flexibility, by allowing for domestic, work and other commitments, allows some 40 parents to be regular members of the group, many of whom attend several times each week. The group has successfully campaigned for the provision of social housing, in the face of rising house prices, and is currently opposing a major motorway development that would slash through their area. The group communicates to the surrounding community, besides of course through informal networks, by means of an entirely self-produced neighbourhood newsletter.

Open-ended length of group

Just as the number attending a self-directed group is not fixed in advance, so the facilitators need to learn not to pre-set the duration of time during which the group will meet. This is the case with the Ronds

Points group described above. It is not easy to move away from the kind of assumption in many professional settings and in the literature (e.g. Zastrow 2009) that has consistently come to associate small groups with a typically time-limited duration of six to 12 meetings. However, more practice has always been undertaken in groups of open-ended length than has commonly been recognized (Henry 1988), usually associated with open membership (Doel and Sawdon 1999; Steinberg 2004).

Often, time-spans are calculated according to the length of commitment groupworkers feel they can make, rather than the exigencies of the group itself:

> Arguably greater weight is often given to the constraints on group-workers, such as the length of student placements, other work commitments, and the duration for which they feel they can sustain commitment to the group, than to a structure related to group development or anticipated to be reasonable for adequate completion of the group's task. (Preston-Shoot 2007, p. 90)

Additionally, Preston-Shoot identifies organizational interests, such as throughput of work and the increasing adoption of off-the-shelf packaged group programmes with their rigid configuration of sessions. Also there is, for some, a fear that long-term groups encourage dependency (Northen and Kurland 2001). This focus on the short term is compounded by the unfortunate tendency to regard any form of 'self-help' activity as able to become member-led after a very short period of time (see Wilson 1995) so that, again, the pressure is towards practitioners' own involvement in the group lasting perhaps only a matter of weeks. In self-directed groupwork, group members themselves decide for how long they find the group to be serving a useful purpose, which frequently extends over a period of years until long-term goals for external change are achieved.

Groupworkers may hand the responsibility for facilitating the group and its work over to members themselves or, if more appropriate, after a time to colleagues, volunteers or community members (subject to the group's agreement). However, groupworkers should expect to be associated with the group for a good few months – and years are certainly conceivable as a number of examples will show. Kristina Berdan, the teacher working with the Youth Dreamers, has been supporting the group for over ten years and her role within the group has changed as the members have become adults and taken responsibility for many of the groupwork roles themselves. Such a long-term commitment makes a team of more than one facilitator especially desirable, so that sickness, leave and job and life changes can be covered. These workers need not all be from the same agency. The adults within the Youth Dreamers, for example, are teachers, parents, community activists and supporters, all with specialist skills that have been required by the group at different times.

The Three 'R's: Rules, Recording and Facilitator Roles

Once a group has come together, as well as the group members deciding for themselves whether they want to attend, making the planning decisions such as where and when to meet in future, and taking responsibility as a group for setting the group's goals, there are a number of other matters to be decided. Once again, they need to reflect maximum involvement of, and control by, group members.

Self-directed groupwork is grounded in the well-established notion of a *working agreement* (Brown 1992; Lizzio and Wilson 2001; Preston-Shoot 2007) between facilitators and members. In the earliest stages of a group's life, this agreement will focus on the facilitative rather than leadership nature of groupworkers' roles. The expectations of members on first joining the group will need to be explored and clarified, as would be the case with any method. It will need to be clear from the start that they will not be telling members what to do but will be handing the responsibility for decisions to them. In addition, the working agreement needs to cover any rules for the conduct of the group, including those relating to confidentiality – who 'owns' and records information about the group and its achievements – and the roles which groupworkers play in relation to those group members who are receiving individual help alongside group membership (including any with a compulsory component). These latter points can be summed up under the three 'R's of Rules, Recording, and Roles of groupworkers who are involved both in individual and in group work. Each will be discussed further below.

Rules

Whereas, in conventional groupwork, it may be appropriate to have rules imposed by groupworkers, rules and norms for the conduct of self-directed groups are collectively determined and recognized by the members, in ways the group itself decides, such as a majority vote or reaching a consensus view. Typical early examples of decisions the whole group can be encouraged to take together, and which can involve important lessons for members in working co-operatively, include choosing a name for the group – which also asserts the members' ownership of the group. Many groups quickly decide on a rule that chairing will be exercised in a non-hierarchical style and that it will rotate around the group. This gives everyone a chance to learn the skills involved and prevents control being vested too strongly with any one individual. Groups also need, early on, to establish their own statement to cover anti-oppressive aims in their working principles, since they will not automatically regard themselves as covered by those the facilitator team has agreed in its pre-planning phase. Issues concerning group decisions about who may join or who is asked to leave have already been touched on in earlier sections under membership. Decisions about control over any budget and spending decisions also need to be taken by the group as a whole. In the past, young people's groups encountered particular issues here, in not being trusted with public money by funders (Harrison 1982). However, this is now much more common-place with some initiatives, such as Youth Bank or Youth Opportunities funding, *only* giving grants to young people's groups. Nevertheless, many individuals or organizations may find the principles on which the group operates hard to understand and may continue to look to the groupworkers to exercise control.

Groups need to establish ways whereby everyone's contribution is valued and everyone has an equal right to participate fully in the meetings. Some participants will have strengths in carrying out tasks and others in studying and reflecting on group process. Status should not reside in how loudly people can shout. We have discerned much commonality in the rules created by groups. For example, both Family Advocacy and Youth Dreamers have the rule that only one person can speak at a time and both stress the importance of listening to each other and treating everyone in a respectful manner. The 'Rules in the Dream House' were created by the young people and are painted on the wall so that whenever someone comes in they can see them. It would, of course, have been perfectly possible for the facilitators to predict that such rules would be needed and to have delivered them to members as an expectation at the first meeting. This, however, would have established a 'them and us' feeling between facilitators and members and would have placed the former firmly in a leadership role. Had facilitators then gone on to say to members: 'This is your group and it is up to you to decide how you want to use it and what you want to achieve', the members would have had no reason to believe that this was actually how they intended to operate.

A group of young people who were being 'looked after' by the local social services and accommodated in residential homes had to tackle the issue of confidentiality between the group and the outside world. The residential staff felt somewhat threatened by the existence of the group and would sometimes 'pump' the young people for information as to what went on there. The group considered this situation and reached the view that they had a right to discuss in privacy matters that concerned them but that, at the same time, there was no point in unnecessarily fostering suspicion of the group's activities. As a result, the members decided that they needed a rule that the content of group sessions was confidential. Such freedom was absolutely essential if they were to have the necessary space to share their adverse experiences of the system of public care for young people and to reach decisions on how to tackle these. The facilitators regarded themselves as bound by exactly the same expectations. So as not to feel that they were being disloyal to individual social workers, however, the members decided to hold occasional 'open evenings' for their field and residential social workers at which the group's progress and plans could be reported on. In this way, the whole group would have a chance to plan what would be shared and how, and, at the same time, support could be enlisted for the group's continued existence from a group of significant adults. Whatever rules a group decide on, overall power resides in the group and not in the rules or the facilitators. Rules that prove problematic can always be changed.

Recording

Another issue that requires resolution at an early stage, and that is related to the above discussion, is the question of recording the group sessions. It is not normally appropriate in self-directed groups for the facilitators to make the usual assumption that they will keep their own record of sessions, for their own use and not to be shared with participants. It is more in keeping with the self-directed approach if either the facilitators maintain a record but share it with group members, in a way that makes it the property of the whole group, or the group members themselves act in this capacity. Members' lack of confidence in writing skills can be tackled by undertaking recording in pairs, for example, or using digital recorders (audio or flip-cameras).

Of course, group recording consists of more than minute-taking. At the simplest level an account only of who attended and the major events and decisions taken at that particular meeting would entirely omit group process from consideration and would also undersell the detail of the group content. What is to be recorded needs to be discussed and agreed in the group. This means that whoever is undertaking the recording, whether facilitator or member, will need to be helped to learn the skills involved in noting both what the group is doing and what it feels like to be in the group at that time. A useful list of points to look out for in group process is given by Douglas (2000). Although usually viewed as the province of professionals, we see no reason why group members should not become skilled in observing and noting group issues and developments. A classic model for recording developed in a self-directed group of young people who were not regularly attending school is set out in Figure 4.1.

Approaching recording in this way means that we would state categorically that it is not appropriate to keep personal files on the members of self-directed groups. The only time when this would happen would be when individual work was being undertaken alongside the groupwork and, in that instance, the file would relate to the latter and not to the member's 'performance' or behaviour in the group.

The uses to which group records may be put obviously include giving groupworkers and members a concrete reminder of what they have achieved. In addition to this, they are likely to be crucial in assembling

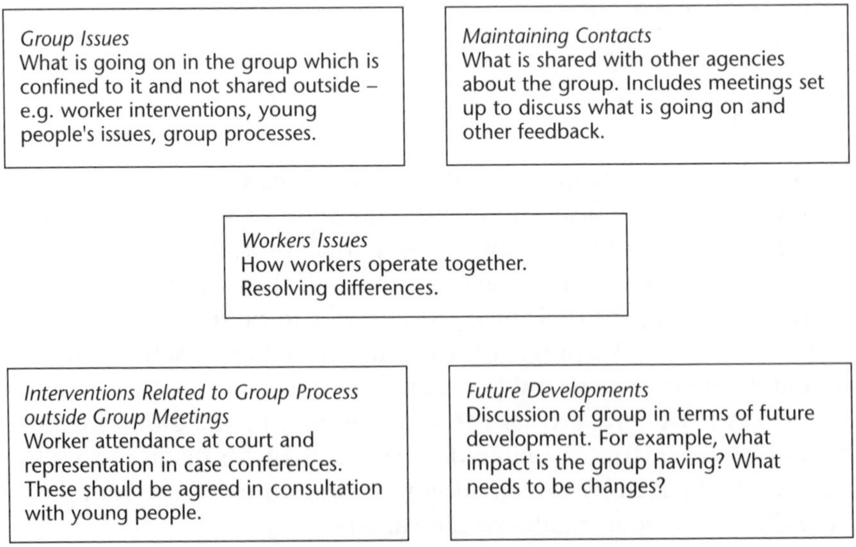

Group Issues
What is going on in the group which is confined to it and not shared outside – e.g. worker interventions, young people's issues, group processes.

Maintaining Contacts
What is shared with other agencies about the group. Includes meetings set up to discuss what is going on and other feedback.

Workers Issues
How workers operate together. Resolving differences.

Interventions Related to Group Process outside Group Meetings
Worker attendance at court and representation in case conferences. These should be agreed in consultation with young people.

Future Developments
Discussion of group in terms of future development. For example, what impact is the group having? What needs to be changes?

Figure 4.1 A model for group recording (Burley, 1982)

any funding bids for the group when it may be useful to back up statements like 'The group has given talks all over the country' with specific
details. Another essential purpose of recording, especially in a field that
is still being developed, as this one is, is to provide a basis for written
accounts of groupwork activity that may encourage others to take on
further work of this kind.

Recording frequently consists of more than a cursory running-record
of the group meetings and of any other meetings or conferences in
which the group is involved. We shall see, in Chapter 5, for instance,
how flip charts can be preserved from group exercises to serve as an 'art
gallery', or 'group memory', and to this we would add further variations,
such as a photographic or more elaborate exhibition on a group's work
to date and a newspaper cuttings collection or on-line folder if the group
has attracted considerable media and social media publicity.

Sometimes such materials are stored and only occasionally referred
back to, to boost group morale or remind the members of the goals and
tasks they have set themselves. Other groups may routinely use records
of the direction they have set and their achievements to date as a framework for their continuing efforts. The flip charts on which all the issues
and plans of action have been brainstormed and analysed, for example,
can usefully be retained and regularly displayed at meetings to form the
basis of subsequent work. The Ainsley Teenage Action Group always
took care to work in this way since they found it empowering to see all
their work as a progression towards a clear set of goals. The methods
used for recording have developed over time, as means of communication have changed. An early example of imaginative recording is
provided by Croft and Beresford (1987), in relation to a group of housing estate residents funded by a local Family Services Unit. They kept a
scrapbook in which anyone could write down their feelings, experiences
and ideas. Groups nowadays may take digital pictures of their hard copy
work and share these and other electronically created material (e.g.
reports), for example, in *google docs* or on a private or public self-created
web-site, such as *wordpress*, or by means of other such programmes.

Roles

Part of the process of negotiating a working agreement with the
members of a self-directed group consists of clarifying which matters it
is proper to bring to the group and which should be dealt with outside
of it. Brown and Caddick (1986, p. 101), in the first recorded response to

the emergent self-directed groupwork model, questioned how it 'incorporates the agency's goals in relation to individual behaviour', with particular reference to social control functions, and also 'whether there is a place within it for individual members to work at their own . . . personal matters perhaps of health, role change or relationship'. Unequivocally, we would answer that a groupworker using the self-directed model would not put any of these matters on the agenda in the group. Individual members themselves are, of course, always free to mention in a group meeting that they are due to appear in court again on Tuesday or have been excluded from school, or that a bruise on their child is being investigated or any other current concern, but this would be because it arose in the course of conversation and not in the expectation that the group would 'down tools' to focus on the matter, as might happen in a group that had a therapeutic purpose. When an individual problem arises spontaneously, it may well be discussed but is often a prelude for either facilitators or other members to refocus on the goals or tasks in hand. For example, in a group held in a penal setting, a number of people wanted to know about parole or visiting arrangements; answers to specific factual questions on these matters, as well as strong expressions of discontent by particular individuals, led into broader discussions of how to 'play the system' for an early release and of the unfairness of the 'system' overall (Badham 1989). What is not appropriate at such a time is for the groupworkers to move into an individualized perspective if it would be at odds with the overall goals of the group.

This is not to say, however, that individual needs are ignored, particularly in self-advocacy groups where it is the individual experience and a commitment to support each other that bring members together in the first place. On occasion, a facilitator does retain a continuing one-to-one professional relationship, sometimes on a mandatory footing, with a group member outside of the group. Where this is the case, it must be made clear to all group members that he or she (or the rest of the team) remains available to offer individual support to all members at times of difficulty. The probation officer who worked with the Ainsley Teenage Action Group left open the offer of individual contact for occasions like this. Some members did indeed ask to see him individually when they felt they needed to do so. As a group develops over time, however, members increasingly offer each other this support both inside and outside the group and, where they feel something to be beyond their scope, will often help the person concerned to seek appropriate sources of external help.

We would not deny that very many group members feel that their personal problems have eased, or that they have become more able or more motivated to tackle them, as a result of their membership of a self-directed group (Cohen and Mullender 2000; Arches and Fleming 2007). These benefits we refer to as 'secondary advantages' of membership of self-directed groups, even though they can, in fact, be at least as notable as the changes achieved through participating in a therapeutic group.

Conclusion

In this chapter we have begun to describe how the achievement of empowerment can be begun through the medium of open planning. What has emerged is that empowering values are demonstrated through a different kind of planning from the traditional, worker-led approach. Recognizing that people themselves have skills and abilities and particularly, that the self-directed model requires people to make decisions for themselves and to take full control of setting the goals for the work, ways have to be found to involve them as fully as possible right from the beginning. The conduct of the group, its recording and control of its resources, are also negotiated by facilitators and members together. The message to be conveyed is that the group belongs to its members right from the start.

For many group members, be they service users patients, students or community members, the degree of power they hold and learn to exercise in the group, in conjunction with the other group members, is their first experience of feeling in control of anything in their lives. Often, everything else, including previous involvement with them by professionals, has appeared to happen to them, or to be done to them, without their own volition and without their views on the matter even being sought or noticed to any great extent. Beginning successfully to assume some control, in and through the group, not only changes the way that others regard the group members, as negative labels are challenged, but also fundamentally alters their own perception of themselves. They slowly come to see themselves as people who have rights and they also gradually develop the skills to exercise those rights effectively. This is fundamental to the concept of empowerment.

The next three chapters will show group members continuing to exercise control, initially over setting the agenda for the group and then in taking action on their own behalf.

5

The Group Prepares to Take Action

The pre-planning and planning stages of the self-directed model, as presented in Chapters 3 and 4, have covered all the preparations for a groupwork process, including getting the participants together with the facilitators on the basis of a preliminary working agreement. This led on from the groupworkers' concern to clarify their own value positions and to translate these into practice through planning in partnership with group members.

The role of the groupworkers now becomes one of facilitating the group members themselves to move beyond joining the group into preparing to take action. This chapter will explore the nature of the techniques and skills that best achieve this. Although utilized selectively, the techniques we recommend are not peculiar to the self-directed approach. What is different here is that their use is imbued with the six underlying values or principles for practice that we set out in Chapter 3, just as is the planning process discussed in Chapter 4.

We will now demonstrate, as was outlined in the framework of the model in Chapter 1, that the facilitators' overall responsibility is to help members move through the steps of answering the questions WHAT?, WHY? and HOW?: that is, to assist the group in stating their problems (WHAT) and in arriving at their own analysis of those problems by comparing experiences and understandings (WHY), prior to deciding for themselves what priorities to set and considering what action to take to achieve their shared aim (HOW). At all times, the facilitators are active in creating a favourable environment for this step-by-step development: by maximizing group members' autonomy, stimulating their motivation, and in encouraging and supporting their own initiatives.

Let us remind ourselves how this stage was presented in Chapter 1:

Box 5.1: The Group Prepares to Take Action

The group is helped to explore the questions WHAT?, WHY? and HOW?

Step 5: The groupworkers facilitate the group in setting its own agenda of issues:
Asking the question – WHAT are the problems to be tackled?
Step 6: The groupworkers help the group to analyse the wider causes of these problems:
Asking the question – WHY do the problems exist?
Step 7: The groupworkers enable the group to decide what action needs to be taken, set priorities and allocate tasks:
Asking the question – HOW can we produce change?

In this stage, therefore, there is a critical movement from exploration, through understanding, to action. All three steps or phases are equally important but we place a special emphasis on the middle one – the WHY phase, simply because it is so often neglected by other authors and practitioners. They often neglect to ask the question WHY themselves and almost never encourage users of services to ask it. In order to emphasize its key place in self-directed work, the more complex understanding – which the WHY question is intended to strive towards – is incorporated as a basic principle of the approach, expressed as the following practice principle:

> *Injustice and oppression are complex issues rooted in social policy, the environment and the economy. Self-directed groupworkers understand that people may experience problems as individuals but these difficulties can be translated into common concerns.*

Practice should reflect this understanding. This principle signals the dangers inherent in moving too rapidly from considering WHAT is wrong to deciding HOW to take action to put it right, without pausing to ask WHY it was wrong in the first place. Such an over-hasty assessment often leads to the assumption that personal inadequacies can be treated as the root cause of most human suffering because it glosses over underlying social factors. There needs to be a vital middle stage that consists of people reflecting on, and coming to an understanding in social structural terms of WHY they face the problems that exist in their lives. Considering WHY an issue exists gives the group the opportunity to break away from perhaps narrow self-blame and to come up with new explanations for problems and ideas for tackling them.

Without this crucial WHY stage, the question HOW? leads to some extremely misleading answers; consideration of WHY is crucial so that any actions agreed upon will address the root causes and not just the symptoms of deeper problems. Participants in self-directed action could, for example, jump straight from the decision that WHAT is wrong is high unemployment to the view that HOW best to tackle it would be to limit immigration, if they did not pause to understand the national and international economic and social forces that create unemployment. Dealing with unemployment requires responses far wider than particular policies on the flow of labour and immigration that turn the spotlight on the victims of problems rather than on the root causes. It is not necessary to become experts on the workings of international economics to see that it may suit certain interests very well to have attention directed to a preoccupation over who gets the few jobs available instead of to budgetary policies that impact on the economic prosperity of the entire area. Similarly, turning to a group of young offenders where WHAT troubles them most is police harassment and lack of opportunities, the expected message from the authorities is that keeping their heads down and their noses clean constitutes HOW to rectify the problem. Yet the examples of the Ainsley Teenage Action Group and Youth Dreamers, given in the next chapter, show that entirely different solutions are possible.

We recognize that, without the question WHY and without the value-base to which it closely relates, it would actually be dangerous to offer this effective and more confident approach to practice that the self-directed model implies. If it were utilized to arrive at misleading answers, as demonstrated above, its impact would be more damaging than merely allowing other ways of working to continue undisturbed. The techniques and the values within the model must always, therefore, be taken together as a package and not disaggregated.

A New Respect and Other Benefits for Group Members

It is only the full and detailed consideration of WHY problems have actually come about, which may take weeks or months and, indeed, be returned to many times over the years in long-running groups, that will prevent people from selling themselves or other oppressed people short when it comes to taking appropriate action. The groupworkers' role in all this is to facilitate this delving deeper and deeper into the causes that underlie difficulties. Facilitators are likely to learn a good deal about themselves in the process, including that they should never underestimate the potential understanding of their peers or those with whom they work.

It is not only the WHY stage that gives a new insight into the hidden strengths of group members (recognizing the *People have skills, experience and understanding* principle). During the initial WHAT stage many group members have the shock of being asked, often for the first time, what they see as their own problems and, once they recognize that someone is actually listening to their answer, they rise readily to the challenge. Some may have engaged in the various forms of pseudo-participation that we discussed in Chapter 2. It is important that neither we nor participants are seduced by its empty rhetoric.

Enabling participants to use their voice (see the principle *People have the right to be heard and define the issues facing them*) and to find a combined confidence (see the principle concerning *Collective power*) frequently opens the flood-gates on pent-up resentments that need to be heard in full. At the same time, it reveals the frankness of expression and resilience against repeated set-backs and in some cases humiliation by those in power. This stage in the group is both humbling and uplifting. It gives one both joy and shame in shared humanity.

The HOW stage, too, during which there is a detailed consideration of all the various remedies to try and apply to the situation, aims to give people a sense of their own positive qualities and abilities, through discovering new responses to situations and developing the skills to deal with them. Instead of being content with everybody else 'blaming the victim' (Ryan 1971), this takes group members into the realm of social issues and opens up new and unanticipated options for action in the public sphere. It can also remove the pressure of self-blame from individuals within the group and offer them the chance to take action for themselves, with positive impact on their personal esteem. Participants gain still more because they value their own efforts, not just in terms of improved knowledge and skills, but also in terms of their activities having very practical benefits for themselves and others.

What we propose to do for the remainder of this chapter is to look in greater detail at the various elements of this stage: asking the questions WHAT?, WHY? and HOW? in preparation for TAKING ACTION on the issues that can emerge. We will examine how these steps might appear in practice and go on to consider some of the questions that arise for the practitioner. We will be drawing attention to a number of activities and exercises that can be used in non-oppressive ways (*Commitment to Social Justice*). We are not attempting to present a comprehensive list but will be outlining those we have found to be effective in our own practice or in that described to us by other self-directed groupworkers. It is notoriously difficult to acknowledge sources for any particular techniques that may now be presented in greatly modified form from the one first created. However, where possible, we will attempt to identify references that will lead readers naturally towards developing their own repertoire. Over the time we have been working, we have come across approaches that are developed and conceptualized well beyond simply recounting practical exercises and techniques. Many of these run comfortably alongside self-directed groupwork and can contribute in a complementary and congruent way to a Freire-inspired approach such as ours. All have been successfully used by the authors and facilitators of the examples in this book.

For example, they can be found in literature on Training for Transformation (Hope and Timmel 1999), Dynamix (2002), narrative therapy (Vodde and Gallant 2002), critical reflection (White *et al.* 2006), Socratic dialogue (University of Wollongong 2006, Pullen Sansfaçon 2010), critical learning (Jones 2009), Appreciative Inquiry (Bellinger and Elliott 2011), the Art of Hosting (http://www.artofhosting.org), Circle Practice (http://www.peerspirit.com) and Open Space Technology (http://www.openspaceworld.org). In recent years, some publications based within the self-directed or social action approach have been produced that include useful exercises to be used within the self-directed process. These include the 'considerations and activities for group building and developing focus' (Fleming 2004), *Act by Right* (Badham 2004, with its accompanying website), 'Stuff You Can Try' section in *Writing for a Change* (Berdan *et al.* 2006) and *Leading for the Future* (Farrow *et al.* 2011). However, this list is not comprehensive, nor should it be considered to be prescriptive. Facilitators need to work at developing their own repertoire for the various stages of the model.

Asking the Question WHAT?

The first area of activity, once the initial working agreement has been reached between facilitators and participants (the point we reached at the end of Chapter 4), is for the group to begin its search for collectively agreed goals. The facilitators' first priority is to find ways of working that will help participants express all the concerns that are uppermost in their lives so they can go on to set their own agenda of issues. This is what we refer to as 'Asking the question WHAT?'

Techniques Used to Elicit, Discuss and 'Own' Participants' Views

Brainstorming is a common technique and a classic one in self-directed groups, particularly at this early stage of needing to encourage the free expression of hitherto unvoiced views. Most people are now very familiar with brainstorming as a way of working, both in practice and in education. However, we give a detailed explanation here to illustrate how well it fits within the self-directed model. Brainstorming consists of posing a straightforward question or presenting a topic to the group and simply recording all the responses that are forthcoming so that everyone present can see what is being written. There is no discussion of the ideas as they are recorded; members simply state or shout out their own immediate reactions, for a set period of time or until they are exhausted, and are discouraged from reacting to other people's contributions at this stage. Some practitioners stop at this juncture but they are missing the main aim of the exercise.

The second stage of the brainstorm is to discuss all the points members have listed, in a search for linking themes and common threads, so that what at first looks like a completely chaotic jumble begins to take on a definable shape. Again, group members are encouraged to express and compare their own ideas, opinions and experiences; these are not filtered out by the facilitators on the basis of age, status, or loudness, for example.

The skills required by the facilitators at both stages of a brainstorming exercise include those of eliciting comments, recording them accurately but succinctly, and 'spotting' what is only hesitantly forthcoming. Here it is useful for one or more of the facilitators to sit amongst the group and to pick up any 'mutterings', so as to be able to draw out the contributions and encourage the most reticent to participate (see Foucault 1978 on silenced voices). As groups develop, group members themselves will be able to act in the recorder or 'rapporteur' role, and some will be able to do this straightaway. The other roles, too, may be taken by group members where appropriate but usually at the expense of that person's full contribution to the ideas that are forthcoming.

Both the recording of ideas (which can be done as words or pictures) and the subsequent work to sort them into groupings can be done on flip-charts or on a blackboard or whiteboard if one is available. An interactive whiteboard makes the record permanent, even more so than it would be on a flip-chart. More imaginatively, as was mentioned in Chapter 4, we have come across the brainstorming technique being used in a totally impromptu way with a natural group of young people on a street corner by a detached youth worker. As previously mentioned, he wrote down what they said were the problems facing them on their estate in chalk on the paving slabs in front of them. More recently we have come across a street worker in Canada who uses an electronic tablet for the same purpose. All discussion exercises should ideally be recorded in some way so that the material they produce will be available to the group whenever it is needed. Digital photographs of drawings and charts can be taken and easily uploaded onto private or open websites and, through constantly evolving and developing software programmes, can provide accountability and also act both as an immediate and permanent record of events.

There are other reasons why brainstorming is a very useful technique at the earliest stages of a group. Individual members are not in undue focus and thus it helps them come to feel at home in the group and has the effect of drawing people together. A number of conditions have been found to assist this to happen:

- suspended judgement on ideas proffered, with no criticism;
- freewheeling, with no limit on the type of ideas – in fact, often the 'strangest' ones can lead the group in new and rewarding directions;
- as many ideas as possible, the more the better;
- cross-fertilization, through ideas being combined and improved in the second stage of the exercise.

A simple framework for forward planning can be introduced on the basis of 'likes'/'dislikes' or 'good and bad' aspects. This was adapted in a group of young people using mental health services into 'snakes and ladders' where the snakes were the downs and the ladders the ups of their experiences of services. Snakes included 'being misunderstood', 'changing psychiatrist every six months', 'taking way too long to get help', whilst ladders (of which there were far fewer) included 'treating me as an individual', 'involving my friend and partner' and seeing 'me as a person not just my eating disorder' (Young Minds 2011, p. 10).

Perhaps no other exercise can occupy quite the place in self-directed work that is accorded to brainstorming, with its opportunities for all group members to participate and its drawing out of so many spontaneous but normally unspoken feelings and views but there are certainly many other techniques that are employed.

Art gallery

Flip-charts are still frequently used in self-directed groups; however, other ways of creating and recording information are used as well, such as the snakes and ladders example above. The Young Minds group also used graffiti boards, Post-it labels, drawings (for example of the 'Ideal Specimen', see Berdan 2006, p. 142), blogging, Twitter and other ways to collect people's views and experiences to address the question 'WHAT are your issues and concerns as users of mental health services?'.

All these techniques produce material that invariably becomes key in later sessions of the group so they should never be lightly discarded. This 'harvesting' of ideas captures the wisdom in the group and can be used to create a tangible collective memory, seeing patterns, making meaning and making this meaning visible and accessible (Fleming 2010, p. 26). Flipcharts and other collected material, like Post-it notes on large sheets, can be displayed on the walls of the group's meeting-room at the start of every session, websites can be set up, newsletters produced and shared. In the short term, this provides concrete illustrative material to remind everyone what the group is working on. Having a visual record enlivens and speeds up the discussion by allowing the group to capitalize on, and to take responsibility for, work achieved so far.

The material produced is recognized as the common property of the group, binding people together through an open, visual history of a campaign. This gives group members a sense of movement in their work and also provides a symbolic focal point with which members can identify. It becomes the group's heritage, a focus for group identity, cohesion and continuity. Crucially, it is also available as a foundation for moving the group on beyond the WHAT stage into asking the questions, 'WHY do these problems confront us and HOW do we intend to tackle them?'

Photographs, films and videos

Fink (2012, p. 45) views visual methods as offering 'creative and participatory opportunities to generate locally produced knowledge about the connectedness of the lived and structural elements of urban life'. Visual representations of ideas draw on different ways of knowing and are particularly useful for group members with specific (e.g. dyslexia) or more severe learning difficulties, or who lack formal schooling. There is a range of graphic methods that let people *show* rather than *tell* about their lives (Richards 2011). Such methods have been used by the Dementia No Limits group, for example, who, through drawing, painting and film, have conveyed to others what their lives are like and the issues they wish to highlight and change within them.

It is often possible to initiate fruitful discussion in a group by showing photographs and pre-recorded material that focuses on similar social problems to those that confront the members themselves. Both documentaries and fictional works with social content may be used. YouTube, photo-sharing sites and other digital media can be a good source of such material in the public domain. Provided that due attention is paid to any copyright issues, material that has been commercially produced for television may be particularly good because it is usually digestible, highly visual, and may already be familiar from members' own viewing. As well as the obvious documentaries, even material from chat-shows and 'soaps' can be used if it comments on a relevant issue such as the position of women (How did this female celebrity make it to the top? Were obstacles placed in her way?) or a topical social issue. Media representation of disabled people or older people (for example, 'Who plays the parts?') may be clearly seen in popular programmes.

The disadvantage of existing material is that there is never a complete fit between what is seen on the screen and group members' own lived experience. It can only ever constitute a jumping-off point. In addition, the potential themes for discussion may crowd in upon one another so that it is hard to retain them all in mind until the end of a programme, unless one is prepared to make liberal use of the pause button. On the other hand, seeing a familiar programme in the unfamiliar setting of the group may inject it with sufficient 'surprise' element to awaken renewed interest, whilst retaining feelings of 'safety' and of everyday relevance in relation to content.

Statement cards

A simple exercise that brings out a richness of material for discussion involves the use of index cards, pieces of paper or Post-it labels. Statements are written on these by the group members (with assistance if writing is a problem). They each write down their own ideas – for example on what they see as the chief problems facing them – one idea on each of five cards. These are then pooled, shuffled and laid out face-upwards in a big space on the floor, or on a large table. Members are asked to read them and to take out three cards, not their own, expressing ideas with which they agree.

The whole group is then asked to find common themes amongst the cards they have chosen, initially by finding someone else who has a card similar to one of theirs and laying both together on the table. Other people can then add cards that match the emerging topics. Discussion opens up across the group around themes that do and don't link up, and around similar and opposing selections of cards. The cards that were not taken up can be drawn into this and, in practice, usually find a place on one of the piles which have been formed.

The facilitators may or may not need to help participants to go and ask what cards other people have drawn and to spot common themes until they get the idea for themselves. They also need to concentrate on noticing and, where appropriate, highlighting to the whole group issues both of content and of process. Content issues include those points on which all or most people agree, and those on which there is the most dissension. From this, members can identify shared interests and matters on which it is possible to move forward straightaway. This is particularly useful where a group has previously been bogged down in disagreement over petty detail and has been oblivious to whole other areas of agreement. Group process issues include members' ability to consult one another increasingly freely as the exercise progresses, to 'hear' the various angles on an argument more effectively and to enjoy the feeling of the whole group beginning to gel together.

The exercise does demand that members should be able to read and have some rudimentary writing skills, as well as being reasonably articulate and able to listen. It is, of course, useful in helping them to develop the skills of offering their own views and listening to one another. In another, more complex variation of the game, the cards are not laid out but are dealt, face down, to the players with a central pile left over, also placed face down. Players then have to decide which of the cards they have been dealt they happen to agree with and which they want to exchange. This involves making quite fine distinctions as to the acceptability of a particular way of phrasing one's own views and assessing whether what one holds in the hand is 'near enough' or should be risked for something still closer. The parallels with real-life negotiating skills are obvious.

In our experience, all groups can find it extremely useful to move away from pure discussion into activities that are fun but which sharpen the clarity of the debate. It is important that all groups, of whatever age, should be enjoyable to belong to as well as having a more serious side. We have used the technique frequently in consultancies and training events as well as in group and project work. The final arrangement can be photographed, typed up or be taped together and afterwards displayed.

The statement-card exercise can also be used in the HOW stage of a group for focusing on what different participants want to do about an issue.

Film poster

Here, group members in small groups imagine that a film is being made of their lives. Group members need to think about what is going on in their lives, both the positive and the negative things. What makes them angry or happy, cross or frustrated? What would be in this film? Once they have discussed this, they go on to think about how to create a poster advertising this imaginary film that would represent the things they have been discussing. Working together, they create a poster advertising the film about their lives. Other than the title they give to their film, the poster should have no words but be made up of a drawing. When all the groups have finished, they display their posters and consider each one in turn. The group that has created the poster are asked to stay silent, while the others discuss what they see in it. Someone is delegated to make a list of the things they say; everything that is said is valid and recorded. Once the first poster has been fully discussed, the group moves on to consider the next and so on. The list created from the discussion of the posters is a list of problems and issues the group members face and can form an agenda for further discussion.

It can be important to reassure people this is not an artistic competition, since many people are not used to expressing themselves in drawing. Nevertheless, it can help articulate aspects of their lives in a different way. This happened when the 'Movie Poster' (Berdan *et al.* 2006, p. 121) was used in the early days of the Youth Dreamers to help young people express what was going on in their lives.

Concluding comments on exercises for the WHAT stage of the process

Inevitably these exercises do not reflect the full range of possibilities for asking the question WHAT? However, they are ones that we ourselves and close colleagues have come to use again and again. In talking to other groupworkers who have sought to develop groups that seek to empower their participants, we have found expressions of frustration that the standard 'games' texts provide little for the early stages of a group beyond 'icebreaking' and 'group-building' exercises. These are often based around constructed or fantasy scenarios; they de-contextualize practice from the real world of group members and, thereby, establish the groupworkers too strongly as directors of the tone, agenda and activities in the group.

The exercises we have described are of proven effectiveness both in breaking the ice and in building the group and they do this through focusing on participants' lived experience. They get straight to the heart of what most concerns group members and, consequently, keep the emphasis on their words, their priorities and their choices. The groupworkers are facilitators and enablers of the activities and the discussion. They do not impose their own topics or insert their own ideas. Every single group member is involved and the facilitators' skill can be used in drawing everyone in: ensuring that quieter members, someone who stammers or another who mentions the things others would like to ignore, are not overlooked or rejected by the rest of the group. The facilitators also need to select exercises that match the abilities of the group, without underestimating these, and that catch people's interest and willingness to engage.

Asking the Question WHY?

As was pointed out earlier in this chapter, working with group members to analyse WHY the issues they have identified exist is the distinctive feature of practice that seeks to facilitate empowerment. Without it, there can be no awareness of wider-scale oppression, no moving beyond blaming oneself for one's problems into greater awareness and the pursuit of social change. To jump straight from identifying WHAT is wrong into the practicalities (the HOW) of achieving change would be to collude with a process in which explanations of the responsibility for problems are usually sought in the private world around individual and family because, in professional situations, this may actually reflect the extent of the practitioner's own understanding or appear to make intervention more feasible or it may accord with the prevailing political or policy landscape. To ask the question WHY? brings social issues into play and opens up new options for action in the public world. It represents the application of the values of empowerment (see Chapters 1 to 3) in practice.

Whether, and how, the question WHY? is asked has its roots in the way facilitators frame their questions and responses during the WHAT phase, as well as in the ways they carry these forward into the kind of discussion that will be outlined in this section. How such framing takes place depends on the assumptions and values that facilitators bring to their work. It is for this reason that the exploration of values was stressed as an inescapable aspect of the first stage of the model. It remains so here, 'You really have to believe in the principles, or it is an empty process' (Berdan *et al.* 2006, p. 95). Asking the question WHY? puts oppression firmly on the agenda and requires that special and subtle attention be paid to the principle regarding tackling oppression: *Commitment to social justice*. Working for social change means systematically dismantling the interlocking systems of oppression, an objective marked out by Mullaly (2010, p. 217) as a key feature of anti-oppressive practice.

We will now move on to looking at some particular techniques that help to raise the question WHY? and hence can help to establish a clear anti-oppressive perspective.

Consciousness-raising

One of the techniques that tends to lead automatically from WHAT into WHY is consciousness-raising. As argued in our opening chapter, the process of consciousness-raising or 'problematization', to use Freire's terminology, is a key aspect of empowerment.

The term consciousness-raising is inextricably connected with the women's liberation movement (DuPlessis and Snitow 2007; Napikoski 2011). In this context, groups of women sat in a circle and spoke in turn about the everyday circumstances and events of their lives. No one remained silent; no one interrupted or passed comment. This made it possible to share things that would have seemed inconsequential or wrong-headed in other, notably male, company. Through this exercise, women learned to recognize and to value their own and each other's experiences and, in turn, to voice these more freely. Gradually, it emerged that women had in common the same feelings of drudgery, duty, guilt, inadequacy and anger at housework, at sole responsibility for child-rearing, and at being taken for granted or abused by men. Issues that individuals had not previously even recognized as such – like who performed tasks in the home or how men assumed women to be stupid and unreliable – were heard repeatedly until the conclusion became inescapable that they affected all women, from all backgrounds. They could not be attributable any longer to individual failings on the part of those women. It was the fundamental relationships between men and women and women's own valuation of themselves that needed to change. In this way, women reframed what really mattered to women under the phrase 'the personal is political' (Hanisch 1969 and 2006).

Similarly, the raised awareness of the Black consciousness movement confronted and reversed the negative valuation of the dominant white society through the slogan 'Black is beautiful'. Likewise, increasing awareness of and militancy against the orthodoxies of the 'medical model of disability' (Oliver 1990) among people with physical impairments and learning difficulties led to the adoption of the 'social model of disability' as a key aspect of campaigns for equal rights to positive experiences and full participation in society. Disabled people were fed up with systemic barriers, negative attitudes and their exclusion from mainstream society that they experienced as the norm.

An example is provided by Family Advocacy Network, a self-directed group in which members are service users and/or carers of, for example, disabled people or people with learning difficulties. Whilst they do pair people with an individual peer advocate with similar experiences/problems, most of their work is done in group sessions. Commonality of experience is really important. For example, one member had cared for his parents with dementia and had found he was fighting lots of mini-battles to get past 'All the people who say "No!"'. He could see others struggling with precisely the same things. The group started informally with people sharing knowledge and experience, for example, of having been to a tribunal, of helping others prepare themselves or of going with them to the meeting. At the group sessions, a member presents their problem or issue or a particular challenge they are facing; then the other group members can speak about it, drawing on their own experience to advise and offer insights. Recognizing the solidarity of others with similar experiences can be uplifting. They have built friendship and support networks through the group which, as well as relieving isolation, have fostered self-confidence, self-esteem and self-awareness. The discussions in the group help members understand that others face the same kinds of problems and obstacles as they did; they recognize the general social oppression of people such as themselves and their own potential power and ability to have control over their lives.

This experience is shared by all oppressed groups, when they come together:

It is great to have a disability community. People in that community know exactly what I am talking about when I say I was called a 'retard' at school. They know because they were called it too. People without disabilities may not understand that because they have never experienced that label. (Jennifer Stewart, Action Hall member, in Calhoun *et al.* 2011, p. 45)

In practice, for facilitators, be they peers or health and social care professionals, to help groups achieve this shared movement from naming private troubles to recognizing shared problems and their structural causes means basing their style of intervention firmly on the principle that recognizes that all members already have skills, understanding and ability. Groupworkers need to develop a non-patronising approach based on the belief that people already know and understand many of the issues surrounding the reality of their lives. They also need techniques for encouraging group members to ask themselves the broader questions. Provided they can do this, health and social care professionals can have a particular contribution to make.

Techniques used to ask the question WHY?

Specifically, at this stage those responsible for facilitation should see that topics come from the group and are kept in play long enough for broader understanding to develop. Just as the brainstorming and other exercises asking the question WHAT? had this purpose, so the ideas which were forthcoming then should now be handed back to the group in a *'problem-posing'* way (Freire 1972) in order for the group to gain more awareness of the total issue. Hope and Timmel (1999) offer the 'But Why?' method. It is an exercise we have found can be readily adapted to any situation or group (Berdan *et al.* 2006, pp. 127–131).

> 'The child has a septic foot.'
> 'But why?'
> 'Because she stepped on a thorn.'
> 'But why?'
> 'Because she had no shoes.'
> 'But why has she no shoes?'
> 'Because her father cannot afford to buy her any.'
> 'But why can he not afford to buy her shoes?'
> 'Because he is paid very little as a farm labourer.'
> 'But why is he paid so little?'
> 'Because the farm labourers have no union.'
> (ibid., p. 79)

Example of asking the question WHY?

Introducing the question WHY?, though the answers may not always extend to global understanding, does consistently widen the areas of concern and potential action that members will identify and hence makes a major difference to the work of anyone involved with a self-directed group. The analysis of group members will extend to external forces and their view of the relevant and the possible, moving out from personal problems to give access to public issues, provided the group-worker facilitates rather than blocks this wider thinking (Berman-Rossi and Kelly 2004). It is important to note that some groups can find this key stage challenging and facilitators need to take care that group members do not become frustrated, leading to feelings of, 'Well, I don't know, do I?'. Once they get the hang of it, asking the question WHY? is a technique that groups often return to of their own volition, time and time again.

The way this can unfold can be encapsulated in an example from the work of the University of Massachusetts students with middle-school pupils. The account is in the words of the UMass Professor and some of her students about undertaking the WHY stage in considering violence in the young people's lives:

When talking with the young people about their lives, community violence and violence in the community have been identified as a significant issue. They have done quite a lot of work on the WHY piece of this, for example, producing a web chart that includes things like racism, competition, unemployment, power.

We spent a day doing a violence poster. It is really important not to rush the process, you need to be flexible and make sure all the voices are heard. The youth did an amazing job with it. We spent a really good session identifying all the factors that contribute to violence. The level of analysis was incredible. They did a free association and named all the things they could think of that caused violence. They wrote down or drew the all ideas/factors on a big piece of poster board. These included:

- drugs/alcohol
- racism
- unemployment
- poverty
- war

- militarism
- homelessness
- domestic violence
- inequality
- lack of hope
- depression
- gangs
- stress
- family break-ups

The youth then drew arrows showing how the different issues were connected and the middle school students explained the connections. All the youth added to the discussion and analysis. The explanations were incisive, and the youth seemed to recognize the cycle of one form of violence causing another, which only reinforces the first form, and so on.

Then we went on in the following sessions to follow up with a picture exercise to have another way of understanding the causes and creating an opportunity for the group to consider the causes of violence in their community even more deeply. We drew a big tree on poster board and cut out lots of leaves from green construction paper. We put tape on the back of the leaves and the youth filled out factors of BUT WHY? to put on the leaves, and taped them to the tree, starting on the top with each round of getting more at causes as we got closer to the roots.

Rather than rigidly going through and creating a poster and tree, our facilitation allowed the youth to express verbally answers to that BUT WHY? question, while using a prop (the poster and tree) to illustrate them and at the same time truly feel their authority over a topic of violence that is felt so acutely in their lives. The BUT WHY? conversation was authentic and formative in our work; the youth showed great knowledge of what is going on in the world and why things are, and how they could be. The conversation became a touchstone throughout the year. I believe taking part in that conversation, the experience of their authority, empowered the youth. There were ripple effects of the BUT WHY? conversation that the youth can still feel and act on today. Asking BUT WHY? led them to want to ask the same of their peers. And so they piloted a survey to find out the views of a wider group of youth. (compiled from material provided by Arches, Boates, Patel and Smith of UMass)

Another example is when a group of older and younger disabled people came together to campaign against discrimination in employment and the lack of employment opportunities for disabled people. The groups met together, facilitated by a practitioner experienced in self-directed groupwork with whom they had had a long association, to analyze the reasons for their frustrations. The facilitator suggested the 'BUT WHY?' exercise. The issue: 'Despite the legislative changes in recent years, disabled people are still discriminated against in the employment market' was written in the centre of a piece of flip-chart paper and the group then created a number of 'threads' of analysis, coming from the central issue, like a mind map. For example:

Despite the legislative changes in recent years, disabled people are still discriminated against in the employment market: But why?
Because employers are still filled with prejudice.
But why?
Because people's opinion is not changed by legislation.
But why?
Because they are subject to other influences.
But why?
Because most images in media focus on health, beauty, youth, etc. Where are the disabled people?
But why?
Because they want to promote unrealistic aspirations.
But why?
Because they want to make money.
But why?
So they can realize their own aspirations at our expense.

A further strand was:

Despite the legislative changes in recent years, disabled people are still discriminated against in the employment market: But why?
We can't always do the jobs.
But why?
Because we don't have the experience.
But why?
Because we are not encouraged to enter many fields and gain qualifications when at school.
But why?
Because teachers are subject to the same influences and have many of

the same prejudices as everybody else.
But why?
Because nobody educates them about this.
But why?
Because they need to learn so many other things to do their job prop-
erly. (example provided by Ian Boulton)

The last line could equally have started with: 'because we lack influence
over the teacher training curriculum and ...'

The group continued with their analysis until all their ideas and
understanding were out on the paper and then used this to identify
points at which they could intervene to start to address the issue of lack
of opportunities for work for disabled people in the area.

The role which all of this indicates for facilitators is one of fostering
and building up a 'dialogue' (Freire 1972): a process of mutual learning
among and with group members. This means threading a way through
the maze of information, experience and feelings which all participants
bring, in order to find broad themes and to keep the flow of discussion
and action going. Hope and Timmel (1999, p. 21) illustrate this as shown
in Figure 5.1.

Problem-posing, asking the question WHY?, involves probing questions of which 'BUT WHY?' is just an opener. Further questions can help
to dig below the surface. These could include: Whose interests are
served? What are the factors influencing this situation? What else is
going on? How are these factors connected to each other? In particular,
the political, economic and social forces should be analysed in detail:
who benefits from the status quo?, who loses out? and in what ways?

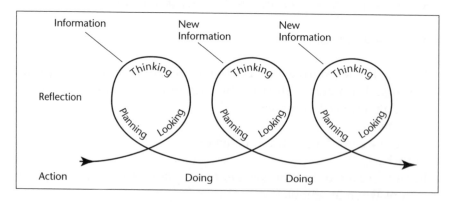

Figure 5.1   The Information–Action–Reflection Cycle (Hope and
             Timmel, 1991)

How do all these things link up? One way of seeing this is as a process in the course of which the layers of a problem or issue are unravelled in a manner similar to unpeeling the skins of an onion until the 'core' is reached (Badham 2004, pp. 45–46). It is on this analysis that action for change will later be based. The single most effective question is 'who holds the power?'

Another exercise that has been frequently used in groups described in this book, to uncover and explore opinions as to the causes of problems, is the 'Four Faces' exercise (Berdan *et al.* 2006, pp. 124–126). In this exercise, the facilitator or group members create a series of five or six controversial statements from listening to the discussions in the group around the issues they have identified. For example, when working with a group of young people some of the statements were: 'Adults need to listen to us if services are to get better', 'Things were better when your mum and dad were young.' Four faces are drawn on to paper – one very happy, one quite happy, one quite unhappy and one very unhappy and each is placed in a separate corner of the room. The statements are read out in turn and each time people move over to the expression that best reflects their level of agreement with it. People gather at the expressions and discuss amongst themselves why they have that opinion and prepare what they are going to say to the other groups. Those standing at each face tell the others why they have chosen this position before the groups in the separate corners debate and discuss the issues and ideas behind each position. The debate can get very lively, and indeed heated, and care may need to be taken to ensure that the discussion is about airing and exploring opinions, not creating conflict (see http://www.right-space.org.uk/content/accountability-nottingham-children-and-young-peoples-trust for a video of the Four Faces exercise and other aspects of the self-directed process).

The result of asking WHY? and asking power-related questions is that people build a picture of the wider social system, on a local, national or international scale, focused around their own place in it. They can then discuss how it is maintained in this form, what needs to change and what can be done to achieve this. The strengths of problem-posing are not simply its simplicity as a technique but also the complexity and inter-relatedness of the resulting analysis, the graphic and comprehensible form in which this emerges and the affirmation that groups can conduct their own structural analysis. There is the added benefit of developing group control over process.

Problem-posing offers an appropriately empowering methodology for an empowering message and does so by starting from participants' own experiences. It is cooperative and hence helps people to arrive at a collective analysis of their own situation. There are often low points when participants see how many powerful forces they have identified as being ranged against them. With facilitation, however, this can also be a turning-point, provided the facilitator has ensured that resources and strengths have been included in the picture in addition to all the problems. Positive features to be highlighted can include networks, friends, allies, people's own strengths and motivations, past successes of the group, other individuals and groups affected by the same negative social forces, and so on. These can all be called on when it comes to planning how to fight back. The facilitator needs group process skills, often shared with the group, not only to read the overall emotional climate but also to encourage the group to look at any blocks that may occur and to deal with apparently contradictory views.

Asking the question WHY? is intended to help group participants feel for themselves that oppressed people are only oppressed because (and for as long as) they do not perceive their common interests or recognize their collective strength. All the exercises in this section are designed to overcome such obstacles to action and the pursuit of change.

Establishing Priorities: Moving to the Question HOW?

Addressing the question WHY? has been directed towards opening out options for action by enabling group members to reach a broader social understanding. The question now arises of where attention should be focused, given the range of possibilities this broader vision will have brought into the group's ambit. They will need to determine priorities, strategies, tactics and tasks.

Feasibility exercises

Following the process of identification (WHAT?) and analysis (WHY?) of issues the group wants to work on, feasibility exercises can then be used to plan the specific action the group can undertake. Thus, the question HOW? is asked by breaking down the issues into component parts that are comprehensible, manageable and can then be allocated as specific tasks.

Table 5.1 Short-term, medium-term and longer-term tasks

	Now	Sooner	Later
By us			
With help			
By others			

Planning grids

The various elements of an issue taken from a brainstorm flip-chart or index cards, for example (see earlier in the chapter: asking the question WHAT?), can be plotted onto a grid in order to identify short-term, medium-term and longer-term tasks and whether additional help will be required to meet them (Table 5.1).

Of course, the 'Now/By others' box (the bottom left-hand box) should not have anything in it. If a plan depends on others taking first actions it is not appropriate. Other decisions facing the group can be plotted in a similar way, for example, onto a 'resources grid' where the specifics of resources the group will need rather than tasks to be performed are explored.

Bull's eye exercise

A similar effect can be achieved using concentric circles, in an exercise described by Taylor and Kemp (undated) (Figure 5.2).

In the course of one or both of these exercises and the discussion they generate, an action plan will have begun to be self-evident. It will consist of a balance of short- and long-term goals, individual tasks and collective action, self-help and areas in which it will be necessary to influence and gain the support of other people. The grid or circle can provide a useful initial means of setting this out. The grid, however, has the additional advantage of not implying that change will come about through some kind of linear progression but shows that it will be affected by forces operating at various levels. It also shows how the course of change, or the outcome of action, cannot be neatly predicted.

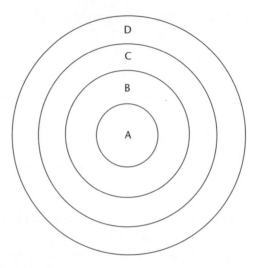

Circle A represents situations than can be changed completely by members;
Circle B represents situations that members can change with help;
Circle C represents situations that members cannot change, but where they can influence
           others to do so;
Circle D represents situations outside the influence of members.

Figure 5.2   Bull'e eye exercise

Force-field analysis

Given these complexities, this exercise, the Force-Field Analysis (see, for example, Berdan *et al.* 2006, pp. 144–145), becomes useful in concentrating on the development of action once a specific goal for change has been agreed. The purpose is to enable groups to anticipate problems and blockages to achieving their goals. The exercise helps groups identify helping and hindering factors.

Figure 5.3 represents the fact that situations always involve dynamic forces. The goal is written in the centre of the diagram, and a horizontal line drawn across the middle. The top half of the diagram represents the positive forces, those that will help and support the desired outcome; the bottom half those working against the change.

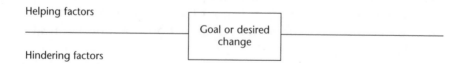

Figure 5.3   Force-field analysis

The group identifies things, people or assets they have that will assist them in achieving their goal. These are written in the top half of the diagram. The most strongly helpful should be closest to the group's goal.

Then the group members identify all the forces they can think of (for example, people, policies, lack of skills or resources) that will stand in their way and hinder them in achieving their goal; these are written in the bottom half of the diagram. Again, the most strongly hindering should be closest to the goal, the weakest further away. The distance from the goal should relate to the strength of the helping or hindering effect.

The next stage is for the group to think of ways to overcome or neutralize the unhelpful factors, and maximize the impact of the helpful ones. The aim is to find ways to pull the helping forces closer to the goal and push the hindering ones further away. The more sophisticated artists may wish to draw in arrows of varying lengths and thicknesses, or of different colours, to show that some forces for or against change have greater or lesser longevity or strength.

The key to the value of the exercise is that, from the force-field pattern, one can identify three possible ways forward:

- to strengthen the forces for change;
- to weaken the restraining or opposing forces; or
- to do both.

Usually, only the first is actively considered as people push stubbornly towards what they want to see happen, with the sole exception of trying to talk others round to their own point of view. The force-field exercise opens up more options and also makes it possible to consider whether strong or rapid movement in one direction will cause a backlash in the other. How fragile is movement towards their goal? Possible actions in each of the three categories can be listed by brainstorming. They can also be considered in the light of further questions such as:

- What is it feasible for us to do as things stand?
- Which opposing forces are weakest or easiest to tackle?
- Which potential alliances are strongest?
- What are others doing?
- Which positive and negative forces can be tackled at the same time?

Clearly there is potential for organizing on a grid the information and ideas thus acquired. See Berdan *et al.* (2006, p. 145) for an example of a completed force- field analysis.

Role play

Role play is also a very useful technique at this 'HOW' stage of a self-directed group. How it is best used will depend on the group and the issue but it enables the group to consider how to present their case to others, what their reactions might be and what the consequences of the group taking particular courses of action might be. It can be productive to re-play the role play a number of times after discussion of each version in the group.

Conclusion: Keeping the Values in Play

Presented in these terms – in the form of exercises that we have found useful in groups to ask the questions WHAT?, WHY?, and HOW? – the final steps of the *Preparing to Take Action* stage of the model might appear rather mechanistic. However, as options for action emerge in response to the question HOW?, it remains essential to challenge the group to consider these in the light of the overall values we outlined for the work in Chapter 3. This includes the commitment to confronting oppression and is achieved by continuing to ask the question WHY?. The result will be that some potential answers to HOW? are favoured over others.

Inevitably, activities and campaigning will be subject to ebbs and flows: unexpected obstacles will be encountered, new information will emerge. As we will see in the next chapter, asking WHAT?, WHY? and HOW? is not a one-off, they are the key components of self-directed groupwork identifying and assessing whatever comes into the path of the group, repeated at every turn, and helping move the group to reach successfully towards its goals.

6

Taking Action

Once priorities have been established by considering and answering the questions WHAT?, WHY? and HOW?, the task is for group members to apply their knowledge and skills collectively to action, still on the basis of the underlying principles of the model and of the analysis they arrived at in answering the question WHY?.

For many groups, this will mean mounting a major public campaign. Others become involved in a long-term series of campaigns focused around one central issue, such as disability rights or the needs of a local community. Still others, such as Advocacy in Action, exist more to create groups and support which may, in turn, become the seat of particular campaigns and activity as they become more established and vocal, for example, challenging the lifelong oppression faced by older Irish men in Nottingham (McGregor 2011). The common philosophy which all such groups share is illustrated by the comments years later of a group member and a parent who became one of the adult facilitators of the Ainsley Teenage Action Group:

> Why did we show up for two hours every week? We were in control, we were in charge. We set the guidelines. When we first started off, we thought we would do it and just not get into trouble — then it carried on, and people started to listen to us. (Group member)

> Saying that, when they was kids, they were tearaways. Now look at them – they've grown into responsible people. In them days, nobody thought they would have made anything of themselves and that club started that off – give them a bit of responsibility and it worked. It worked with the ... mob. (Father of group member and facilitator, cited in Arches and Fleming 2007 pp. 40 and 42)

It also indicates how far people can progress as a result of being a member of a self-directed group.

In the outline of the self-directed model in Chapter 1 we pointed out that the whole process of WHAT, WHY and HOW may recur several times. This means, inevitably, that more than one round of action is likely to be needed before the goal is achieved. In each action phase the broad tasks that a group undertakes tend to cover: collecting the information to make their case, mobilizing support, heightening the visibility of the issue they are fighting for through use of the media and inviting key personnel from public bodies to meet them and, if necessary, raising enough funds to run the group and the activity or campaign. Responsibilities for all this work have to be assigned, as well as for additional tasks that arise periodically, such as running public meetings, creating a website or writing an entry for a blog.

There is an extensive literature covering and debating community campaigning (from Alinsky in 1971 through Butcher *et al.* 1980, Henderson and Thomas 1980 and 1981 and Dominelli 2007 to Ledwith 2011 and beyond) and it is outwith the scope of this work to review it. Instead, we offer an extended group example – the Ainsley Teenage Action Group (ATAG) – which was first described in Mullender and Ward's original *Self-directed Groupwork* (1991) but which remains of interest because some of the inaugural members are still activists in the area and can look back on what they achieved. The ATAG example is supplemented with accounts of other, more recent groups to provide illustration of action and campaigning techniques in practice and of some of the other themes we have explored thus far. They provide real examples of the Taking Action stage in a group where groupworkers facilitate the process.

These examples illustrate the development and application of knowledge and skills by group members to achieve goals they have fixed for themselves, facilitated by groupworkers and with the background support of a consultant. In each case the whole process is set firmly within the values outlined in Chapter 3. Where possible, we have used the words of group members themselves, thus according well with the principle that enjoins us to give a voice to those who would otherwise be unheard.

The Ainsley Teenage Action Group (ATAG)

A group of teenage young men had offended together on the council estate (an area of dense housing rented at that time from local government) where they lived. One or two had served custodial sentences while others were under the supervision of the probation or social services, had been fined, or simply had not been caught. Their offences had been mostly related to break-ins at local business properties and the disposal of stolen goods. Their probation officer, along with a youth development worker and a volunteer (one of the present authors), decided to make themselves available to support the young people to work together as a group to pursue the young people's own goal of obtaining and running youth-run leisure facilities on the estate. Rather than the usual course of action, of taking the young people out of their community and putting them through programmes based on professional assessment of their needs and of the risk they might pose to the community, the aim was to help the young people themselves to understand and to deal with the issues, on their own home ground, in their own group.

The groupworker's role: facilitation in practice

The groupworkers established themselves as a trustworthy and reliable presence in the lives of the young people, working consistently to the principles in Chapter 3 in that, for example, they refused to accept members' negative labels and sought their own definitions of the problems they faced. They were committed from the outset to the possibility of the young people taking action on these issues through the group. The groupworkers continually affirmed, acknowledged and respected what the young people brought to the group, encouraging them to find their own strengths and take their own decisions; in short, treating the young people as adults not as children. Their role was to facilitate not lead and, henceforward, we will refer to the members of the groupworker team as facilitators.

For a group to become self-determining, it is necessary for the facilitators to create a relaxed informal setting in which the members feel comfortable and confident. As the Ainsley Group gained momentum, ways had to be found to create an environment where there was a relaxed informal attitude on the one hand, and as much participation as possible on the other, without exercising undue control. Being used to being told what to do, members found it hard to discipline themselves and to control their own sessions. In the early days, some lacked the confidence to participate at all, while others dominated aggressively and gathered cliques of supporters. The facilitator team might have been tempted to use individuals as allies to try to achieve more control, but they did not consider this acceptable, ethical or, in the long run, likely to be effective.

The use of structured exercises (as outlined in the last chapter), suggested by the facilitators and taken on by the group, helped to some extent but was by no means the whole answer. Eventually, a system for managing these problems emerged naturally. The members came to allow themselves a 'relax' session at the beginning of each meeting, followed by getting down to 'business'. This became an accepted part of the routine as one of the members stated at the time:

> When we meet at the club, the first half hour we just sit round, have a drink and just generally chat between ourselves. Then we get down to sorting out how we can get one step closer to getting the club and any paperwork that needs doing. Any leaflets for handing out, we'll do them at the club.

Sometimes the 'relax', or general discussion time, took up the whole session and no formal 'work' was done. What the facilitators discovered, however, was that in these informal sessions a lot of 'business' was in fact sorted out among the young people themselves, often pulling together discussions that had taken place outside club meetings: on the street or at school. After this, the business sessions, when they took place, were productive – sharp and decisive – and exercises were used discerningly, to meet group purposes rather than the facilitators' concerns about control. The team had to recognize and accept that, on occasions, the members took decisions independently and without their awareness. They needed to tune into the wavelength of this informal but very powerful decision-making process, whereby members might reach their own separate conclusions and not feel the need to communicate them. This really tested the team in their determination to facilitate the group in owning its own decisions and goals.

Consultancy for the facilitators

Already, this account has involved some hard decisions for the facilitators and the necessity to develop a new style of working and learn to make new kinds of judgements. Consultancy sessions (see Chapter 3 and Mullender and Ward 1993) were essential for untangling these questions and achieving clarity about the right way forward. In the early days, much consultancy time was spent on analysing detailed interventions in the group (who said what to whom) but, as the group developed, more time was spent looking at the wider issues affecting the group and the nature of facilitation itself. This seemed to coincide with the young people increasingly taking over the process of decision-making (as outlined above), then running their own brainstorms in the group and recognizing the need to set their own plans of action.

The facilitators were in no doubt that it was invaluable to meet with an objective outsider who stood at some critical distance from the day-to-day goings-on of the group and who could ask pertinent questions and challenge them to find answers. It helped prevent the work drifting or idling, assisted the handling of anxieties brought on by happenings within the group or pressures from outside (such as the rest of their workload or agency views about the direction the group was taking), and stopped conflicts of opinion or style from becoming too personalized. Through these shared efforts, the groupworkers were able constantly, in the face of consistent external pressures to do otherwise, to reaffirm their commitment to young people being their own spokespeople, making their own decisions and taking action for themselves.

Teachers wanting to be self-directed facilitators face particular challenges as school is not always a place where adults and young people work together in an equal partnership and support and consultancy within the school may be hard to find. A group of teachers in the USA worked round this by having annual consultancy sessions at a Summer School with members of the Centre for Social Action where issues, challenges and successes were given careful consideration. The rest of the time they relied on email contact to discuss any issues as they arose.

Boundaries between consultancy and the group

In view of the belief (expressed in the principles set out in Chapter 3) that group members should control the agenda of action, it was important that the consultancy focused on group process and not group content. The latter, in terms of group aims and tasks to be achieved, should be up to members to decide and regulate. Facilitators should not slide into prejudging these issues by airing them too fully in consultancy sessions. This is particularly the case where the facilitators are also education or health or social care practitioners with relationships with group members outside the group as well as within it.

As outlined in Chapter 3, the boundaries between consultancy and group sessions were interestingly explored by the ATAG facilitators and members when the notes from a consultancy meeting were seen by a group member. It was agreed that the notes be brought along to ATAG meetings and made available to any member who was interested. In addition, some group members attended the consultancy sessions on a few occasions. Being aware, by this time, of what was discussed in the meetings, they were able to pick up on things they particularly wanted to discuss. This reflects the members beginning to cross the boundary into sharing or taking over responsibility for group process. We shall see in Chapter 7 that this forms part of the next stage of the self-directed model and can be expected of, and encouraged in, mature groups.

One reason why the involvement of group members in consultancy meetings did not pose particular ethical problems in ATAG, and why there was not a hidden agenda for the young people to uncover, was because the aims for self-directed groups do not include individual change. Consultancy sessions do not focus, therefore, on possible thera-peutic or risk management benefits of group membership or on profes-sional assessments of individual functioning or risk of further offending. The only authentic reason to consider individual levels of participation in the group is in relation to members' potential contribution to select-ing and achieving the goals which they themselves have set. Facilitators might, for example, notice that one person has been particularly with-drawn but that they have recently become more involved, showing more initiative than usual. This might be mentioned outside of the group and discussed in terms of how to encourage this new-found confi-dence. In this way, performance and behaviour of group members are related to group process by those whose function is to facilitate the process of the group. This kind of development would most likely be mentioned in the group as well, so that both facilitators and members can draw out the best from each other. This is not to say that group members do not experience individual benefits from belonging to a self-directed group; they most certainly do (Cohen and Mullender 2000).

Division of tasks: new approaches to compulsory requirements

As was mentioned at the beginning of Chapter 3, the ability to co-work effectively, often across professional boundaries, is a fundamental skill in self-directed work. Such collaboration requires, for example, well-devel-oped communication skills directed to the tasks in hand, full recording of group process, adequate back-up from a consultant, and the ability to channel the lessons, both from what is recorded and from the professional support mechanisms, back into the groupwork itself. In the Ainsley group, the team was concerned primarily with helping the young people to decide issues and courses of action. However, early on, it became apparent that the group needed a reference point or, as it was termed, a 'key worker': one member of the team who would take primary responsibility for certain tasks outside the face-to-face work with the young people. This ensured that the young people had a contact point between meetings, and that agencies and outside bodies had a port of call if they could not link directly with the young people themselves – though the key worker's role would then be to make this link. Also, the role ensured that tasks the team undertook to do between meetings were carried out. This role was taken on by Colin, the Probation Officer.

In this role, he was also able to undertake other tasks which were part of his wider responsibilities for some group members: these were to record the fulfilment of supervision conditions, prepare court reports and, in some cases, offer family support. It would not have been appropriate to deal with these matters formally in the group because the agreement between facilitators and young people was to focus on issues and problems which concerned them collectively. On the other hand, as the group developed, individuals increasingly chose to discuss personal matters there and the fact that court reports were being prepared provided a useful jumping-off point for important discussions about offending, the courts, the police, and the young people's experiences generally. To all intents, the resultant reports were products of group discussions.

Although it did not happen at Ainsley, in other groups, the group members and facilitators not from the probation service contributed to court documents, commenting on local conditions and the work of their group to change these, which were appended to the official report containing an account of the offence and relevant personal details. These were accepted, and comments from the judiciary suggested that they helped engender a view of the young person before them which put strengths before deficiencies. This provides a practical example of the principle, *People have the right to be heard and define the issues facing them* being applied through the work of the group, since negative labels have been challenged in one of the most difficult forums of all – the courts.

Groups associated with school, even if meeting after school, face similar issues. In the minds and experience of the young people, a school may not be associated with their being respected or listened to or seen as a place where they can set the agenda. Although their schools have a heavy investment in formal educational content and outcomes, teachers using the self-directed model have found that if they 'divest from the product; concentrate on the process' (Berdan *et al*. 2006, p. 95), they can achieve 'powerful conditions for learning' with students 'many of whom were not engaged in traditional school activities' (ibid., p. xix). From the considerable experience now of self-directed groupwork in schools in the USA, a key feature does seem to be the teacher's/facilitator's uncompromised commitment to the principles and process of self-directed work and their ability to consistently put these into practice.

These examples also illustrate the fact, discussed previously in Chapter 4, that the voluntary membership of self-directed groups does not necessarily preclude group involvement being offered to those under compulsory supervision or who are subject to monitoring or investigation, provided there is no actual or implied requirement that they will join the group. Some groups, however, have preferred to avoid involving practitioners who are currently employed in the agency responsible for group members. Others place great emphasis on remaining entirely independent of any service-providing agency.

Asking the Question WHY?: Policing on the Estate

Let us now turn to the actual collective activities of ATAG. The process the group went through was to ask the questions WHAT?, WHY? and HOW?. One particular feature of their discussions gives a clear illustration of the difference it made to their ensuing actions when they asked the question WHY?

In the group's first year, the number of police arrests, prosecutions and court appearances for Ainsley young people reduced dramatically. During this period there were no official reports of group offences of burglary, theft, or taking and driving away vehicles. However, during the second year, the teenagers attending the group, when discussing 'WHAT were their concerns now?', started giving vague, frustrated accounts of conflict with the local police, about being harassed and arrested in their neighbourhood for no apparent reason. Police arrest referrals to the probation service were beginning to increase and the nature of the offences were violations of public order, such as threatening behaviour, breach of the peace and abusive language; in other words, they were always offences that the police themselves can define as such. It was also noticeable that police arrest action was confined to two or three officers.

The young people began to ask themselves WHY this was happening? Here, they take up their own story:

> About five or six months ago, the police activity on the estate was large. I think the reason for this was, when we was together on the estate, we always used to keep together – perhaps about ten of us. We used to actually split into two, the younger ones and the older ones, and we used to hang about on the estate and people used to get annoyed by the presence or the noise, and the police used to come down more or less every night, clearing us off. But, instead of just coming and asking us to move, we got a lot of lip, and we got pushed around a lot and, well, we resented this.

Feelings were running so high that a group of four teenagers stoned an unoccupied police car. This incident became the main focus of the next group meeting and the members decided to make representation to the sub-divisional police headquarters, to invite the senior officer responsible for police operations in the area to meet them: 'Well, what we decided to do was we contacted the local police station, because the main source of trouble was one officer.' They role-played in advance how they thought the meeting might go and then, on their own, visited the police station, thus illustrating our remarks earlier in this chapter about facilitators not needing to negotiate on behalf of group members. 'About five of us went up, but, when we got up there, they was not showing much willingness to help us, so we actually had to write a letter. We invited the Chief Inspector down to tell him the problem.' They circulated interested adults, asking them to give support at the meeting:

> Well, he did a lot of talking, but we did manage to get our point over and we emphasised that this one officer was mainly to blame for the trouble, and he said he would see what he could do about it. Subsequently, this police officer was moved off the estate which is really a great thing for the estate because, since then, the trouble has gone down, and there hasn't been so much police activity on the estate.

The Chief Inspector, a high ranking police officer, not only moved one officer but introduced a community liaison constable to work with the group and to help with the campaign for a youth-led club, the term adopted by the young people themselves. He made a bargain with the young people that if he made these policing changes and adopted a lower police profile in the area, he expected the group to play their part and reduce the number of incidents and residents' complaints. There was clearly a good deal of mutual respect between the group members and the Chief Inspector. He personally attended their monthly committee meetings, put forward points raised by the members and was at times their advocate. Further conflict with the operational police was minimal.

We may contrast this with the more common response to young people who offend: expecting them to examine *their* behaviour on the assumption that it must need changing for the better (British Youth Council 2011). It also provides a stark example of facilitators encouraging a group to set its own goals, here to change policing behaviour, rather than these being determined by outsiders.

Digging deeper for underlying causes: asking 'WHY?' again

The changes agreed by the police dealt with the contentious spate of recent arrests but they did not deal with the reasons why the group had come to police attention originally, before the group was established. The group's view on 'WHY this had occurred' was that they had had nothing to do and nowhere to go. They now had the group to attend but that was only a temporary measure for a few young people and did not tackle the problem itself. Longer-term action was needed.

Moving into action

> We decided we would have a go at getting youth facilities for the teenagers of the estate. As one of the first things, the group agreed to get a petition to see if the majority of the estate agreed with us that there are not enough play facilities. We collected over 400 signatures from residents.

The petition was preceded by a distribution of leaflets around the area, announcing the existence of the group and its intentions. Both the leaflets and the petition forms were drawn up by members.

The next stage was to meet their elected representatives. This idea arose accidentally, when the group took the petition to the Lord Mayor's home, not realizing that he lived in the same area as themselves; this is not entirely surprising as the role of Lord Mayor of the City of Nottingham is honorary and lasts for only one year, so could easily go unnoticed by young people. Through him, they made contact with their own elected local government representatives (councillors):

> We sent them a letter inviting them to come down to Robert Shaw Primary School where we held our meetings. We wanted them to come to look at our petition and give us help. When they came, we told them about the estate and about the good points, but especially that there is nothing to do for young people. We said that we had been in trouble and are not angels. They agreed with our aims and made plans for us to meet the Sheriff [another honorary position held by a locally elected representative], to present our petition.
>
> The press were told about our petition and came to one of our meetings to find out what we were meeting for. We talked to the pressman about the club's problems and having no place where we can meet. The two councillors were also present and they told him that they supported us. They also said we had a good chance of getting the wasteland down by the bridge for a youth hut, which is what we would like to start with. The following week the press cameraman came and took some pictures of us

The newspaper article and the picture, presenting the group in a positive light, made quite an impact locally, and members quickly saw the value, not simply of publicity but of representing their cause and themselves. They immediately produced a news-sheet, the *Ainsley Youth Express* (*AYE!*) detailing their activities in a series of short articles. Some of these articles (in part reproduced above) were by members who had been written off by teachers as illiterate. Here there are strong echoes, once more, of the principle, *People have the right to be heard and define the issues facing them* and the need to challenge negative labels. On completion of the draft, and after discussing the general lay-out and subtitles, four members went to a local community print shop, laid out titles and subtitles and printed off the news-sheet.

Their next step had the same 'outreaching' purpose and it tackled negative labels head on:

> We organised a jumble sale to gain our respect back; because people on the estate did not like us ... We also had a raffle of goods given to us by firms we had written to. This and the jumble sale raised £55 ... People who came also saw a display of our work: a model and a map with photographs of the estate.

Groups can find it a challenge to translate thoughts into action plans and it may take them several attempts to develop clear plans of things they are going to do in order to achieve their agreed goals. The UMass group used a web-group (*Google Groups*) to smooth out logistics and share information, work and links. They found it was excellent for creating mutual accountability and equality – 'we were all on the same platform and had access to the same information'.

Techniques for action: fund-raising and community arts

The jumble sale had required considerable practical and coordinating effort. An unusual aspect of work surrounding the jumble sale was a photographic display. For the display a small group toured the estate taking photos of features they regarded as significant with regard to their aim of getting a club, for example, graffiti, 'Keep Off' notices, and areas of unused land, mounting them on display boards at a group meeting. Other self-directed groups have also used community events in a similar dual-purpose way, both to raise funds and to generate awareness of, and support for, their campaigns. The Youth Dreamers have an annual 'Fun Fest Block Party' as well as one-off events such as a Christmas party. These raised a much needed $6000 in 2011.

McDonnell (2011) writes about the significance of arts for promoting democratic citizenship and political participation. Drawing on the philosophical writings of Mouffe (2005) and the work of Rancière (2007) on aesthetics, she highlights the potential of arts, as both representation and performance, in providing opportunities for and experience of democratic learning and political action. In relation to photography in particular, Ortega-Alcazar and Dyck (2012, p. 109) argue that photography enables participants to position themselves in a detached way from the things they experience in everyday life, to reflect upon them from a different perspective and, thus, to gain new understandings.

Many groups have used arts and community art as part of their group-work process. The Youth Dreamers has an established record of producing art with and for the community, for example, creating street-light banners with positive messages, designing mosaic stepping-stones to make pathways in public open-spaces and creating a book of poems about their city: *Baltimore We Love You*. They view these events as being important for establishing a mutual and reciprocal relationship with the community they live and work in. For No Limits Dementia, art work is a crucial element of their group and how they get across their messages about dementia to a wider audience.

Such 'community arts' techniques are an effective way of making abstract issues concrete and visual for the group as well as for those they need to convince with their arguments. They also give members a short-term project to carry out collectively as part of a longer campaign. This means they can experience the satisfaction of successfully completing a task and getting positive feedback on their work. Items produced can be wide-ranging and may include illustrated leaflets, newsletters and reports, photographic or video material, posters and models, the last being particularly useful for campaigning on housing or planning issues and in any fight to get a community or youth centre. In recent years, local authorities have become more willing to involve young people in the planning process than at the time of ATAG. Many regularly consult directly with young people, mainly on planning and service provision decisions that have a particular effect on them (Fleming *et al.* 2007).

ATAG: finding their collective power

A difficult period ensued for the ATAG group when local adults, at the instigation of the local council, tried to change the rules mid-stream and take over the campaign and during which the young people learned some hard lessons reflecting the obverse of all six of the Principles set out in Chapter 3. The parents and councillors seemed unable to see beyond their negative stereotypes. They would not listen and they did not want to consider the wider problems underlying the situation the young people were in. Above all, and despite their good efforts on improving their image, the young people still keenly felt their status as an oppressed group owing to prejudice against the young and against offenders: they are so readily dismissed as 'hooligans' or 'delinquents'.

Such ups and downs are commonplace in long-running groups such as this. Although initially knocked off their stride by this experience, the group took a breath and critically questioned and reflected upon what was happening. After much discussion, and supported by the facilitators, the young people looked again to themselves for collective power and rediscovered their own momentum and sense of purpose by refocusing on their original goals. They kept their overall aim in sight by running youth club sessions in the school where they held their own meetings and, since by this time some of them were aged 18 or over, they were able to win back control of the club's steering committee and funding.

Their building was finally opened five years after the group began. Purpose-built, it was a simple but weather-proof shell with mains services, ideal for lively activity, which the members equipped themselves. Attendance regularly reached a hundred. The older group members took responsibility for the day-to-day running, supported by regular discussions with one of the facilitator team.

Over a period of years, then, the young people had exposed the real nature of the problems they faced (WHAT) and had organized with others, combining analysis (WHY) and action (HOW), to tackle these effectively. In taking action, they had utilized campaigning techniques that may be more familiar to community development workers, planners and youth workers than to health and social care or related professionals. Crucially, however, they had done this in order to solve a problem – offending – which, as they well recognized, was not only a problem to the community in which they lived but also was, ultimately, of no advantage to themselves, a factor which usually goes unappreciated in media, political and even academic debate about youth offending.

The Youth Dreamers in the USA have faced numerous such set-backs and challenges in their ten-year campaign for their youth centre. Kristina Berdan, the teacher/facilitator, recounts one:

When we went to zoning (planning permission) and previously supportive neighbors showed up to oppose us, students had a new WHAT. Students realised that it wasn't just the problem of getting our zoning passed but the bigger problem of elders in the community fearing teenagers. We worked on WHY this was and then identified HOW to work through it. Students called upon a Community Conferencing organisation to lead a mediation between the youth and the residents to discuss and address their concerns. The Law students helped the Youth Dreamers prepare for zoning and we rehearsed by having a mock board of students from another class watch and vote. We returned to zoning, as did the opposition, but because of our hard work and training, we met the zoning law requirements.

They had won, but the Dreamers didn't feel like winners. In our reflections, they shared the need for the residents to know and understand the group in order to be a part of the future youth center. Myresha stated, 'It did not feel like we had accomplished our goal. I wouldn't want them [the residents] to move away but [rather] to be closer to us ... even to come to the youth center to volunteer.'

Since that zoning appeal hearing, the Dreamers have worked hard to build positive relationships with residents, which has included having students in our summer art program, create mosaic house numbers for them, making and delivering Christmas wreaths, holding an annual block party and securing a grant to collect oral histories from the life-long residents. At the end of one interview for this project, a resident shared, 'I was opposed to you going in there; but I've watched you all ... Maybe you can save the kids with what you want to do.'

Overall, the Ainsley Teenage Action Group members discovered that they could become more powerful in questioning other people's attitudes towards them, and in analysing and tackling the issues that dominated their lives. They were supported to take the initiative into their own hands by taking their own decisions in the group, finding the strengths they needed amongst their own members, learning the necessary skills and acquiring the necessary knowledge and resources to pursue their campaign.

Without question, the young people learned in a very practical way how to run a fairly complex organization and to take responsibility for it. In so doing, they learned to take responsibility for their own actions – taking decisions, sticking to them in the face of pressure from officials, councillors and other adults, and facing the consequences. On the surface, this may carry echoes of the neo-liberal discourse of personal responsibility and enterprise, glibly advocated in media and political rhetoric and effected in current policies. However, the context in which this self-responsibility was developed and the objectives sought and secured, are a far cry from those envisaged by opinion-formers and policy-makers.

In the process, the young people came to distinguish between supportive and oppressive adults: how to include the former and exclude the latter. In examining what they did with their time, the young people realized the problems in their neighbourhood. They became aware of the concentration of power in the established institutions and within adults at a personal level and how these come together effectively to disempower young people, and working-class young people like themselves especially. They came to appreciate that society does not allocate resources fairly, to young people or to other powerless groups and that planning and policing policies often do not show much concern for those they most affect. However, they learned, also, that this state of affairs and those who uphold it can be challenged. Consequently, they grew in confidence and experience and earned new respect from their families, the local community and the public authorities. The work they undertook, with the support of the facilitators, was carried out on their own terms and focused on their own goals. The group itself, rather than the groupworkers, took the credit for their own success. The participants found this self-directed process, as much as its outcome, to be an empowering one.

Postscript

Although the issues confronted by the Ainsley Teenage Action Group have a current feel about them, in fact the group actually took place some 30 years ago. In our view this is a sad reflection of the timelessness of perceptions and prejudices about young people, their behaviour and the 'problem' that they are seen to be, similar to those chronicled by Geoffrey Pearson in his classic text, *Hooligan: A History of Respectable Fears* (Pearson 1983). Toynbee, bemoaning the attitudes to young people revealed in reactions to the 2011 urban 'riots' in the UK, referring to Pearson, observes: 'each generation grows up into respectable parents ready to be terrified by the next one' (Toynbee 2011).

Despite the 'timeless' nature of the issues, we thought carefully whether to present the Ainsley group in full again in this text to illustrate the ACTION stage of self-directed groupwork. There are numerous current examples we could have used as a detailed study (as the examples throughout the book and the case studies at the end indicate). We decided we preferred to revisit the example of Ainsley that was also showcased in the 1991 volume of *Self-directed Groupwork*. We did this for two main reasons. First, and importantly, it is a strong example of the application of the self-directed groupwork model with both the principles and the process clearly and overtly embedded in the work. Moreover, the account offers an exceptional level of detail regarding the process the group followed, drawn from our own records, publications and the transcripts of a television documentary made about and with the group (BBC 1981). Even so, we were concerned that under the present *modus operandi* of the English Probation Service it is most unlikely a probation officer would be able to play the central role in the way Colin Butcher did in this project, although close liaison with such a scheme would be feasible and, indeed, good practice (Ward 2008; Ministry of Justice 2011). However, of the other two facilitators, one worked for a voluntary sector youth participation project, not unlike some contemporary projects, and the other, a university lecturer, took part on a purely voluntary basis. Hopefully they would be there today.

The second factor that influenced our decision to use Ainsley is that, perhaps uniquely, the members of ATAG have been followed up and interviewed about their memories of the group and its impact on their lives, 25 years after the group took place (Arches and Fleming 2007). We think that the following extracts from these interviews speak for themselves, both to justify a retelling of the ATAG story and also to reinforce the efficacy of the methodology:

> Basically we were all hanging out on the streets and getting up to no good. Police used to come round and we would taunt them, throw stones at their cars, and generally get up to no good. Back in those days, the fires were all coal fires and we would climb the drainpipes and put slates across the chimneys and smoke the houses out. Now you think back, it's horrible, but to us it was a joke. I think the residents wanted to get rid of us because we had nothing else to do.

> Why did we show up for two hours every week? We were in control, we were in charge. We set the guidelines. When we first started off, we thought we would do it and just not get into trouble – then it carried on, and people started to listen to us. We used to think, councillors coming down to get more votes, and this police officer's coming, we never thought we would get what we got. We carried on … we achieved a lot – just from persevering … and getting a youth hall.

> No one had an individual role – it was like this group thing and … to talk to us and break us into groups of three or four – and think what could be better for this estate – things like that. We all stuck together – the girls as well as the guys stuck together – never let each other down. That still stands to this day. The thing was that it was mixed, there were black, white, Asian – it was a small estate and we were all together.

> By sitting down and talking and working it out together, you can solve the problem. You can't have one person going one way, and one another – you are not going to solve anything.

They recognized the approach and the principles that informed it, in the way the adults worked with them:

You [the facilitators] were just on the sidelines. We did what we wanted to do without people being in charge. You let us get on with it basically.

I think we just learnt to communicate – that's what I think it is: talk seriously, not loudly – not wind each other up. Brainwork – made us think we are somebody. Don't listen to what the teachers or the parents or police say to you.

The experience of being part of the group was felt to have had significant consequences for some of them: 'Without the group, I probably would have ended up in jail.' And a number considered that the experience of being part of a self-directed group and part of a value-based approach had influenced the type of people they had grown up to become and affected how they related to others both at home and at work:

Yes, I think it has helped me in the job I'm doing now – I'm a supervisor – I listen to people at work now – if I hadn't had this experience I would have thought 'I'm right and that's it.' I listen – like when we first started, I didn't listen, 'We want this and we want that' – there was no negotiation.

You do talk to your children differently, especially if they got in trouble, I got boys and when they do things that I did, I understand. I used to get told off, staying in and grounded. I didn't do that with my boys … Yes, it worked: he's 17 and didn't get in trouble.

When I was young I was treated like a baby, but now I treat youngsters like an adult … When we started the club, I got a better understanding.

You're more sensitive to other people's needs, aren't you? You can see what they are going through.

I'm just working hard – I've got a 12-year-old son now – and I know from what I went through to get this and that … I am trying to show him values. If you work hard and try something, you can achieve your aims … I was part of something … I was part of making something work by sticking together and persevering – you can change people's lives. I'm proud of that.

7
The Group Takes Over

Following an initial round of taking action, groups inevitably pause to take breath. This next stage begins with the group reviewing what it has achieved, coming to see links between the range of issues addressed thus far, and identifying new areas to be tackled. The group then continues with more collective action, joining or establishing new campaigns. Members turn to their own group meetings for confirmation of the wider understanding they have reached and to consolidate their shared strength and conviction. By this time, they will have redefined their experience from one of personal inadequacy and self-blame to strength and determination, through the achievement of doing something about the external factors that have contributed to their oppression. By making these connections, they realize they have a right to a different style of services and to more control over their own lives.

The group, having been facilitated up to now to analyse issues and set its agenda of action, takes over increasing responsibility for ensuring that this is done, as well as for group process. Increasingly, not only the work of the group but its understanding of collective power based on Freirian 'conscientisation' (Freire 1972) is under group control. Mature self-directed groups become models to those who may be able to join together to take action in a similar way. External facilitators and, sometimes, founder members move gradually into the background and take on a different kind of role. Ultimately, both parties may judge the time to be right for them to leave the group altogether, although experience is that this is can be hard to do in practice and can on occasion lead to a group ending or negotiating the facilitators' return. Evaluation of the group and of the facilitators' performance in it is, consequently, of key significance at this time.

The themes that will be covered in this chapter, then, are making the connections, using the media, evaluation, changing roles and withdrawal of groupworkers or founder members moving on.

Making the Connections and Creating Change

We refer to the process of evaluating past achievements, making connections between issues, and planning for the future, as reformulating the questions WHAT?, WHY?, and HOW?. It is an exercise that happens numerous times in active groups and that, indeed, becomes a continuous process. Reformulating 'WHAT' means asking 'What are the problems we still face?'; 'What worked and didn't work?'; 'What is still left to do?' In so doing, the group members are naturally led into reformulating 'WHY'? – that is, asking themselves why such a range of issues or problems still exists, why some things were successful and other not, and recognizing, understanding and defining the links between them. As they continue to develop their understanding of the external causes of their issues and concerns – causes that relate to prevailing attitudes about group members and resourcing and organization of provision – groups also see ways in which they can take action to tackle aspects of these causes in order to bring about change. This we describe as reformulating 'HOW?': 'How can we best act on our renewed understanding to achieve our goals and demands?'; 'How can we make our group function more successfully?' As the group continues its progress – and it is now evident why self-directed groups are not short-term groups – this reformulation of WHAT, WHY and HOW becomes a continuing process throughout the life of the group. It leads on, in a cyclical process, through action and reflection, back into what, why and how as represented in the Information-Action-Reflection Cycle set out in Chapter 5. As campaigns and actions continue, understanding and awareness grow in parallel.

Members' developing understanding of the injustices they face, and of their own relative powerlessness, will slowly grow into a broader comprehension that they and others beyond their immediate group share the experience of social oppression. They come to see change, and action to achieve it, not as a local concession but as an absolute right and they come to conceptualize in a new way their area of concern (Weyers 2001, p. 50). They recognize the need to make links with people in other places and to take further action, often at a regional or national level. Group members now wish to alter the way that things are 'done to' them without their permission and to alter, too, the attitudes held by others about them.

Disabled people, for example, within a wider debate on attacks on public expenditure (Oliver and Barnes 2012), recognize they can no longer be prepared to tolerate, let alone to be grateful for, inadequate, stigmatizing and paternalistic forms of service delivery. They have the right to receive a proper standard of service and support. Indeed, they may well wish to take over the control of the support services and to develop those that enable their full participation in a predominantly non-disabled world and, hence, to take control over their own lives (Beresford *et al.* 2011). 'Taking over' does not mean seizing the power to exploit those one has been exploited by in the past but gaining the power to direct one's own life and one's own affairs. Taking the first decisions for oneself breeds the desire to go on taking decisions and to extend one's sphere of capabilities as far as it can go. It also engenders the demand to be seen as capable and able to control, not to be patronised, not to be dismissed as incompetent or uncomprehending and not to be left out when the really important decisions are made or the real power is exercised (Taylor *et al.* 2007).

The facilitators' role, now that a first round of externally directed activity has been successfully concluded, becomes one of facilitating the group to analyse what it has achieved - what worked and why – but also to acknowledge blocks they experienced, why these occurred and how the group managed them; to identify the problems they still face and the extent to which they still fall short of being fully accepted into society and given equal treatment. The facilitators may go on to help the group plan and carry through its next project or campaign, recognizing that the overall goals of at least some of the group members will have moved up several notches and will be directed at achieving a more fundamental level of change beyond short-term advantages or the satisfaction of immediate individual need, important though these are. Group members will by now be generalizing from what has happened across to other issues that confront them. This phase of empowering practice is characterized by group members making connections between achievements and experiences so far, broadening out to wider concerns and, finally, moving towards TAKING OVER whilst the facilitators move into the background.

The springboard for these developments is often the tangible success or desired change. These can take many forms, such as groups acquiring their own resources or facility. Examples include the young people's facilities of Youth Dreamers or ATAG; No Limits Dementia providing their own support; achieving the banning of mosquito devices; and Young Minds in the UK and Action Autonomie in Canada both directly influencing the prescription and delivery of mental health support. In all cases, the real issue is one of beginning to have some control. In the case of the Youth Dreamers, it is not just the fact of having a building that matters, but of running and managing it themselves. When the Youth Dreamers started out as a small group of students wanting to provide a safe space for other young people in their neighbourhood, the teacher who worked with them honestly expressed doubts about their ability to be able to do this (Cary *et al.* 2004, p. 66). The young people worked tirelessly over ten years to achieve their goal, motivated by being 'part of making a future for the youth of today' (ibid., p. 67). They learnt much in the course of doing this. At the start they did not know what a 'grant' (funding application) was, but now group members can write business proposals, letters of enquiry to foundations and numerous grant applications. Whilst in conventional classes the young people had been reluctant to revise and improve their work, in the group they developed the commitment and staying power to accomplish these tasks. As, one of the founder members of the group says:

> We reflect a lot as Youth Dreamers; not everything we strive for we obtain, so we have to evaluate and reflect on what things worked and what things didn't in order to set new goals and make progress towards achieving them.

He goes on to say that the work of the group has

> shown many people, youth and adults alike, that young people are not the cause of problems which adults have to rectify but that they have the capability to come up with remedies that will solve some of the problems themselves.

Members are clear the group has had a considerable impact on them as individuals, in terms of the skills they have developed and the individual achievements associated with this. It has also had an impact for young people more widely in the community, seeing what young people can achieve and, for the community as a whole, both in having the resource available and also because of their developing respect for the group. Again, the member quoted above says: 'It is not about giving or doing something for the community; it is about having a mutual reciprocal relation with the community.'

One vital feature of the Youth Dreamers has been how the 'seasoned' Youth Dreamers support the integration of 'fresh' Youth Dreamers and how they work together, both to keep the vision alive over a very long period of time and also to allow new ideas and developments to be incorporated. Over time, the young people are taking more and more control and responsibility for the actions of the group (quotes and material from Lawson, pers. comm. 2011).

No Limits Dementia have achieved considerable change in how people with dementia can express things that are difficult to talk about in their lives through their art work, both at real and virtual exhibitions, their website and a film. Reaching outwards, they have worked to realize improvement in support for people with dementia through meetings with key government ministers and policy-makers.

Coalitions of Disabled People have achieved some enormous successes, having come together in a tangible and visible form through the establishment, for example, of Centres for Independent Living (NCIL UK 2011), where advice is available about every aspect of life as a disabled person. From the outset, such centres have been based on the actual experiences of disabled people who are living independently in the community (DCDP 1986; Davis and Mullender 1993). To this end, disabled people from throughout the UK successfully fought against the ingrained paternalism of local authorities to gain control of substantial funds for service users to run their own facilities. This has latterly been translated into the personalization agenda with individual control over funding and an individualized dilution of service user control, leaving disabled people open to abuse (Thiara *et al.* 2012). It is important not to lose sight of collective influence and collective power in influencing social agendas and keeping people strong.

Achievements like those outlined above appear to mark the threshold between the 'taking action' and 'taking over' stages of the model. The acquisition of their own resources, be these finances, buildings, websites or films, for example, provides groups with the demonstrable success that can act as a foundation and springboard for further and extended action. The scope of activity, aspirations and horizons can move from an original local campaign to a national and, in the case of the Derbyshire Coalition of Disabled People, an international movement (Disabled People's International 2011) when groups link up with other people in the same position as themselves and, through a 'multiplier' process, share their experiences and enthusiasm and assist and advise their peers to develop their own organizations and campaigns. Thus, in the course of its particular campaign to secure funding for a Centre for Independent Living in its locality (Davis and Mullender 1993), the Derbyshire Coalition of Disabled People became an active affiliate of the British Council of Disabled People (BCODP 2011) and, through this, in turn, an active participant in Disabled People's International (Disabled People's International 2011), a grouping of organizations from nearly a hundred member states of the United Nations. Disabled People's International has campaigned to alter attitudes at the global level, including through its consultative status to the UN. This formal recognition and the benefits of coming together on an international basis have spurred on vigorous activity across the world. In this context, the European Region of the Disabled Peoples International, like its World Council, has propagated the idea of Centres for Independent Living to which representatives from DCDP have actively contributed. Following negotiation with and pressure from the Disabled People's International, the European Union has adopted measures that lend support to independent living initiatives (Hurst 2005), and the Derbyshire Centre itself received a European Social Fund Grant.

The local young people's group that campaigned against 'mosquito' devices (instruments that emit a high pitched noise, too high for adults to hear, aimed at deterring young people from gathering in certain public areas) on city council properties in their city made contact and links with groups of young people in other cities to share knowledge and experience and strengthen each other's campaigns. As part of their campaign, they linked with national children's rights organizations and spoke with local and national politicians. When they were successful with their local campaign, they developed an action plan based on detailing the work they had undertaken and made it available to other groups of young people to use if they wanted. The campaigns gained the support of the Children's Commissioners in England and Scotland (BBC 2011) and this specific group was used as a case study in *Positive for Youth*, a document produced by the Parliamentary Under-Secretary of State for Children and Families in the UK Department for Education (Department for Education 2011, p. 68).

Having said this, it is important to record, as well, a more cautious reflection on the 'multiplier' effect. Action Autonomie is an organization of mental health survivors in Montreal, Canada, that campaigns against the dominant position of the medical profession in mental health diagnosis and, in particular, against the use of ECT (electro-convulsive therapy – electric shock treatment – a form of treatment that can have severe side effects and should only be used, if at all, in a very few cases) in psychiatric treatment in the city's mental hospitals. In the course of its campaign it has become affiliated to local, Canada-wide and international coalitions campaigning against the abuse resulting from the medical model of mental health and, as they see it, its characteristic attachments to 'chemical', i.e. drug, and 'electro' therapies. They have observed, however, that in such coalitions there is a requirement to achieve consensus among groupings that come with different backgrounds and reflect different nuances in analysis of the issues. This, they have found, frequently dilutes and dampens the erstwhile sharp-edged focus of the campaign as they have developed it in Montreal, such that some of their own members have become disillusioned with the coalition and drifted away from this form of mobilization. They suggest that this may be a built-in feature of such social movements (Todd and Taylor 2004) and may blunt their potential to be drivers of social change and, paradoxically, play to the advantage of dominant and oppressive professions and institutions.

Another feature of this phase in the development of self-directed groups can be the initiating and staging, for instance, of events for interested members of the public and relevant professionals. The Youth Dreamers regularly organise events for members of their local community and professionals. No Limits Dementia organized the exhibition of their art work, while members of the Te Aroha Noa Community took part in organizing a 'Party in the Park' in Palmerston North, New Zealand, both to build community and to develop relationships with council officials (Handley *et al.* 2009, p. 11).

An interesting debate that takes place within self-directed groups involved in such interventions is whether changing attitudes is of any use if it leaves control of services untouched. Often, meeting directly with front-line workers and working face to face, to thrash out the practical detail of the impact of such attitudes on practice, can be more productive than protracted and exhausting negotiations with senior management (Barnes 2008). Yet it has to be combined with the latter if it is to lead to any redistribution of power.

In contrast, Advocacy in Action has deliberately sought to keep small. Due to past experiences of having almost lost direction when they had both funding and paid staff, they now do not accept funding as they reject the control that so often comes with it. They prefer to be an independent group and appreciate the fact that this keeps things personal. This approach has not limited their impact or ability to achieve change, though, as evidenced through the production of the *Arise You Gallant Sweeneys* film about Irish men returning home (McGregor 2011). Advocacy in Action has also helped to set up disability rights groups in Italy and Slovenia, as well as having one of its members become the first person with learning difficulties to be a visiting lecturer at a university.

Techniques for Action: Using a Range of Media

One of the most effective ways for groups to move from local action onto a wider canvas is through the use of the media. This is the area that has perhaps most changed since we first wrote. Now, alongside conventional media, largely controlled by others such as local and national newspapers and radio and television companies, the rapidly growing and evolving user- controlled social media are available to all who want to use them.

Many mature self-directed groups have become very comfortable and skilful at using websites, blogs, Facebook groups and Twitter to promote and publicize themselves and their causes and activities. Advocacy in Action chooses not to have a website or use electronic communication. However, many of the other groups do: Te Aroha Noa (http://www.tearohanoa.org.nz), Youth Dreamers (http://www.youthdreamers.org), No Limits Dementia (http://www.nolimitsdementia.com), the Asian Pride (http://www.asianprideproject.org), to name just a few. Many use both public and private Facebook groups and Twitter.

The group that succeeded in getting mosquito devices banned in certain areas is an example of the use of both user-controlled and professional media. There was a core group of about six or seven young people who undertook much of the analysis, planning and action and they met both face to face and virtually. In this group they were united in their opposition to the mosquito devices and worked together as equals, took turns in doing things and shared responsibility. The core group used Facebook groups to attract interest and gauge young people's opinions about the devices and, through such social media, they made contact with a wider group of about thirty young people. Using email, Facebook and Twitter which most members could access via their mobile phones, making it a very rapid form of communication, the members also gauged opinions of an even wider group, for example, other students and friends. All advocated the ban. In this way the core members established that there was widespread support for a ban and also made contact with a diverse group of young people who could be part of a two-way conduit of information for the action. The group similarly engaged with professional media. They wrote letters to the local paper, were invited to take part in debates on local radio, were interviewed for local television news and had articles about their campaign in local and regional newspapers. There was also information on other groups' and organizations' websites, for example, a local young people's issues-based website. The campaign ultimately got coverage on the BBC News national website (BBC 2011).

Harry, one of the group members, says that, in the main, they felt they were treated very fairly by the professional media. In a debate on local radio with an elected local government member, he felt he was treated equally. However, he did say that sometimes public reaction was not so positive. For example, very negative comments about young people were posted on the local newspaper's website under articles about their campaign. The campaign took about six months from its commencement to the decision to ban mosquito devices. The group feels the Council would never have instituted the ban without the young people's campaign, which they started themselves and which was entirely their idea.

Twitter has proved itself to be a powerful medium for groups to bring about change. It has been credited with having played a significant part in bringing about political change in, for example, Moldova (Smolar 2012) during the period one of the authors was working there, support-ing, using self-directed methods, the development of social services institutions. Twitter has been a significant strand in the strategy of disability groups to challenge proposed changes to Disability Living Allowance in the UK. At one point hundreds of thousands of people, including celebrities and politicians, tweeted the link to their report *Responsible Reform* (undated) which forced mainstream media to discuss the issue, helped crystallize public opinion and, for the time being at least, created political upset (Butler 2012).

Some groups have created films based on their lives and have sought to have an audience for these. The Long Distance Gang is a group of older Irish men that is part of Advocacy in Action. The name comes from the fact they used to follow work, particularly in the construction indus-try and often walked long distances to find it. They would meet and play music, sing and share stories about their lives – drink was an important part of all the men's lives. The idea to plan a trip home to Ireland arose from these conversations and over a long period of time, they planned the trip back to Ireland. They received funding from Arts Council England as they planned to make a film of their journey. They learned to use a movie camera and also had to get used to being filmed; they agreed the film would belong to the group itself. The trip was very emotional and many very personal things happened whilst they were away. On return, they took another 18 months to finalize the film, all being part of making decisions about what went in and stayed out, how they would construct the story, the use of music and all the details. The journey was one of healing and validation and they were very proud of it and wanted others to see the film. The film entitled *Arise You Gallant*

Sweeneys is available on DVD and has been shown to groups within the Irish community and at the local independent cinema a number of times. It has been reviewed by a national newspaper (McGregor 2011).

One danger with the media is that they will attempt to construct a 'story-line' within their standard perspective of what will attract and hold the interest and attention of reader, listener or viewer; that is, within the current discourse, to use a post-structuralist term. The advent of 'reality TV', which in fact is highly staged and has blurred the distinction between fiction and reality, has, arguably, increased the pressure on journalists and directors to find a 'good story', while reinforcing many social stereotypes and turning 'subjects' into 'objects'. Just as ancient Rome used bread and circuses with physical danger and death to please the masses, so psychological dissection and torment are used on popular television in our own time. In these circumstances, it can be hard for members to convey to a reporter that the group finds their tone patronising and that the group's work represents a belief in the rights of a particular constituent group, not a wish for charity, pity or condescension. On the other hand, particularly when it comes to the local press, the pressure to find interesting material, tight deadlines and a lack of journalists to follow up stories, mean that a well-crafted news media release or, indeed, feature story is highly likely to be published in the form submitted: an opportunity not to be passed over lightly (Rose 2005). Radio is also extremely news-hungry, often with local reports every hour, and should not be neglected as a well-followed source of information.

Thus, using all forms of media requires care and skill, as does ensuring that the group featured in the press or on television is represented in a way that will not be damaging to the group itself and that will convey the desired message, as opposed to being merely newsworthy. Asking for a veto on transmission, and getting this in writing, can be important in the case of a whole programme. This is because a danger in programme and film-making that is not controlled by the group can be of meeting someone else's agenda and preoccupations at the expense of either the group's objectives or the empowerment process. In the past, a number of groups have had particularly negative experiences with television directors which, in one case, almost broke up the group. A group of grandparents had given considerable time to the preparation of a training film, only to find that its input was juxtaposed with contradictory views from another party and did not have the impact they wanted. Another group found that they were being expected to behave in all respects as the director wanted them to, to the point where they became deskilled and lacking in confidence, and lost their sense of direction as a group. They also found that conflicts broke out between group members over how this situation was to be handled which could not be resolved because the group no longer had the privacy in which to do this.

There is a further danger of being distracted from the group's issues. The sheer time and attention the media demand may temporarily disrupt the local campaign. In the context of an endemic celebrity culture, the prospect of gaining public profile can be dangerously seductive. However, people from marginalized groups are not always represented in ways they can accept in the media: one of the groups facilitated by the university students in America chose to challenge the negative and, as they perceived it, racist way they had been presented in the local media. Asking the questions WHAT?, WHY? and HOW?, with the assistance of the exercises in problem analysis, evaluation and prioritizing covered in Chapter 4, are essential tools for weighing up the pros and cons and taking an informed decision before engaging with any form of media. They can help groups to demand both a more positive portrayal of themselves and their campaign and also a coverage of their own issues rather than current preoccupations with, for example, demonizing young people or portraying all disabled people as 'brave' and 'courageous'.

Not all groups rely solely on internet and electronic communication. RondsPoints, the parents' group in Montreal, publishes a twice-yearly magazine that is distributed widely around the district. Attractively formatted and illustrated, it is produced entirely by members of the group using both personal and the local family centre's computers, with printing and binding undertaken at the centre. Besides raising awareness of the existence of the group and encouraging new members by coverage of the group's activities and campaigns, each issue contains a mix of items of entertainment and local interest with other pieces offering practical help and information for parents in general. The magazine is important as a symbol and representation of the identity of the group. In similar fashion, Action Autonomie produces a magazine, *La Renaissance,* three times each year, which is published in both paper copy and electronically on the organization's website (www.actionautonomie.qc.ca).

Changing Roles: Handing Over to the Group

As we have progressed through the stages of the model, we have seen members taking on more and more responsibility for the group. They increasingly share both groupwork and practical tasks with the original facilitators, who may be paid workers or other, perhaps founding, group members, all learning and developing together. The facilitator encourages group members to believe in the capabilities they so obviously possess and are increasing over time. The groupworker's task thus changes from an emphasis on structuring the decision-making process to creating space and opportunities for group members to work autonomously. Whilst much of this section discusses groups with an outside facilitator, the issues are also relevant in many self-run groups where roles can also change over time. Different group members come to the fore and use new-found skills and confidence. There can be less reliance on key individuals, who perhaps had a role in establishing the group initially, as ownership becomes more widely held and as a larger number of people take responsibility for both tasks and group maintenance.

An example of this change of direction took place with a neighbourhood-based group of young people in Nottingham. On the first occasion that the group members ran a summer holiday activity scheme, the facilitators had to assist members with all aspects of the planning and running of the scheme, using the 'taking action' techniques outlined in previous chapters. The next time round, the groupworkers stayed in the background and played a more advisory role. In direct terms, they only needed to provide or to point members towards, for example, information on sources of funding, regulations relating to play schemes and on the practicalities of running their scheme. This left members free to consolidate and extend the skills and awareness they had developed previously. This process is also visible in the Youth Dreamers. As the young people have become more knowledgeable about writing applications for funding, contacting potential supporters, contributing to meetings with adults and also confident enough to facilitate after-school sessions for other young people by themselves, the role of the supporting teacher has retreated more into the background until she is seen as a resource to be called on by the group as needed (Berdan *et al.* 2006, p. 35).

To be sensitive to these changes and to adapt their practice accordingly, facilitators need to be on their toes: using evaluation processes and continuing debriefing and consultancy to stay alert to the way the group is evolving. The very same questions that lie at the heart of empowerment work form the framework of evaluation:

- WHAT are the issues and problems members currently face?
- WHY do these problems exist?
- HOW can we as facilitators enable members to achieve change?

Of course, as always, in order to keep the work progressing non-oppressively, these questions must be guided by and asked within the framework of the statement of principles that underpins all self-directed groupwork (Chapter 3).

At this stage of a self-directed group, the groupworkers are occupying a far less central role. Group members themselves will have become increasingly skilled in relation to both group task performance and group maintenance or 'process'. Consequently, they take much more of the responsibility for moving the group forward than hitherto. There may still be times when the facilitators move to the fore again temporarily. For example, a group may hit the doldrums for a period, or it may become static simply because members are enjoying the performance of tasks for their own sake rather than as a means to an end, or because the social pay-offs of group membership have caused them to lose sight of their longer-term aims. Generally, however, in a group that has 'made it' through to this stage, such episodes are short-lived. A brief return to the use of earlier planning and action techniques will normally get the group back on course. As Astarte from the Youth Dreamers says, 'If we can't go through trials, we can't move forward and be strong' (Berdan *et al.* 2006, p. 36).

As groups mature, they become able to spot and handle problems like these over group 'process' by themselves. They become increasingly secure in the authority of their own knowledge base (Munn-Giddings and McVicar 2007). A good example of this is provided by the experiences of one women's self-help and action group. In campaigning for the resources to set up a women's centre, the members had found their strength and identity as a group to be a crucial asset. Then, when the group became transformed into the steering group to establish the centre, some members were frightened by the complexities of acting as employers and left the group. Members realized from this how much support and development a new member would need before she could join them as a full partner in their current responsibilities and they knew that they did not have the time or the capacity to offer that level of support during this period. Consequently, they took the decision themselves to close the group to new members until the centre opened. The concern was that, if anyone had joined the group at this time, without massive support that could not be offered during this period, she could have become perplexed by the talk of constitutions, job descriptions, and other aspects of employing and managing staff. This would have been a confidence-sapping, not a confidence-building experience. The Youth Dreamers similarly recognize the different levels of support and contribution members can both need and offer and that it is possible for young people to be involved at a range of levels: from simply using the centre or taking part in one-off events, through to facilitating sessions on a regular basis and eventually becoming members of the Board. Young people can move between these levels of involvement and responsibility as they gain experience and confidence, and often are both giving and receiving support at the same time.

. . . And Withdrawing

Although we have constantly stressed the open-ended nature of involvement in self-directed groups, it is eventually the case that the facilitators, especially if they are professionals or from outside the group, may need to judge when it is appropriate to withdraw completely from the group. Even if they were the initiators, they do not necessarily need to continue for ever. However, letting go of something you have been so close to is not easy. Furthermore, the process of handing over needs to take place carefully and over quite a long period of time.

When a group is contemplating becoming self-sustaining, then action and direction, like participation, require formal and explicit structures based on democratic principles. These include delegating responsibility and distributing authority to those best able to handle it, rather than to the most popular or most dominant individuals. Various groups have chosen to rotate or share tasks amongst all members. The group itself needs to determine who will exercise power and authority on its behalf and who will have access to information. To ensure that this transition does not entail becoming oppressive in the process, both power and knowledge should be shared as widely as possible, whilst also recognizing that things have to get done. There is no one clear process of how power can be transferred in professionally-initiated groups to the members (Seebohm *et al.* 2010). It is a two-way process. As the members gain more autonomy, the groupworker, too, must be preparing to release control and move out of the 'central person' role (Preston-Shoot 2007 pp. 146–150). This needs to be done in a skilled and measured way, giving attention to both practical and relationship aspects of the group's functioning. Rather than a uniformly-paced withdrawal, as would be the case in structured conventional groupwork, letting go involves the skill of gauging when the group has become sufficiently self-motivating and self-resourcing for the facilitators' contribution to its functioning, at both task and emotional levels, no longer to be essential. Unless the group has become resourced from elsewhere or has achieved its purpose and is drawing to an end, it is crucial for the facilitators to make a realistic assessment of the group's strengths and functioning at this time, not dependent on a pre-determined idea of what is appropriate in general terms.

This stage in a group's life needs to be viewed flexibly and there are a variety of ways in which members can be supported towards more shared and distributed power. Strategies can include the facilitators coming only to alternate meetings, then, in consultation with members, every third meeting and so on. At this stage, at the end of each meeting, when plans are being made for 'what next', part of the discussion could be whether the facilitator needs to attend the next meeting or not. Two common misconceptions can be traced in groups that claim to be self-directed but yet follow a scheduled number of weeks of facilitation and then do not long outlive their workers leaving. Firstly, withdrawal cannot be built into the planning of a group in advance and, secondly, it is not a 'once and for all' activity. This shows that groupworkers who may have been attracted by the efficacy of the WHAT, WHY, and HOW process in beginning a group and engaging the motivation of members may not fully have understood or adopted the statement of principles of self-directed groupwork (Chapter 3), out of which 'open-ended length' (Chapter 4) and withdrawal only by negotiation and in agreement with members will flow.

CIFAN is a group of North American public organization workers who are unhappy about the directive and authoritarian management approaches that are being introduced into their workplace. A trade union officer found out about the self-directed groupwork process and, after a brief introduction into the approach, decided to apply it to a series of three meetings she was convening. Far more than the expected number of workers came along and attendees engaged animatedly. An agenda for action was formulated at the end of the third (HOW) meeting and roles and responsibilities were delegated to small number of volunteers. Follow-up meetings were called but were poorly attended and the campaign did not gain momentum. Besides not appreciating the risks of telescoping the 'preparing to take action' stage (Chapter 4), the facilitator saw the self-directed approach as a strictly time-limited intervention, most probably based on assumptions arising from other areas of her work. In the brief initial preparation she had not sufficiently 'taken stock' (Chapter 2). Members had had an initial experience which, on all accounts, they experienced as positive and empowering but the premature termination of self-directed facilitation cast them adrift. The campaign was then led by self-appointed leaders and got nowhere.

Despite a less empowering beginning, Friends in Action groups for mental health services users remodelled more successfully from a staff-run to a self-run basis (Bates and Steven 2011). Whilst these groups could not initially have been considered self-directed, some of them did ultimately become so. Some important lessons can be drawn from the process of this transition from professionally-run to self-run. These include that any move to less dependence on professional involvement must be done in discussion, negotiation and agreement with group members. A major challenge to being self-run is the absence of belief people have that they can indeed manage without worker support (ibid., p. 21). So that capacity and self-confidence can develop, the group must dictate its own pace and timescale, members should be able to take on as much or as little as they can handle and workers must 'check-in' occasionally with the groups as they move to independence.

Another positive example of moving towards self-facilitation was an annual neighbourhood music festival that gradually became a self-sustaining event over a period of ten years, during which time the facilitating youth worker moved into a background consultative role. Although many of the bands that played in the early festivals remained involved in its organization, a new generation came forward to take responsibility and new performers were found every year. Every year there was a question over whether it would happen but it always came together in the end. The healthy aspect of this instability was that it forced those remaining to undertake new recruitment. This required fresh publicity and open meetings. It put responsibility for the event back within the local community, avoiding it becoming the slick operation of a small clique.

Similarly, in ATAG, once the youth facility was underway and running successfully, it was decided with the young people that two of the three original groupworkers should withdraw. The probation officer remained involved in a supportive role, dictating neither pace nor decisions to the group members. He saw himself, rather, as being there to support them in their decisions and to help them move forward if they got stuck.

Pre-judgements about withdrawal make no more sense in groupwork than they would, in our view, in work with individuals. Self-directed groups tend to be long-term and to require an extended process of withdrawal as well as of development. If the facilitators leave prematurely or too quickly, the group will be badly shaken and may even fold. This is a measure of the very long journey that group members have experienced up to that point and of the 'to and fro' nature of the model, where it is often necessary to revisit earlier stages.

Evaluation

To avoid any misjudgements, the skill of evaluating performance must be central to all the stages of the self-directed approach. It is important that groupworkers and members learn the skills involved in evaluation, and establish the necessary responsiveness to constructive criticism and suggestions. Evaluation helps to consider whether the self-directed approach has been effective or not, and what has contributed to that performance. While evaluation has become much more common in practice in recent years, it tends to be mainly focused on outcome rather than process and to be driven by funders' and sponsors' interests (Pullen Sansfaçon 2011). To be effective, evaluation needs to be emphasized from the start, to resist such a narrowing of focus and not to be seen as predominantly a feature of the group termination stage, as can be the case in conventional groupwork (Preston-Shoot 2007; Zastrow 2009).

Evaluation of the group process

Maintaining the emphasis on full participation of group members, the evaluation of the group will be conducted jointly by groupworkers and members. In any approach that aims to be member-centred, joint evaluation must be a key constituent. The facilitators in self-directed groups have to be prepared to open the purposes and objectives of their activities, and likewise the values these are intended to represent, to detailed scrutiny. Both members and facilitators need to develop evaluative skills, so that they are able to comment on their own and each other's work to date and to become more effective as a result.

The broad questions to be asked in reviewing and evaluating the group's work to date cover all the steps in the earlier stages of the model: whether the group was planned in an open and shared way; whether, with appropriate facilitation by the groupworkers at all points, the group succeeded in setting its own agenda of issues and analysing why the problems on this agenda existed; whether they decided clearly what action to take, and effectively broke it down into a series of tasks that were then shared out between themselves and carried through efficiently. At the same time, there needs to be consideration of whether members' expectations have been met in the group, whether it has achieved its aims, whether members have found the method used to be an effective and appropriate one, and whether changes or further developments are required. An essential backdrop to answering these questions is the principles for self-directed work set out in Chapter 3. By looking at what happened in the light of these principles, the key question of whether the group has been an empowering or oppressive experience for members will be addressed.

The process of evaluation itself does not stand apart from this scrutiny. The question should be asked, here too, as to whether it is carried out in a way that is thoroughly collaborative with group members. The issues discussed in relation to consultancy and recording in Chapters 3 and 4 have clear resonance here. After each meeting the workers, who facilitate the RondsPoints group at the Famijeunes centre in Montreal, meet with colleagues to evaluate and discuss the morning's session and to provide hand-over information to those who will facilitate the following day. Although group members have not been explicitly invited to join in this de-briefing – something which the facilitators intend to remedy – members are still within earshot as they chat and prepare to leave. They show by their side comments, salutations and 'waving to us as they pass the window' that they are thoroughly relaxed with what is going on. Group members are, though, explicitly involved in periodic evaluation through contributing to the agency's annual review for its funders and in their write-ups about the group in their twice-yearly magazine. The young people in the after-school group facilitated by the UMass students undertake a quick evaluation of each session and this information is then drawn on for an overall evaluation at key stages in the group's life and is also used to inform reflection during the classroom consultancy between group meetings.

It is important to bear in mind that both group task and group process should feature in the evaluation. Co-operative working of the sort involved in self-directed groups takes place at the meeting-point between the need for task achievement – that is, for doing something concrete and visible – and the needs of individuals and of the group. The inter-relationship between establishing a secure and empowering emotional climate, on the one hand, and effectively carrying out practical tasks, on the other, will no doubt emerge from this process of review and evaluation.

Reflecting this inter-relationship, as influenced by the particular values of empowerment reflected in the six principles of self-directed groupwork, certain issues will come to the fore in considering how far the group's aims have been achieved. For example, have members gained more choice and greater control over aspects of their lives and challenged the forces that are oppressive to them, constraining their potential and life chances? Are they being treated with greater fairness and responsiveness by existing facilities, services and institutions, indicating a change of approach in significant people towards members? Not everybody in an organization or geographical area who had previously devalued or discriminated against the group members is likely to have changed their views, opinions and behaviours. However, any such changes can begin a process of *positive* 'labelling' among those who have the power and capacity to block or open up opportunities. In saying this, we are very clear that such labels or images are not characteristics of the members nor is it their responsibility to change, rather that responsibility lies with the oppressor; for example, challenging homophobia is the responsibility of heterosexual people (Cosis-Brown and Cocker 2011; Fish 2012). However, one measure of the success of empowerment work is to see the labellers, the image-makers, beginning to change. It is behaviour as much as attitudes that counts, as reflected in provisions, resources and procedures. If taken as the primary focus, attitudes can provide an excuse for liberal posturing which merely marks continued oppression and discrimination in practice.

To be consistent with the values of empowerment, any gains made by group members on their own behalf, often in the form of new or changed facilities or service provision, should also be available to people outside the campaigning group. The Dream House, for example, is open to all young people and serves as a resource for the whole community. How far are the new facilities under democratic control and seen by the wider community as 'theirs'? It is no use acquiring provision by the sweat and toil of group members that becomes merely a reflection of the oppressing institutions they have been challenging, nor simply to replace one group of oppressors with another, perhaps more insidiously because it can be masked as devolved control but merely be doing the authorities' job for them on unchanged terms. Once again, we must be on the alert for pseudo self-directed practice, adopted because the techniques can so effectively engage people to address a task. As described earlier, such educational methods as problem-based and enquiry-based learning may purport to be grounded in Freirean educational principles but are entirely devoid of political context and goals: Freire's pedagogy, when translated and transferred into the mainstream, invariably gets stripped of its critical edge (Zuniga 2011). If the ATAG youth hut, or the Dream House, had not been widely used and democratically run by local young people, they would offer little improvement over existing facilities.

What we have not included here is explicit evaluation of group mood or 'problems' (Zastrow 2009, pp. 105–118), defined in terms such as 'flight', 'apathy' and 'inadequate decision making'. There are two interconnected reasons for this. Firstly, in empowerment work, such features are of no relevance in their own right; the work is externally, not internally focused. Secondly, such factors cannot be measured in isolation or independently but would need to be assessed as part of the progress of work towards the group's main objectives. Hence, they are subsumed within such questions as those raised above about achievement of goals, such as the acquisition of more resources and members experiencing less oppression, discrimination and devaluing behaviour.

There are examples that illustrate this in the life of the Ainsley Teenage Action Group. Members became demoralized, with a dropping off of attendance and enthusiasm, when it appeared that control of their campaign to get a youth hut was being taken over by a committee dominated by adults, set up in that form on the insistence of the County Council Youth Service as potential funders. Similarly, they were disorientated, with decision-making effectively neutered, when a local councillor, whom they had come to view as an ally, described the group members as 'offenders' in a newspaper interview. Among members, there were conflicting feelings of furious anger and deep hurt. It was task-focused activities, using techniques outlined earlier, that enabled them to overcome such setbacks by analysing the issues that underlay the events and planning to take action to deal with them.

Evaluative Techniques

Techniques for carrying out group evaluation, then, include all those that were listed in Chapter 4 as suitable for focusing on goal selection and task performance. These are equally appropriate for this re-assessment of the group's progress and of the remaining issues it should tackle. Preston-Shoot (2007, pp. 181–186) and Sabo-Flores (2008) provide details of further techniques that may be adapted. The use of techniques may be different at this stage of the group from the earlier stages since the facilitators have by now receded more into the background. The group members are more likely to conduct their own thought showers, write out their own statement cards, draw their own grids, and so on.

The UMass students use an evaluative exercise called 'Roses and Thorns' where group members are asked to identify something that they liked about the day's session, represented by the rose. The thorn is something they feel the group could improve on. This reflection time gives them a sense of contribution on an individual level where other group members are paying attention to what they say. The student facilitators encourage the group members not to repeat comments. By gaining a range of opinions, the comments serve as the start of a discussion about the group and how things are going. One technique that we have found particularly effective in our own practice is the concentric circle exercise, outlined for another purpose in Chapter 4. In the context of evaluation, the circles can be used to represent a target and the greater or lesser achievement of aims, with the 'bull's eye' obviously representing 100 per cent success. Members, either individually or as a group, can plot on the circles the point any particular task has reached. Different judgements of this can be compared over time or, even more graphically, the sheet of paper can be marked periodically with arrowed lines going inwards or outwards, showing the progress of action towards its goal. The target can be divided into sections to represent different aspects of the group process. A rather less nuanced way of representing this is with traffic lights, where green indicates that the goal has been completely met, amber partially met, and red as yet unmet.

Evaluation of the members

Unlike traditional practice, self-directed groupwork does not involve an individualized evaluation of each member's progress in the group. The goals of the intervention concern the group as a whole and their achievement or otherwise is measured at that level. Although there is no doubt that individuals develop both practical and social skills (Cohen and Mullender 2000), it is axiomatic to the approach that these are seen as secondary and not primary outcomes. It is our view that this must be so. So strong are wider social pressures towards 'blaming the victim', that to allow personal developments to have undue significance would be a dangerous step back towards patronising and pathologizing orientations.

Evaluation of the facilitators

In traditional groupwork, the groupworkers normally evaluate their own performance. At the most, they may seek limited comments from members to feed into this process, typically through a closing evaluation exercise at each meeting. An example of this would be a round of 'Resent and Appreciate' whereby each member in turn is asked to say one thing they resented or disliked about that week's session and one thing they liked or appreciated. The groupworkers might keep notes on the responses and feed these into their own subsequent evaluation of the group. In self-directed groups, though, the underlying belief in partnership makes it far more important to carve out a central role for the members throughout the process of evaluation, including the evaluation of the facilitators.

In Chapter 6, we gave an example from the Ainsley Teenage Action Group that demonstrated how facilitators undertaking an evaluation of their own performance with their consultant were challenged to include the group members. In the process, they re-examined their views on the matter and discovered that there was a fundamental contradiction between their talk of openness in the group and their separation of their own learning from what they expected of group members.

Since we first wrote, it has become much more common and, indeed, good practice for users of services to be involved in the governance of organizations, particularly in the voluntary sector but also in some areas of state health, social care and education services (Badham and Wade 2008; Care Services Improvement Partnership 2008; Fleming *et al.* 2010). This may be through patients' forums, service user groups or school councils, for example, and can lead to direct participation in the selection of staff and the management of their performance. Action Autonomie, like other groups portrayed in this book, describes itself as a partnership between paid employees and activists. The board of the organization meets monthly and is made up of eleven survivors (drawn from various strands of the organization's work) and one worker representative. Twice a year, the board meets with the whole worker team, the focus of one of these meetings being to agree the 'business plan' for the organization for the year ahead. Action Autonomie is funded predominantly by a grant from the Quebec Province's 'Secretariat for Autonomous Action'.

The kind of issues that are considered in the facilitators' performance, just as much as the way this is done, should reflect the central tenets of the self-directed approach. Hence, values will need to occupy a key place in what is being evaluated as well as in how it is measured. There might, for example, be a detailed examination by the group members and self-reflection by the groupworkers themselves, of the 'fit' between the facilitators' expressed value position, as reflected in the statement of six principles, and the way they have actually related to group members. It is by no means uncommon for professionals to talk about working in partnership while, in fact, constantly reinforcing their own more powerful position. Conversely, facilitators may find that they have been able, over time, to move closer to what empowerment requires from their practice or to reach a more mature manifestation and realization of their values.

It can, of course, be most instructive to chart this development. Detailed points to consider might include the extent to which each facilitator, and the groupwork team together, have been able to become more open with group members: better able to help them set their own goals; increasingly alert to what is a 'normal' response to adversity through group members' eyes; more aware of the need for, and more effective in, fighting for improved resources, both through and outside of the group; and generally more skilled in this type of groupwork. Beyond this, each facilitator may fruitfully consider the extent to which their wider practice, including with individuals, has changed as a result of their involvement in the group. Have they moved towards a more open and shared style in all their work, for example, and have they shown greater willingness and ability to refer people on, when they feel ready, to other self-directed groups or projects in the community?

Thus, the values of self-directed groupwork and its associated methods and techniques cannot be compartmentalized. Self-directed groupwork becomes, as facilitators' own understanding and awareness grows through practice and evaluation, a 'life-style choice'. Preston-Shoot, who reviews self-directed groupwork in highly complementary terms and integrates much from it into his proposed directions and practices for 'effective groupwork', makes a similar point:

> groupwork knowledge and skills will have little beneficial impact on research, organisational leadership, staff development and involvement with experts by experience, unless they become integral to each practitioner's mindset and approach to their work. (Preston-Shoot 2007, p. 188)

Conclusion

The impact of self-directed groups that run their course through to maturity is both deep and far-reaching. On meeting people who have belonged to such groups, it is clear what an effect their involvement has made (see, for example, Arches and Fleming 2007, and Centre for Social Action 2011, and also the many quotes from group members in book chapters, articles and films on the approach). Self-directed groupwork has provided a framework for understanding, and experience and skills for handling, the personal and wider relationships of the society in which group members are living, even in the face of unemployment, poverty, racism, and all the other oppressive aspects of contemporary society.

The groups also provide an opportunity to experience 'an alternative culture' (Sennett 2011), in which people are able to pool ideas and grow together towards an understanding of how they and others like them are oppressed, but also of how they can fight back, and support one another during the emergence of a new way of thinking and responding. In our society's dominant neo-liberal culture (Hall 2011), people are expected to vie against and outdo one another (Sennett 2006). The self-directed approach has helped to show that people with, on the surface, very different priorities and values can cooperate and rely upon one another, whilst working toward genuine improvements and change.

Finally, in 'taking over', groups make an impact far beyond members' immediate lives and surroundings. They provide ideas and support to others to aim for similar achievements. Their success and visibility make space for new groups to go in the same direction, and thus contribute significantly to developments that can enable real empowerment to spread more widely.

8

Spreading the Reach and Moving Forward

We have aimed in this book to reach groupworkers, be they paid workers, volunteers or peer members. We have argued the relevance of the self-directed model across organizational settings and have considered the necessary transformation of conventional working practices to reflect a set of essential practice principles. These have been translated into a five-stage model which has been explored in some depth. In this closing chapter, we shall review the strides self-directed groupwork has made into new areas since we first wrote about it and will look to the future. What contribution might self-directed groupwork make over the next 20 years?

Over the past 20 years, we have seen self-directed groupwork, often under the wider auspices of social action (Fleming 2009), permeating and demonstrating relevance and results in areas only tentatively signposted when the model was first framed: in education and training, in research and evaluation, in project and service development, and in management and organizational practice. We had always believed that the self-directed model had an immensely wide applicability (Mullender and Ward 1991). Indeed, there is no reason, in terms of its ability to encompass the complex causation of contemporary social problems and to provide a methodology for tackling them, why self-directed groupwork should not be the norm for people seeking to create change in many contexts, leaving currently more accepted approaches on the periphery.

The group, of course, is an essential feature of this landscape. As in the direct practice described and examined in the previous chapters, what we have shown the approach has to offer is not merely a new configuration of descriptive features or a new menu of techniques. Rather, it is a clear statement of the principles from which flow methods of working

161

together and interacting with other people. In particular, there is a distinctive collaborative commitment to achieving group aims, goals and purposes on issues recognized, identified and owned by the group members themselves. Both this commitment and the values from which it springs are a world apart from those to be found, explicitly or implicitly, in much current work. We shall now explore the adoption of self-directed groupwork, often under the wider auspices of social action, in education and training, in research and evaluation, in project and service development, and in management and organizational practice.

Education and Training

The links between the self-directed approach and education, training and learning should be clear. The influence of Freire's (1972) writings, on the development of the approach, ground it within a learning framework from the start since he was an educationalist whose work was adopted by other professions. Peer education and 'bottom up' learning have an obvious egalitarian value-base that is sustained beyond the end of any specific period of training.

We have undertaken training based on the self-directed model in a wide variety of settings and with a diverse range of participants, including health workers, teachers, youth workers and youth offending teams, social care workers, police officers, local communities, young people and researchers, throughout the UK and in America and in Eastern and Western Europe (Fleming 2004). The self-directed approach has also been used by others in educational settings, for example, teachers in a variety of American schools (Berdan *et al.* 2006) and in universities (Arches 2012), as well as to inform widely disseminated training materials produced by other organizations (see, for example, Badham 2004; Woodcraft Folk 2010).

With groupwork at the core of any training, most commonly the self-directed approach is used to enable people to learn experientially about the approach itself: learning through both the content and the process of the training. The aim is to help people make their practice more relevant to service users or peers and the programme is broadly based around the stages in the process:

- WHAT are the issues and problems we face?
- WHY do these problems exist?
- HOW can change be achieved?

Again as in the model itself, this involves considering what role we can play in enabling people to achieve change, how we can develop practice that supports people to achieve that change, and how we can act to change our way of working and reflect on and review what we have done. In the same way as in self-directed groupwork itself, the trainers facilitate rather than lead. They work to create a learning environment where people are listened to, can contribute their ideas and are encouraged to set out plans for acting on their suggestions with the aim of developing reflective practice. One participant reflected at the end of a week-long training event: 'The greatest strength was the way in which we experienced the process of Social Action through particular strategies. We came to an understanding of Social Action in an authentic, process-based way' (Fleming 2004, p. 38).

An example of social action training is a programme of training sessions with people working with young people in three Ukrainian cities. We made it very clear from the outset that we did not come in with solutions or answers to Ukrainian problems. We offered the framework, but the actual content was to be theirs. The courses were experiential. All the exercises and techniques used on the course could be used with young people themselves. Each course had three parts: the first was a week-long workshop and involved the identification and exploration of 'what' were the problems confronting young people, then understanding their causes and 'why' they existed, and finally examining different models of intervention. This involved identifying the value-base they wanted to work to and developing ideas for working in partnership with young people to identify and address the issues they faced, that is, the 'how' of the selected response. Time was then spent on developing action plans. The second part of the course covered the next six months, during which participants attempted to put their action plans into practice and to adapt and use the learning from the course in their work. The third and final part was another visit from the facilitators to review progress, reflect on and share the learning from what had actually happened in the work, and establish networks and mechanisms for continuing support and peer consultation among participants.

The Ukrainian youth social workers developed many projects with the young people with whom they worked as a result of this training. These included new initiatives in residential institutions for young offenders, the development of groups of disabled people enabling them to have more control over their lives, work with the police, contacting and working with street children, work with young men and young women on issues of violence and relationships, and self-help groups for young parents. Another consequence of this programme was that the book *Self-directed Groupwork* (Mullender and Ward 1991) was translated into Ukrainian, under the auspices of the European Union's TACIS Scheme for the development of civil society institutions in the former Soviet Union. It became, and continues to be, a key text on training courses in the social welfare field.

A further illustration of using the self-directed approach as a methodology for teaching and learning, this time in a higher education setting, is the UMass Service Learning Class. This class uses the approach to develop transferable self-directed facilitation skills among university students (Arches 2012). *Self-directed Groupwork* (Mullender and Ward 1991) and *Writing for Change* (Berdan *et al.* 2006) are core texts. Following a period of in-class experiential learning, as part of an after-school programme one afternoon a week, the UMass students then facilitate a self-directed group with young people at a secondary school located in a disadvantaged area of Boston adjacent to the university.

These examples illustrate how the self-directed approach can be applied to learning and skill development on a wide range of topics, in different cultural settings and in all stages of training and development. The boundary of the term 'training' is very permeable and the issues discussed and the examples described in other parts of this chapter in relation to research, to project and service development and to organizations, clearly overlap and interlink.

Those who use self-directed groupwork within a wider, social action framework are clear about the broader educational opportunities this creates for students. Members of the Youth Dreamers said they learned more and completed more work in the group than in their other classes (Cary *et al.* 2004), while their teacher lists the skills and knowledge they have gained from their involvement as covering improvements in English language, maths, social studies, technology and real-world skills (Berdan 2006). This is despite the fact that members of self-directed groups are often those who have found conventional education a challenge. Often, teachers remark that group members do more within the group than in their classes, asking the facilitator 'How do you get them to do all that work?' Her response is: 'I don't. They do' (Cary *et al.* 2004, p. 72). The young people explain that they are working on a project they choose; they feel their voice is being heard, that their opinions matter and that they are working to make change happen in the community. These are the key reasons why they participate so actively and work so hard (ibid.). It boils down, essentially, to mutual respect.

Research and Evaluation

In the course of developing and refining the self-directed groupwork model in practice, we quickly realized the application of the principles and process to research and evaluation (Everitt *et al.* 1991, 1992; Ward 1992). From this developed a particular approach to research, underpinned by self-directed principles and process, that has become known as 'social action research' (Ward and Fleming 1999, Fleming and Ward 2004). The six principles of self-directed groupwork were reworded with the focus on research rather than practice, but their essence is unchanged (Everitt *et al.* 1991, 1992; Ward 1992, Fleming and Ward 1996).

Social action research is participatory in that it seeks not only to discover meaning but to explore its properties with the people who are the focus of the research. Those who might traditionally be considered 'research subjects' become research participants and engage collaboratively with the researchers in a process of gathering, refining and interpreting data. The notion of empowerment is closely aligned with this approach (Abu Samah 1996/7) as participants can and should be involved in all stages of the research process: deciding the parameters of the research, its framework, the questions and who should be involved; collecting and analysing the data; presenting and using the information gathered.

There are three distinctive aspects of social action research. First of all, social action research involves starting from the ideas and understanding of all those affected by or having an interest in the area of study. This does not mean including only patients or service users, for example, but all those who have an interest in a particular research project. As with self-directed groupwork, social action research involves respecting and viewing people positively as 'knowers': the experts in their lives. It involves a realization that research, just like empowerment practice, is a process of learning, development and change and that the researcher is a practitioner, as much as a researcher, in facilitating that process.

Secondly, in a similar way to self-directed groupworkers, social action researchers set in motion a process of participation and engagement. They work with interested parties to shape agendas, make decisions and control outcomes. This involves a relationship between researchers and participants that is non-hierarchical and recognizes everybody as having an equal but different contribution to make to the research process. Social action researchers need to be experienced in participative ways of working and to be committed to working in partnership. Thirdly, social action research involves a responsibility not to leave the participants or

Table 8.1 Framework for social action research

Taking stock	Identifying a research topic
	Forming the research team
Taking off	Planning the research strategy
	Identifying respondents
Preparing to take action	Engaging respondents
Taking action	Collecting data
	Analysing data
	Writing up
Taking over	Dissemination and action

the stakeholders stranded at the end of the research process, having learnt a great deal but not knowing what actions can be taken to change the things they have discovered. Social action research involves groups and communities moving from understanding and knowledge into action (Table 8.1).

An early research project we undertook using the self-directed approach was an evaluation of a project supporting families at risk of having children removed into care (Fleming and Ward 1992). As with the practice model, the research approach developed and gained refinement over time. A key advantage of the approach is that it not only generates deep and rich descriptions and explanations of situations that give clear insights into problems and issues, it also engenders knowledge, skills and structures that can be sustained after the research involvement is over. Social action research has evolved from working with people to ensure their perspectives and their voice are heard in ways they think are appropriate, to finding ways of their having a more and more active part throughout the research project, including taking action on the results as a necessary conclusion of the research process. Partnership and genuine participation throughout the research process mean engaging and supporting people to be active co-researchers and evaluators on projects. Examples include young people working as peer evaluators in the evaluation of a teenage pregnancy project (Fleming *et al.* 2009) and the employment of young people in age-exempt posts as

Associate Research Assistants at the Centre for Social Action (Fleming 2012a). These features are, of course, not unique to social action research but owe an enormous debt to feminist research (see, amongst a wide literature, Du Bois 1983) and have a very great deal in common with participative action research (see, for an example that teases out the stages, Dullea and Mullender 1999). There are also extensive sources on involving children and young people to an increasing extent in research (see, for example, Mullender *et al.* 2002). Thus, we can regard social action research as a framework that like-minded researchers can use to ensure that they establish their value-base very clearly at the beginning of the project and that they work in a collaborative way with the research participants throughout. The focus on acting on the research findings – taking action, in fact – is a vital part of the approach.

A fully fledged illustration of social action research is the Childcare Research Project, in which the Centre for Social Action was commissioned by a neighbourhood liaison group to work with it to develop and undertake a piece of research on the issues of training, education and employment opportunities in a particular urban neighbourhood (Fleming and Ward 2004). Members of the commissioning group included representatives of community and statutory organizations already working on these issues: health visitors, a further education college lecturer, members of residents associations and voluntary groups, play workers, community workers and youth workers. Discussions at the group's meetings had centred on barriers to the take-up of educational and employment opportunities already in existence in the area. The group suspected that a lack of affordable and quality childcare was a significant obstacle. It was agreed to carry out a research project investigating childcare needs amongst local communities, collecting views and experiences from parents and children. The neighbourhood liaison group became the steering group for the research.

The Centre recruited local people as researchers. They were very active in developing the parameters of the research. Their local skills and knowledge were important and local people remained integral to the whole of the research process. Those appointed were provided with training, in the course of which appropriate methods for information collection were developed. Consideration was given to the topics to be explored, who to include, and where and how contacts might be made. A set of carefully worded open questions was created, piloted and refined, to enable respondents to present their perspective based on their own experience.

The researchers, alongside a steering group, decided on five ways of collecting information:

1. group interviews with children, aged from 6 years old upwards;
2. group interviews with adults;
3. long individual questionnaires for adults;
4. long individual questionnaires for children and young people;
5. short questionnaires for adults to be completed on the street, outside the school gate, in the park or at the post office.

The range of data collection methods encouraged a breadth and depth of information, reflecting local people's experiences.

The researchers spoke to a total of 514 people, of whom 375 were adults and 139 young people. Once the primary information collection was completed, data analysis commenced. A whole-day meeting with the researchers led to the identification of a number of themes and approximately 30 initial code categories, which were honed down through further analysis. The researchers were keen for categories to include the breadth of data collected, which extended beyond the initial interests and focus of the commissioners of the research.

The findings were a surprise to the commissioners who, at the beginning of the project, had had clear ideas about expected outcomes. However, they were committed to finding out what local people thought. In fact, they mentioned bigger things than had been expected, identifying broader issues such as the cost of provision, the condition of the parks and lack of support for parents. Some members of the steering group were surprised by local people taking such a step back and highlighting more issue-based findings than had been expected. Children and young people, it was discovered, were not saying 'We want a swimming pool and an ice-skating rink', as had been anticipated by some but, instead, were seeking places to go where they would not be bullied, and parks where there were no dog faeces or syringes under the swings. Bullying and racism were big issues and flexibility and responsiveness in any provision were considered to be important. The needs of young parents, although they were a minority in the sample, were especially clearly expressed. They felt there was little support for them outside the generic parenting services. A number of young parents had been in public care and had no family support. Also, as interviewers were approaching anyone with a child on the street, a number of grandparents were unexpectedly included in the respondent sample. Some grandparents were fostering or had children living with them full-time and reported receiving very little personal support.

In collaboration with the steering group, the researchers produced an initial report in the form of a newsletter incorporating the views collected into themes agreed by both groups. It set out what children and young people had said, what adults had said, what children and young people would like and what adults would like. It then listed 13 agreed themes that people were asked to rank in priority order, firstly, as personal preference and, secondly, in terms of the needs of the community as a whole. This was a means of involving the wider community both in the analysis and the prioritization of issues and proposals for action. It also gave local people an opportunity to see their own personal experiences in the context of those of the whole community.

Returns from 400 newsletters showed that racism and bullying were major issues for both parents and children. The final report of the Childcare Research Project became an action plan, and the steering group became the Childcare Development Group. It increased the number of local people in its membership and took on board the action plan, working on a number of key issues. Many of the action points arising from the research were taken forward to create change in the area. For instance, the local community centre applied for money to fund subsidized places for both their after-school club and their playgroup. Parents' and children's reported reluctance to use parks – due to dog excrement, syringes, the presence of people consuming alcohol, and a whole range of other things that did not make it conducive for people to play or meet there – led to a clean-up campaign by the City Council, while a local group of parents applied for funding for a scheme called 'Play in the Parks'. Through this initiative, play workers were employed to run after-school and holiday sessions to encourage children back into the parks.

Social action research has been undertaken in a variety of settings and with a wide range of partners, stretching from villagers in rural Malaysia (Abu Samah 1996/7), emerging democracies in the former Soviet Union and parents of gender-nonconforming children in Canada (Pullen Sansfaçon *et al.* 2014 forthcoming) to numerous projects across the UK. An action-research project in partnership with the Ukrainian Institute for Social Research focused on working to create more child-focused services in post-communist Ukraine, particularly in residential and foster care (Fleming 2000), while the Nottingham Social Action Research Project (SARP) explored the relationship between inequalities, social capital and health in local communities (Fleming and Boeck 2005).

The Centre for Social Action worked with a group of foster carers to investigate children's contact with birth parents (Fleming 2005). The findings led to meetings between the foster carers and the social services department to draw up and implement an action plan based on the research. Actions carried out, resulting in changes to practice, included joint training on contact, with foster carers as trainers of social workers and other parents, a feasibility study for contact centres, and a meeting with a family court judge to discuss court practice in relation to decisions about safe contact. A further project for the Centre, working with young people as co-researchers, was a critical review of local government youth engagement structures (Fleming and Skinner 2007) that encompassed eight beacon local authorities across the UK. The recommendations to improve practice were disseminated widely to local authorities by the Local Government Improvement and Development Agency (IDeA). Further reports of research projects and evaluations are available on the Social Action Centre's website (www.dmu.ac.uk/csa).

Given the action-based nature of the social action research approach and the question-posing focus of self-directed groupwork, it is not surprising that the boundary between the two activities can sometimes be blurred nor that many groups specifically undertake research as part of their groupwork activities. There are clear links between practice and research. Indeed, these are reinforced as the process moves beyond investigation, analysis and evaluation towards plans for new and/or improved services and action to achieve these. This has been the case with No Limits Dementia, for example, who have worked in partnership with 'academic' researchers in pioneering research on the campaigning efforts of people with dementia (http://www.nolimitsdementia.com/, Bartlett and O'Conner 2010).

We are concerned not only about the potential for empowerment through research, but also reflexively about the importance of research for empowerment practice and, in this respect, we are seeking to fuse traditions (Gould 1999). The process of social action research requires a high level of practice skill by the researcher and mirrors self-directed groupwork. But, at the same time, it promotes a thorough and defensible research methodology as an essential feature for good practice, in so far as inquiry, intervention and evaluation re-express the 'cyclical process of information-action-reflection which can become a working routine' (Dullea and Mullender 1999, p. 85).

Consultancy on Project and Service Development

When we turn to the development of new services, once more, boundaries are not clear-cut. Self-directed practice itself often leads to the creation of new resources; training activities based on it similarly lead to action plans, research likewise identifies things that need to change and methods for achieving this.

The point we wish to make in this section is that self-directed groupwork has been used when we have been called in as consultants formally to work in support of organizations, teams and individuals in developing and setting-up services and projects. It fits well with any move away from a 'one-size-fits-all' view of services and offers methods that ensure the outcomes are not 'more of the same'. Much work in regeneration and in health and social care has been criticized for not engaging communities that will be affected. Self-directed groupwork focuses on engagement and, because of this, on the ownership by community members and service providers of any change created. In this way the method can provide a sound and practical way forward for many organizations where they are genuinely concerned for the participation of their stakeholders (Fleming 2012b).

Self-directed groupwork has been utilized on a wide range of projects and by various organizations and groups, for example, by a counselling service for those who have experienced sexual abuse, by a group of disabled people wanting to articulate how they feel about their facilities, and in establishing and evaluating projects for young homeless people. At the outset of a project, there is no way of knowing what the outcome will be. Because of the participant-centred nature of the approach, it is left up to the community or group to define the issues of concern and then to lead the enquiry/consultancy in the most appropriate direction as they define it. The partnership of the Centre for Social Action with the National Writing Project in the USA, for example, evolved in this way as a service development commission to the Centre for Social Action. Outcomes have included the Youth Dreamers and many other school projects, which feature strongly in this text, as well as in the book *Writing for a Change* (Berdan *et al.* 2006), which was awarded a prize by the American Society of Educational Publishers.

The self-directed approach to organizational and service development has been especially well received in Eastern Europe and the former Soviet Union. In Russia, for example, members of the Centre for Social Action have, over the years, worked in partnerships on projects as wide-ranging as the development of a national restorative justice scheme, transforming childcare services in the Sverdlovsk region and in a Disability Equality Project in Samara. In this last project, the approach was used to introduce local groups of disabled people to the principles of the social model of disability and to facilitate the development of action plans for their campaigning and lobbying of decision-makers to take on board the issues disabled people identified as important and, hence, to improve access to resources.

Closer to home, the model was used in a long-standing partnership with a housing association to work with young people and develop practical action to address their concerns (Centre for Social Action 2000). The project was initiated in response to the challenges the high proportion of young people on many housing estates presented for estate managers, in recognition that sometimes adults involved did not know how best to work with young people or engage with their energy and enthusiasm. The project entailed working with managers, tenants, residents associations and, of course, young people on three different estates. Whilst responses varied, the work of the young people in partnership with supportive adults achieved provision of new resources and, in two estates, continued after the end of the official project. Self-directed groupwork was also used to inform and facilitate the development of a network of organizations to promote and support the engagement and development of young people as researchers (Fleming *et al.* 2007) and, through the facilitated involvement of policy-makers and practitioners, the development of a framework for a community cohesion strategy in a large English local authority (Boeck *et al.* 2007).

Organizational Issues

We have found that self-directed groupwork can easily be applied to management roles in a range of organizations. Gray and colleagues (2008) address the impact of the introduction of a modernizing agenda to social services that has increased top-down 'business-focused' managerialist approaches to the organization, development and delivery of services. Recognizing that this has not been popular and that it is seen as a threat by many front line workers and service users, these authors argue that social workers must find ways of working within the new agenda to uphold the values and cultural heritage of social work. Adopting a perspective that resonates strongly with self-directed groupwork, they promote a 'communities of practice' approach (Wenger 1998) and the development of 'learning organizations' (SCIE 2004) as offering real opportunities for building bridges and reconciling 'managed' and participatory approaches to social care. Groupwork theory and expertise, where embedded with values of engagement and empowerment, can provide the repertoire of principles, understanding and skills that the leaders of such learning organizations and communities of practice would require. Groupwork's knowledge base is not only relevant for running groups but provides a conceptual framework from which to understand the dynamics, developments and processes involved in other aspects of practice. For example, if we look at ... work with organizations, an understanding of groupwork theory and practice is directly relevant. (Trevithick 2005, p. 99)

For one of the authors, in the course of a career that culminated in higher education management, it became increasingly clear that the values, knowledge and skills of a self-directed group facilitator were central to successfully inhabiting the new world of management. For example, the management team frequently needed to decide whether to consolidate existing provision or bid for new developments. The self-directed perspective meant, in practical terms, ensuring wherever possible that widely representative working groups were set up but, if time did not permit, at least that direct consultation took place. It meant involving outside stakeholders as fully as possible, for example, potential students, employers of graduates and also, in many cases, service users. Besides the values behind these processes, each of these contexts involved group facilitation. It was found that direction and decisions often became self-evident and achieved wide ownership. The result was a team that was not only very successful in its 'business' but, in parallel, had demonstrably high morale and commitment.

Set out in such bald terms these practices seem self-evident. However, in the context of a continuous seeping of new managerialism into the culture of public organizations (O'Reilly 2011), with universities being no exception, they do come to mark a different approach, one guided by an empowerment discourse and signified by a genuine concern for, and promotion of, people working together as group members. Where this works well, desired outputs and outcomes can flow naturally out of people working and interacting in groups. Then, targets and outcomes, structures and procedures no longer need to be the sole pre-occupation but, rather, are a consequential product of effective group facilitation. (See also Badham and Wade 2008, on 'Style of Leadership'.) In this vein, Pam Ward (2008) discusses self-directed group learning during the training of dental students (McHarg and Kay 2008) and how it can impact on their practice as clinical team leaders. She argues that, if contextualized in professional values promoting patient choice and interdisciplinary teamwork, self-directed learning can transfer into an empowering style of practice as clinicians, as clinical team leaders and as collaborating members of inter-professional healthcare organizations.

Pullen Sansfacon and Ward (2012) also argue for the importance of groupwork and, implicitly, a self-directed orientation, to inter-professional practice. They see this as being constrained by a business-orientated, managerialist discourse that dominates inter-professional arrangements and most current conceptions of team structure, team development and team management. This is compounded by issues about the authority, the relative contributions and the status of the professions within inter-professional arrangements which, in practice, have meant that medical practitioners, where present, take on leadership roles and, in their absence, professions line up according to the pecking-order of the medical world. These authors maintain that an alternative discourse, grounded in groupwork, when applied to inter-professional collaborative working could contribute to the promotion of equal relationships between the team members and models of communication that are respectful of different professional knowledge, values and skills.

It is not only managers who need to engage with organizational issues. This is the case for all professionals, especially in the public and not-for-profit sectors. There are specific challenges to being a practitioner seeking to undertake self-directed groupwork within an organization. It is easy to write, as we have done in earlier chapters, about engaging with people, be they patients, service users or any other groups of people determined to achieve social change on issues identified and owned by group members themselves, through a more empowering style of involvement. It is far harder, we realize, to make the necessary changes in practice and all that surrounds it, even when the need for change is obvious to practitioners and participants alike.

In theory, many organizations will be hospitable to empowerment given, as we stated in Chapter 2, how fashionable the term has become. Agency culture often starts with a very positive philosophy about human dignity and meeting needs. Then, under the accretions of paperwork, pressurized workloads, risk assessments and focus on outputs, to say nothing of frustrated service users and intractable resource problems, the rhetoric and reality begin to diverge (Pullen Sansfaçon 2011). Organizations are proficient at absorbing and diluting new ideas in accordance with their own norms and people who use the services can find themselves feeling frustrated and powerless in dealing with an agency whose mission is ostensibly to support them and yet which feels anything but supportive.

Pullen Sansfaçon (2007, pp. 2–4) describes how she experienced this while she was working for a voluntary organization in Quebec, Canada, that provided food and clothing for Native Canadian people experiencing poverty. One of her objectives was to set up a group that would enable service users to define the issues they faced and eventually to create alternative activities and resources that would replace the need for accessing basic food and clothes through the organization. She decided to set up a group of users that would work to incorporate the principles and process of self-directed groupwork. Since part of the organization's funding came from local government, her line manager was a qualified social worker from the local authority. She quickly realized that adopting an anti-oppressive practice framework and trying to challenge inequalities at both the social and structural level would not be straightforward. Using the self-directed groupwork model, she adopted the role of facilitator. After a few sessions of collective cooking (a project that emerged from the self-directed groupwork process), members of the group wanted her to take some food home that they had cooked collectively. However, her line manager called her in for a meeting and assertively told her that she would have to keep her distance from the group and adopt a 'more professional role', the rationale being that a social worker should not accept gifts or benefit from their intervention (Ordre Professionnel des Travailleurs Sociaux du Québec (OPTSQ) 1993). The upshot was that she did take the food home, on the grounds that it did not constitute a gift of significant monetary value, and later left to undertake a doctorate on the ethics of self-directed groupwork.

A different kind of organizational hindrance to the development of any group-based approach is the tendency to see groups as a kind of optional extra. As noted earlier (Ward 2009), groupwork is only regarded as a basic part of the job for specialist practitioners in limited areas of public sector work, such as fostering or alcohol misuse, or as the result of individual specialism or interest. This is all the more regrettable since, in many professional contexts – such as hospital-based nursing, teaching, and residential work, to name a few – there are 'groups' of patients, pupils, or residents already to hand. It never ceases to disappoint us how little appreciated is the notion that groups are a natural and normal, arguably predominant, aspect of everyday living. Even more concerning is that groups may often be viewed by hard-pressed managers and time-starved staff as a threat to be countered, rather than an opportunity for creative engagement and mobilization. It demands a special effort to step back and consider the potential of the group as a group. Once that leap of conceptualization has been made, the possibilities for empowering intervention become virtually endless.

Certainly, some workers *have* experienced problems in persuading their agencies or managers to permit this shift to a group-based approach based on a broader social analysis. Often, however, as our examples have demonstrated, those service users who may be seen as 'difficult' to work with or as 'sensitive' – as are many of the oppressed groups for whom self-directed groupwork has proven to be relevant and successful – are precisely those for whom management may be ready to accept an alternative approach that may have something new to offer. Any fresh ideas that can enthuse staff to try again may be welcome in an organization, and particularly ones that can be shown to have been successful elsewhere. Whether for these reasons or others, whilst not without initial scepticism, probation management was supportive of the Ainsley Teenage Action Group (see Chapter 6) and schools have accepted incorporation of the self-directed approach into their compensatory writing-skills programmes (Berdan *et al.* 2006).

Of course, potential groupworkers who do refuse to turn back when they confront organizational roadblocks run straight up against issues of power. In this respect, the keystone of self-directed groupwork – that responsibility for determining the purposes and goals of the group should lie with the group members – is both a help in eventually finding a path through the quandaries of power dilemmas, and a reason why staff at all levels may initially lack the courage to attempt to employ or support the model. It can look like very unsafe ground. However, it is necessary to decide whether to be a channel for the achievement of essential change, on behalf of and in conjunction with service users, or whether to ally with the obstacles to that change. If the organization demands that its staff 'be realistic' about what it is possible to change, then whose reality is to be preferred – theirs or that of service users? In such circumstances, it is often helpful to return to the principles for practice set out in Chapter 3 and to remind oneself why these seemed so important when considered in the safety of abstract discussion. Faced with the reality of organizational policies, these values become more, rather than less, vital. It is not possible to show respect for people without being prepared to challenge the forces that oppress them, even if this includes one's employing organization. Feeling the collective strength of the group and hearing the views of group members, reaffirming one's original intent and pressing forward for change, should be enough to boost any flagging resolve.

Where, in an organization, staff have to fight to get the self-directed approach itself and anti-oppressive ideals accepted, they also need to form alliances with other like-minded colleagues to achieve progress. They may have to struggle to be taken seriously and for their proposed developments not to be stifled. Persuading a whole team to try the approach or to lend its support is one way of finding collective strength. It also ensures that groups do not fade away when particular enthusiasts leave, thus damaging the credibility of this way of working, and that the values underpinning the work can be carried across into other areas of work, including individual contact. Workers can look for support outside their own agency as well as establishing a self-directed support or consultancy group for individuals across teams, agencies or disciplines. Where the organization cannot offer inspiring supervision, then setting up a peer support group or a formal or informal consultancy arrangement, whether within or outside the organization, can all be invaluable, as can attending relevant conferences, courses and practice exchanges and participating in on-line networks.

Support groups can themselves use the self-directed approach to ensure that decisions are the shared responsibility of the whole group and that members feel empowered and justified in pursuing their own issues. Furthermore, all the techniques described in Chapter 5, such as the force-field analysis, can be used to assess and bring about the necessary process of winning more support. The chief problem encountered by those who are trying to introduce self-directed groupwork has been isolation. Networking is the obvious answer to this. It assists in developing the skills required not only to practise self-directed work but also to handle organizational constraints. A group of people with experience of self-directed groupwork can be drawn together who are able to offer support, ideas and, ideally, consultancy to one another, to set up cross-fertilization of knowledge and skills and, in turn, to help new groups to develop. In this way, the approach continues to grow and develop, to become more widely known about and used, and to be more effective in its results.

Important allies who should never be forgotten if a campaign becomes inevitable to protect the approach once it is in use in an organizational setting, are the group members themselves. Our experience of occasions when group members have had the opportunity to speak to managers about how helpful they have found self-directed groupwork to be, and how they want to see it retained, has been startling. Group members typically do not mince words and they are the supreme experts on why the group is needed and what it has achieved for them. Group members also have the immensely powerful weapon always at their disposal of threatening to attract adverse publicity against the organization, which paid staff cannot do. Indeed, group members have a generally much wider sphere of operation open to them and we should not be afraid to let them fight on their own behalf, whilst never goading them on to do so if this does not arise naturally from the group.

Conclusion

Self-directed groupwork is an approach that can readily be adopted by all those who share the aims of social justice and emancipation. It is a people-centred model and, at the same time, is rooted in anti-oppressive values and a vision of structural social change. The principles and values that underpin the social movements of black, Asian and minority (BAME) people, of women, of lesbian, gay, bisexual and transgendered (LGBT) people, and of disabled people, and all related struggles, are embedded in it. Practitioners and activists are challenged to combine their own efforts with those of oppressed groups without colonizing them to achieve change. Group members, assisted by the facilitation of groupworkers, chip away at the forms of inequality that lie at the heart of oppressive social arrangements and which affect them all, across boundaries of diversity and intersectionality.

However, those who talk about empowerment must be clear about their responsibility *and the skills* they possess if they are to support effectively those seeking their own empowerment. Nothing is more inexcusable than raising expectations and creating commitments that then flounder because groupworkers do not know how to deliver their contribution. Self-directed groupwork is, therefore a highly disciplined and skilled approach requiring training, support and consultancy. Just as the model has been tested and modified since we first formulated it, it will continue to be refined in the light of continuing practice and experience.

The importance of values in marking out the distinctive nature of the approach and of each stage has been highlighted throughout this book. These values, in binding together in a complementary way the knowledge, skills and experience of group members and groupworkers, form an essential platform for this systematic, structurally grounded challenge to the degrading and stigmatizing conditions that are the practical manifestations of oppression.

Self-directed groupwork transcends conventionally defined boundaries between disciplines. Practitioners and activists in many settings can work in an empowering way if they fashion their practice in a manner that is congruent with its principles and value-base, formulated within an understanding of wider political perspectives and if they then translate its implications into their practice. They can transpose well-intentioned, committed but, sometimes, undisciplined work into a dynamic and refined approach that can sustain a clear commitment to social change objectives and stand up to critical scrutiny. Asking the questions 'WHAT?', 'WHY?' and 'HOW?' lies at the heart of this process.

This volume has shown that self-directed groupwork is alive and well in peer, volunteer and professionally facilitated groups addressing a diverse range of issues and across many countries. We have seen 'how' the values and methodology have taken root in other disciplines. Self-directed groupwork continues to sustain the mind-set and practices needed to achieve social justice through social action and community empowerment.

However, while acknowledging and celebrating these achievements, there is a continuing responsibility to invigorate, revitalize and galvanize to meet new challenges. This is all the more important in times of austerity, in an increasingly hostile and regressive political, social and economic environment. In such times, it is vital to re-engage with the core vision and mission and to re-energize open and honest collaboration with community members and users of services as partners in change. This is likely to be uncomfortable as it challenges and even threatens established practice and leadership, 'businesses' based on contracts not local need, organizational and professional power rather than common ownership of process and solutions. Organizations and all people within them need to think about doing things differently for the sustainable benefit of the community. Such reframing of what we do and why we do it in turn impacts upon relationships and behaviours of all involved wherever people meet together, privately and publicly.

What this book shows is the leap of faith taken by adopting the underpinning principles. The consequent practice of self-directed groupwork can make a difference that goes beyond what might previously have been seen as possible. It liberates opportunities never previously seriously considered. It means going beyond a culture represented by targets and outputs to developing a different ethos in the way people interact, work and, indeed, live together. This is not a technical exercise. It calls upon professionals, volunteers, peer activists and in fact anyone who finds themselves in a position where they are facilitating and supporting people to achieve change, to think again about the basics of 'what' they are doing, 'why' they are doing it and 'how' to go about their involvement.

To sustain such innovation requires engaging in an alternative culture with an established history, turning conventional practices on their head. Process comes first, with the confidence and expectation that 'product' will emerge from this. Instead of planning and then involving, it means starting off with engaging with people and moving thence to planning. It involves a double-sided value commitment: on one side, to push towards greater social justice; on the other, albeit pulled back by fear, reluctance and conventional wisdom, to surrender and share power.

For many, this is will be a journey into the unknown but, once engaged in self-directed groupwork, groupworkers, activists, researchers and managers can find, as the myriad of examples in this book have shown, that it is a process that works. Our purpose is to enable people who have not yet taken the steps outlined above now to have the confidence to do so, to try it for themselves – and to make a difference.

In the words of Chinwe Obijiofor, an American teacher who used in her classroom the groupwork approach outlined in this book: 'Instead of being a "Rebel without a Cause"; I am now a rebel with a method!'

Appendix I
Group Examples

Major group examples which recur throughout the book are summarized here in alphabetical order. Whilst we have benefited from reading about and talking with members of a wide range of groups, we have drawn particularly on the eight detailed below. We were thrilled to find that some of the groups that were examples in the first edition are still active, and Advocacy in Action is included again as its members are still active and committed to group work. All examples, with one exception, were active at the time of writing. For all groups we have given a brief description of the group and also indicated where further information about the group can be found.

Action Autonomie

Action Autonomie is an organization of mental health survivors in Montreal, Canada, which campaigns against the dominant position of the medical establishment in mental health diagnosis and, in particular, against the use of ECT in psychiatric treatment in the city's mental hospitals. It is structured and run on collective principles ('Le Collectif') and its statement of values (*Paroles et parcours d'un pouvoir fou* *) runs very close to the Six Principles of Self-directed Groupwork. In the course of its campaigning it has become affiliated to local, Canada-wide and international coalitions campaigning against the abuse resulting from the medical model of mental health and, as they see it, its characteristic attachments to 'chemical', i.e. drug, and 'electro' therapies.

Action Autonomie, like other groups portrayed in this book, explicitly describes itself as a partnership between paid employees and activists. The board of the organization meets monthly and is made up of 11 survivors (drawn from various threads of the organizations work) and one worker representative. Twice yearly the board meets with the worker team, the focus of one of these meetings being to agree the 'business plan' for the organization for the year ahead. Action Autonomie is funded predominantly by a grant from the Quebec province's 'Secretariat for Autonomous Action'.

The organization has developed a number of strands of activity substantially carried out in self-directed groups, including a women's committee, the ECT campaign committee and the member counsellors' committee. Members are trained to 'animate' (facilitate) groups for survivors, for mental health professionals and for students in which issues such as confinement law, access to medical files, patients' rights, welfare services and confidentiality come to be addressed. Another strand of the organization, again led by survivor members, is the production of a journal three times each year, *La renaissance*, which is published in both paper copy and electronically on the organization's website. *La renaissance* presents consistently a critical perspective on legal, treatment and services issues but, in addition, reproduces articles of interest on mental health drawn from the wider press. It is credited with introducing issues to the Montreal medical and policy establishment which have led to changes in practice.

  * *Guide pour une réflexion et un dialogue sur l'appropriation du pouvoir individuel et collectif des personnes utilisatrices de services en santé mentale.*

Further information

www.actionautonomie.qc.ca.

Advocacy in Action

Advocacy in Action started in 1989, when a social work assistant facilitated contact between a group of individuals. Some of them didn't like being locked away, some people didn't like the disparity in how good people's lives were; they also all recognized that working individually things were not going to get better, they would need to work together as a group. They were united by a strong belief in each other and anger that things were not as they should be. The aim of the group was, and still is, to come together and enable disadvantaged people to have a voice.

Originally many group members had learning difficulties. Over the years membership has come to include people who were excluded, for example, homeless people, street beggars, people who are service eligible, even though they may not actually be able to receive or use the services that are on offer. Members now include people from the Irish community, carers, asylum seekers, and people with mental health issues. They are brought together by their shared experience of exclusion and being on the edge. They are all equal within the group.

Groups within Advocacy in Action are very active with a wide range of activities. In addition to supporting each other, group members teach on 18 professional training programmes at undergraduate, postgraduate and PQ (post qualifying) level. They conduct research and have done development work in northern Italy and in Slovenia and had workers from Delhi come to the UK to look at how to involve people in both education and action.

They also do a lot of general community work, for example, Friendly Irish Action, working with older Irish people which led to the Long-distance Gang coming together (the group written about in this book).

Further information

Golsing, J. and Martin, J. (2012) *Making Partnerships with Service Users and Advocacy Groups Work: How to Grow Genuine and Respectful Relationships in Health and Social Care*. London: Jessica Kingsley.

McGregor, J. (2011) 'A long way back', *The Guardian*, 30 April 2011, available at: http://www.guardian.co.uk/film/2011/apr/30/return-irish-exiles-film-jon-mcgregor (accessed 23 April 2012).

Listen to me – a life here, report of research project undertaken by AiA, available at: *http://www.leicester.gov.uk/your-council-services/social-care-health/older-people/listen-to-me-I-live-here-report/* (accessed 23 April 2012).

Arise You Gallant Sweeneys, DVD available from outsidefilm@mail.com.

Ainsley Teenage Action Group

The Ainsley Teenage Action group (ATAG) is the only example not active at the time of preparing this book, and was also included in the first edition. It was one of the range of early groups key to the development of the self-directed groupwork approach. ATAG was a group of friends on a council estate in Nottingham who were getting into trouble with the police. Their probation officer along with two other workers worked with the group. The young people identified both relationships with the police and lack of leisure facilities as the issues they wanted to address and worked on these over a period of time. Ultimately they acquired a youth facility in their neighbourhood and for a time were actively involved in its running. However, it was burnt down some years later and not replaced.

Further information

Chapter 6 of this volume.
Arches, J. and Fleming, J. (2007) '"Building our own monument":a social action group revisited', *Practice*, 19(1): 33–47.

No Limits Dementia

No Limits Dementia is a service user-led group for people with dementia. The group is an advocacy group and mutual personal support is an important aspect of the group, as are lobbying and campaign work. Members have, for example, met with the Secretary of State for Health to discuss their experiences and suggest improvements to support and service provision.

In addition, members have taken part in research and group members have used art work to help communicate about those things that are difficult to speak about. This has led to an exhibition No Limits – Reimagining Life with Dementia. The exhibition explores the individual and collective strength of people living with this condition and brings to life ideas around community, empowerment, and friendship. They also have established a website and are working on a film.

Further information

Bartlett, R. and O'Conner, D. (2010) *Broadening the Dementia Debate: Towards Social Citizenship.* Bristol: The Policy Press. Available at; http://www.policypress.co.uk/display.asp?ISB=9781847421777 (accessed 23 April 2012).
Inclusive Research Network http://www.inclusiveresearch.net/ (accessed 23 April 2012).
International Collaboration for Participatory Health Research, available at: http://www.icphr.org/en/publications (accessed 23 April 2012).

No Limits – Re-imagining Life with Dementia, available at: http://www. nolimitsdementia.com/ (accessed 23 April 2012).

SupportNet

The SupportNet Project is a time-limited project in two neighbourhoods in Nottingham, exploring how self-directed support can develop when a local community starts to imagine a different type of care and support. The project had strong leadership throughout from the Portfolio-holding Councillor and the City Council's Director for Community Inclusion. It was overseen by a multi-agency Steering Group, comprising senior City Council managers and Councillors, along with representatives from key stakeholder agencies.. It was agreed that the project would focus on all three levels of 'prevention', not just on those eligible for social care. There was a commitment to working in a truly participative way with local communities. The worker team comprised two full-time community development workers with part time project management – with strong support from a local resident as 'citizen leader'.

The theoretical and practice base of the project combines 'asset-based' and 'hosting strategic inquiries' approaches to civic engagement, inviting wide and intentional participation through community dialogue. It was based on a commitment to working in a truly participative way with local communities, in the spirit of co-production. The workers employed a range of means to find out what is important to local residents in terms of being able to live their lives to the full and to engage all stakeholders (the whole system) in creating change together to move towards the visions of the future that they see.

The important issues that were identified were transport/access; things to do; information and communication; making the best of Personal Budgets. Each of these had a 'theme group' of residents and relevant professionals, working together to create change.

Further information

Fleming, J. (2010) *SupportNet evaluation report*, available at: http:// bit.ly/eLgslR (accessed 23 April 2012).
http://www.thinklocalactpersonal.org.uk/_library/Resources/Personalisa tion/EastMidlands/Workstreams/CommunityCapacity/Event3Sept2 10/SupportNet_Nottingham_CaseStudyFinal.pdf.

http://www.dmu.ac.uk/Images/Support%20Net%20Evaluation%20repor
t%20-%20%20final_tcm6-71088.pdf (accessed 23 April 2012).

Te Aroha Noa Community Services

Te Aroha Noa Community Services work with families and run a range
of services to support parents and their children such as playgroups,
fathers groups, educational groups and community campaigns, for
example, anti-violence campaigns.

The Te Aroha Noa approach facilitates understanding the ways in
which families and whänau embark upon and sustain themselves
through ambitious change journeys. It provides a framework for considering value-related aspects of practice as well as particular intervention
techniques and strategies that create change. It encourages reflections
and works in an integrated and holistic way very similar to self-directed
groupwork.

The project provides a safe, neutral space that is well resourced to meet
the developmental needs of young children and to support their parents.

Many parents have gained confidence to seek out further opportunities for their own development and to address personal issues that
restrict their capacity to be the parents they wish to be.

Further information

http://www.tearohanoa.org.nz (accessed 23 April 2012).
Handley K, Horn, S., Kaipuke, R., Maden, B., Maden, E., Stuckey, B.,
Munford, R., and Sanders, J. (2009) *The Spinafex Effect: Developing a
Theory of Change for Communities*. Wellington, NZ: Families
Commission Innovative Practice Fund No. 4/09 February 2009.
Available at: http://www.familiescommission.govt.nz/research/the-
spinafex-effect (accessed 23 April 2012).
www.nzfamilies.org.nz (accessed 23 April 2012).

University of Massachusetts Service Learning Programme

This project is a community/University partnership, focusing around a
service learning class at the University of Massachusetts Boston campus.

Self-Directed Groupwork is taught in a university service learning class, where they have readings, discussions and reflections and write assignments. The university students then go into a school once a week to work with middle school students in sixth grade as part of an after-school program. The young people are aged between 11 and 13 and the school is in a deprived low-income area of Dorchester, a suburb of Boston adjacent to the campus. Each week there can be between 5 to 10 middle school students in the class. The university students rotate the role of facilitator amongst themselves and also do small groupwork with the young people. Usually they all have a role within the session.

Back in class, the students reflect on the process and the role of the facilitator. They read sections of the book, compare what happens with what is written in the book and also with what they had wanted to happen. They reflect on why those things happened and plan for the next week.

Further information:

Arches, J. (2012) 'The role of groupwork in social action projects with youth', *Groupwork*, 22(1): 59–78.

Youth Dreamers

The Youth Dreamers are a group of students in Baltimore USA, in grades six through college who decided in 2001 that they wanted to open a youth-run youth centre. The mission they created for themselves (revised in 2010) is as follows:

> Youth Dreamers, Inc. provides a unique safe haven with opportunities for youth to accomplish personal goals, develop leadership potential, and participate in improving their communities.

They started as a school elective course of nine students. They talked about issues in their community and what they wanted to change. They identified that young people did not have anywhere to go after school and decided to create a youth-run youth centre and offer positive activities for young people in the community.

For years they worked to get support and funding for this project and were successful in getting support from local people, politicians and were awarded many grants large and small, including $75,000 from the Department of Housing and Community Development, $70,000 from Senator Barbara Mikulski, and $50,000 from the Harry and Jeanette Weinberg Foundation. They have written about their work and had articles published in the local press, in *Groupwork*, and contributed a chapter to a book about social action in education.

They achieved this goal in summer 2010 when the Dream House opened and now offers a variety of programs at the centre. A Board of Directors of eight youth and eight adults continue to guide this youth-led project. Students have done and continue to do pretty much everything, with guidance and support from adults.

Further information

http://www.youthdreamers.org/.

Berdan, K., Boulton, I., Eidman-Aadahl, E., Fleming, J., Gardner, L., Rogers, I. and Solomon, A. (eds) (2006) *Writing for a Change: Boosting Literacy and Learning through Social Action*. San Francisco, CA: Jossey-Bass.

Cary, C., Reid, C. and Berdan, K. (2004) 'Involving school students in social action in America: the Youth Dreamers Group', *Groupwork*, 14(2): 64–80.

Appendix II
The Centre for Social Action

To foster the self-directed groupwork approach and to encourage the development of its intellectual expression and of critical enquiry, the Centre for Research and Training in Social Action Groupwork (subsequently honed down to, simply, the Centre for Social Action) was founded at Nottingham University, UK, by the original authors, Mullender and Ward. Fleming is the present Director of the Centre which is currently based at De Montfort University, Leicester, UK. Starting off, informally in the 1980s, as little more than a repository of materials accumulated in the process of formulating the self-directed groupwork model, the future centre quickly became a hub through which social action practitioners, undertaking innovatory social action work utilizing the self-directed model, from across the country could source and connect with practitioner colleagues and with like-minded academics. It accumulated information on projects and also practice materials which could be disseminated and shared. For those in the vicinity of Nottingham, it provided a central point for meeting together and, importantly, a 'clearing house' for support and consultation. Its structure at this time was entirely informal.

In these early days much was gained from a link between the University social and community work course, the student training unit at Nottingham Council for Voluntary Service and Nottingham Young Volunteers, a third sector youth action organization. Besides providing placements for students in self-directed groupwork in a wide range of settings and opportunities for praxis and reflection on the evolving methodology, the people involved became a core activist group for networking and dissemination.

The diversity of backgrounds of those involved meant that, from virtually the outset, this 'hub' carried a perspective and pursued interests which extended beyond the self-directed groupwork model although sharing its values, its core practices and critical orientation. As stated in

189

an entry to the *Encyclopedia of Social Work with Groups* (Fleming 2009, pp. 275–277), the work of the Centre established a distinctive, but compatible and complementary, identity from self-directed groupwork:

> Social Action is an approach, that predominately, but not exclusively uses groupwork. It is informed by and has some overlap with Self-directed Groupwork, as it uses Self-directed Groupwork as an element – however, it is a distinct form of practice ... Whilst using Self-directed Groupwork to inform the Social Action process, the Social Action approach has also advanced Self-directed Groupwork in a range of disciplines, for example training, research and education. Examples would include groupwork being used as the basis for a training methodology (Fleming 2004), and as the basis for training for community workers and community activists in Peru. Social Action has been used to inform transformational change in children's services in Russia and Ukraine (Fleming 2000) and the development of more student-led learning in the US through a partnership with National Writing Project (Berdan *et al.* 2006). Social Action has also been used to develop community cohesion and enhance the understanding within communities as to what social capital means to them (Boeck and Fleming 2002).

In acting as a clearing house, the Centre for Social Action quickly found itself engaged in the development of social action on a much wider terrain. Sporadic requests to talk to interested individuals, groups and teams expanded to more formal consultancy and training contracts. International contacts put the Centre on to an even wider canvas. In order to manage a burgeoning portfolio it was accorded official standing within Nottingham University. It subsequently transferred to De Montfort University, Leicester.

At De Montfort, the Centre for Social Action has established a profile as a centre for research, training and consultancy in the field of public participation in youth and community work as well as health and social care. Its key focus is on the realization of people's human rights as enshrined in the Universal Declaration of Human Rights. It does this through a commitment to partnership working and to the active involvement of people in decisions concerning their communities, services and lives (www.dmu.ac.uk/csa).

Thus, the Centre for Social Action, with social action methodology underpinning all of its work, bridges applied social research, service and policy evaluation, consultancy, training, and information services to the field. In particular, the Centre has developed its own distinctive approach to applied social research, with a special emphasis on involvement of users as co-participants at all stages of the research process. The Centre, substantially through the publications of its staff and people working with it, has become recognized internationally as a leading contributor to the development of a research framework consistent with 'user empowerment' (Fleming 2005, 2010, 2012a, 2012b; Fleming and Hudson 2009; Fleming and Boeck 2005; Fleming and Ward 2004).

Beyond the Centre itself, other organizations have also adopted social action as a methodology for training and service development work. Examples drawn from these areas work feature throughout this book.

Appendix III
Principles and Stages of the Self-Directed Groupwork Model

	Taking stock	Taking off	Preparing to take action	Taking action	Taking over
All people have skills, experience and understanding that they can draw on to tackle the problems they face					
People have rights, including the right to be heard, the right to define the issues facing them and the right to take action on their own behalf					
Problems are complex with substantial roots in social policy, the environment and the economy, not personal inadequacy					
People working collectively can be powerful					
Workers are not leaders but facilitators. Their jobs is to enable people to make decisions for themselves and take ownership of whatever outcome ensues					
Workers are committed to social justice					

References

Abels, P. and Garvin, C. (2010) Standards for Social Work Practice with Groups (2nd edition). Alexandria, VA: Association for the Advancement of Social Work with Groups.

Abu-Samah, A. (1996/7) 'Empowering research process: using groups in research to empower people', Groupwork, 9(2): 221–252.

Adams, R. (2008) Empowerment, Participation and Social Work. Basingstoke: Palgrave Macmillan.

Alinsky, S. (1971) Rules for Radicals. New York: Vintage Books.

Anderson, J. (1996) 'Yes but IS IT empowerment? Initiation, implementation and outcomes of community action', in B. Humphries (ed.) Critical Perspectives on Empowerment. Birmingham: Venture Press.

Arches, J. (2012) 'The role of groupwork in social action projects with youth', Groupwork, 22(1): 59–77.

Arches, J. and Fleming, J. (2007) 'Building our own monument – a social action group revisited', Practice, 19(1): 33–47.

Badham, B. (ed.) (1989) '"Doing something with our lives when we're inside": self-directive [sic] groupwork in a youth custody centre', Groupwork, 2(1): 27–35.

Badham, B. (2004) Act by Right: Skills for the Active Involvement of Children and Young People in Making Change Happen. Leicester: National Youth Agency.

Badham, B. and Wade, H. (2008) Hear by Right: Standards Framework for the Participation of Children and Young People. Leicester: National Youth Agency. Available at: http://hbr.nya.org.uk/files/1-Hear%20By%20Right%202008.pdf.

Banks, S. (2006) Ethics and Values in Social Work. Basingstoke: Palgrave Macmillan.

Barker, I. and Peck, E. (1987) Power in Strange Places: User Empowerment in Mental Health Services. London: Good Practices in Mental Health.

Barnes, M. (2008) 'Passionate participation: emotional experiences and expressions in deliberative forums', Critical Social Policy, 28(4): 461–481.

Bartlett, R. and O'Conner, D. (2010) Broadening the Dementia Debate: Towards Social Citizenship. Bristol: The Policy Press.

Bates, P. and Steven, K. (2011) S2S, Staff-run to Self-run: How People Using Health and Social Care Services Can Take Control of Their Own Groups from the Staff Who Have Run Them in the Past. London: London Borough of Barnet.

Bauman, Z. (2000) Liquid Modernity. Cambridge: Polity Press.

BBC (British Broadcasting Corporation) (1981) Grapevine, programme 3. London: BBC Community Programmes Unit. (Television programme).

BBC (2011) 'Teenagers should challenge use of mosquito devices', BBC News website, 20 December 2011, available at: http://www.bbc.co.uk/news/uk-politics-16273076.

BCODP (2011) My Blog, available at: www.bcodp.org.uk (accessed 26 November 2011).

Beddoe, L. and Harrington, P. (2012) 'One step in a thousand-mile journey: can civic practice be nurtured in practitioner research? Reporting on an innovative project', British Journal of Social Work, 42(1): 74–93.

Bellinger, A. and Elliott, T. (2011) 'What are you looking at? The potential of appreciative inquiry as a research approach for social work', British Journal of Social Work, 41(4): 708–725.

Benefits and Work (2008) 'Concern over poor disabled access for compulsory interviews', London: Benefits and Work Publishing Ltd, available at: http://www.benefitsandwork.co.uk/news/latest-news/992-concern-over-poor-disabled-access-for-compulsory-interviews (accessed 23 December 2011).

Berdan, K. (2006) 'Reflections on the Youth Dreamers', in K. Berdan, I. Boulton, E. Eidman-Aadahl, J. Fleming, L. Gardner, I. Rogers, and A. Solomon (eds) Writing for a Change: Boosting Literacy and Learning through Social Action. San Francisco, CA: Jossey-Bass.

Berdan, K. (2011) Personal communication to Fleming.

Berdan, K., Boulton, I., Eidman-Aadahl, E., Fleming, J., Gardner, L., Rogers, I. and Solomon, A. (eds) (2006) Writing for a Change: Boosting Literacy and Learning through Social Action. San Francisco, CA: Jossey-Bass.

Beresford, P. (2010) 'Public partnerships, governance and user involvement: a service user perspective', International Journal of Consumer Studies, 34(5): 495–502.

Beresford, P., Fleming, J., Glynn, M., Bewley, C., Croft, S., Branfield, F. and Postle, K. (2011) Supporting People: Towards a Person-Centred Approach. Bristol: Policy Press.

Berman-Rossi, T. and Kelly, T. (2004) 'Using groups to teach the connection between private troubles and public issues.' in C. Caron, A. Fritz, E. Lewis, J. Ramey and D. Sugiuchi (eds) Growth and Development through Group Work. New York: Haworth Press.

Bierley Youth Action Project (1997) 'The first three years reviewed and revealed: a journey through the joys, sorrows, celebrations, learning, achievements and philosophy of a young people's social action project in Bradford', unpublished report.

Blacklock, N. (2003) 'Gender awareness and the role of the groupworker in programmes for domestic violence perpetrators', in M. Cohen and A. Mullender (eds) Gender and Groupwork. London: Routledge.

Boeck, T. and Fleming, J. (2005) 'Social policy – a help or a hindrance to social capital?', Social Policy and Society, 4(3): 259–270.

Boeck, T., Fleming, J. and Kemshall, H. (2006) 'The context of risk decisions: does social capital make a difference?' Forum Qualitative Sozialforschung/Forum: Qualitative Social Research, 7(1), Art. 17 ISSN: 1438–5627, available at: http://www.qualitative-research.net/fqs-texte/1-06/06-1-17-e.htm.

Boeck, T., Glover, M., Harrison, L. and Johnson, M. (2007) Leicester Community Cohesion Assessment and Evaluation Framework. Leicester: Leicester City Council and Centre for Social Action, De Montfort University. Available at: http://www.dmu.ac.uk/faculties/hls/research/applied-social-sciences/csa/publications/index.jsp.

Boeck, T., McCullough, P. and Ward, D. (2001) 'Increasing social capital to combat social exclusion: the social action contribution', in A-L. Matthies, K. Narhi and D. Ward (eds) The Eco Social Approach in Social Work. Jyvaskyla, Finland: SoPhi 58.

Boehm, A. and Staples, L. (2004) 'Empowerment: the point of view of consumers', Families in Society, 85(2): 270–280.

Bottoms, A. and McWilliams, W. (1979) 'A non treatment paradigm for probation practice', British Journal of Social Work, 9(2): 159–202.

Bourdieu, P. (1998) Practical Reason. Cambridge: Polity Press.

Breton, M. (1991) 'Toward a model of social group work practice with marginalised populations', Groupwork, 4(1): 31–47.

British Youth Council (2011) Our Streets: The Views of Young People and Young Leaders on the Riots in England in August 2011. London: British Youth Council. Available at: http://www.byc.org.uk/media/74716/byc_our_streets_report.pdf.

Brodie, E., Cowling, E. and Nissen, N. (2009) Understanding Participation: A Literature Review. London: Pathways through Participation, available at: http://pathwaysthroughparticipation.org.uk/resources/literaturereview/ (accessed 12 February 2012).

Brown, A. (1992) Groupwork (3rd edition). Aldershot: Ashgate.

Brown, A. (1996) 'Groupwork into the future: some personal reflections', Groupwork, 9 (1): 80–96.

Brown, A. and Caddick, B. (1986) 'Models of social groupwork in Britain: a further note', British Journal of Social Work, 6(1): 99–103.

Bunker, B. and Altan, B. (2006) The Handbook of Large Group Methods. San Francisco, CA: Jossey- Bass.

Bunting, M. (2011) 'Our market-shaped way of life has no time for the elderly or the art of caring', Guardian on Line, available at: http://www.guardian.co.uk/commentisfree/2011/oct/16/market-no-time-elderly-caring#history-link-box (accessed 16 November 2011).

Burley, D. (1982) Starting Blocks: Aspects of Social Education Group Work with Young People. Leicester: National Youth Bureau.

Burnett, R. and McNeill, F. (2005) 'The place of the office-offender relationship in assisting offenders to desist from crime', Probation Journal, 52(3): 221–242.

Butcher, H., Collis, P., Glen, A. and Sills, P. (1980) Community Groups in Action: Case Studies and Analysis. London: Routledge and Kegan Paul.

Butler, P. (2012) 'How the Spartacus welfare cuts campaign went viral', Guardian Society, 17 January 12, available at: http://www.guardian.co.uk/society/2012/jan/17/disability-spartacus-welfare.

Calhoun, A., Whitmore, E and Wilson, M. (2011) Activism That Works. Black Point, Nova Scotia, and Winnipeg: Fernwood Publishing.

Campbell, J. and Oliver, M. (1996) Disability Politics: Understanding Our Past, Changing Our Future. London: Routledge.

Care Quality Commission (2011) Experts by Experience: Guidance and Information. London: CQC.

Care Services Improvement Partnership (2008) High Impact Changes for Health and Social Care: An Inspirational Collection of Organisational Initiatives Which Are Changing Health and Social Care Services and the Lives of People Who Use Them. London: Department of Health.

Cary, C., Ried, C. and Berdan, K. (2004) 'Involving school students in social action in America: the Youth Dreamers Group', Groupwork, 14(2): 64–79.

Carniol, B. (1992) 'Structural social work: Maurice Moreau's challenge to social work practice', Journal of Progressive Human Services, 3(1): 1–20.

Centre for Social Action (2000) Youth Agenda: A Good Practice Guide to Working with Young People on Their Home Ground. Leicester: Centre for Social Action, De Montfort University.

Centre for Social Action (2011) Centre for Social Action: Working for the Community, available at: http://www.dmu.ac.uk/faculties/hls/research/applied-social-sciences/csa/ (accessed 27 November 2011).

Chamberlin, J. (1988) On Our Own: Patient-Controlled Alternatives to the Mental Health System. London: MIND. [Originally published in North America in 1977.]

Cohen, M.B. and Mullender, A. (2000) 'The personal in the political: exploring the group work continuum from individual to social change goals', Social Work with Groups, 22(1): 13–31. (Reproduced in 2005, Social Work with Groups, 28(3/4) and simultaneously in Malekoff, A. and Kurland, R. (eds) A Quarter Century of Classics (1978–2004): Capturing the Theory, Practice and Spirit of Social Work with Groups, pp. 187–204.)

Cohen, M.B. and Mullender, A. (eds) (2003) Gender and Groupwork. London: Routledge.

Coleman, J. (1994) Foundations of Social Theory. Cambridge, MA: Harvard University Press.

Collins, P.H. (2000) 'Gender, black feminism, and black political economy', Annals of the American Academy of Political and Social Science, 568: 41–53.

Cosis-Brown, H. and Cocker, C. (2011) Social Work with Lesbians and Gay Men. London: Sage.

Croft, S. and Beresford, P. (1987) 'We live here and we know the problems', Community Care, 16 July, pp. 12–13.

Davies, B. (1979) In Whose Interests. Leicester: National Youth Bureau.

Davies, B. and Gibson, A. (1967) The Social Education of the Adolescent. London: University of London Press.

Davis, K. and Mullender, A. (1993) Ten Turbulent Years: A Review of the Work of the Derbyshire Coalition of Disabled People. Nottingham: Centre for Social Action, University of Nottingham, available at: http://www.leeds.ac.uk/disability-studies/archiveuk/DavisK/TEN%20TURBULENT%20YEARS.pdf (accessed 26 November 2011).

de Castella, T. (2012) 'Beveridge Report: from "deserving poor" to "scroungers"?', available at: http://www.bbc.co.uk/news/magazine-20431729 (accessed 8 January 2013).

Denzin, N. (2001) Interpretive Interactionism. London: Sage.

Department for Education (2011) Positive for Youth: A New Approach to Cross-Government Policy for Young People Aged 13 to 19. London: Department for Education, available at: http://media.education.gov.uk/assets/files/pdf/p/positive%20for%20youth.pdf.

Department of Education and Science (1969) Youth and Community Work in the 1970s: Proposals by the Youth Service Development Council. London: HMSO.

Department of Health (1989) Caring for People: Community Care in the Next Decade and Beyond. London: HMSO.

Department of Health (2007) Putting People First: A Shared Vision and Commitment to the Transformation of Adult Social Care. London: Department of Health.

Department of Health (2011) Health and Social Care Bill 2010–2011. London: TSO.

Department of Health, Hong Kong (2008) Promoting Health in Hong Kong: A Strategic Framework for Prevention and Control of Non-communicable Diseases. Hong Kong: Department of Health.

Derbyshire Coalition of Disabled People (1986a) The Quiet Revolution: The Struggle for Full Participation and Equality: A Brief Review of the Background and Work of the Derbyshire Coalition, 1981–1986. Clay Cross, Derbyshire: DCDP.

Derbyshire Coalition of Disabled People (1986b) Welcome to the Coalition. Clay Cross, Derbyshire: DCDP.

Disabled People's International (2011) Constitution of Disabled People's International, available at: http://www.dpi.org/lang-en/documents/index?page=4 (accessed 26 November 2011).

Doel, M. (2006) Using Groupwork. Abingdon: Routledge.

Doel, M. and Sawdon, C. (1999) The Essential Groupworker. London: Jessica Kingsley Publishers.

Dominelli, L. (2002a) Anti-Oppressive Social Work: Theory and Practice. Basingstoke: Palgrave Macmillan.

Dominelli, L. (2002b) Feminist Social Work Theory and Practice. Basingstoke: Palgrave Macmillan.

Dominelli, L. (ed.) (2007) Revitalising Communities in a Globalising World. Aldershot: Ashgate.

Dominelli, L. (2008) Anti-Racist Social Work (3rd edition). London: Palgrave Macmillan.

Dominelli, L. (2010) Social Work in a Globalising World. Cambridge: Polity Press.

Dorling, D. (2010) Injustice: Why Social Inequality Persists. Bristol: Policy Press.

Douglas, T. (1976) Groupwork Practice. London: Tavistock.

Douglas, T. (2000) Basic Groupwork. London: Routledge.

Du Bois, B. (1983) 'Passionate scholarship: notes on values, knowing and method in feminist social science', in G. Bowles and R. Duelli Klein (eds) Theories of Women's Studies. London: Routledge & Kegan Paul.

Dullea, K. and Mullender, A. (1999) 'Evaluation and empowerment', in I. Shaw and J. Lishman (eds) Evaluation and Social Work Practice. London: Sage.

DuPlessis, R. and Snitow, A. (2007) The Feminist Memoir Project: Voices from Women's Liberation. New Brunswick, NJ: Rutgers University Press.

Dynamix (2002) Participation Spice it Up. Swansea: Dynamix Ltd.

Easton, M. (2011) 'It's not the "squeezed middle", it's the poor', available at: www.bbc.co.uk/news on 11 October 2011.

Eliasoph, N. (2011) Making Volunteers: Civic Life After Welfare's End. Princeton, NJ: Princeton University Press.

Erben, R., Franzkowiak, P. and Wenzel, E. (2000) 'People empowerment vs. social capital: from health promotion to social marketing', Health Promotion Journal of Australia, 9: 179–182.

Everitt. A., Hardiker, P., Littlewood, J. and Mullender, A. (1991) 'Practitioner research', Social Work and Social Sciences Review, 3: 15–22.

Everitt, A., Hardiker, P., Littlewood, J. and Mullender, A. (1992) Applied Research for Better Practice. Basingstoke: Macmillan.

Farrall, S. (2007) 'Desistance,' in R. Canton and D. Hancock (eds) Dictionary of Probation and Offender Management. Cullompton: Willan.

Farrow, A., Badham, B. and Davies, T. (2011) Leading for the Future. London: Woodcraft Folk.

Fink, J. (2012) 'Walking the neighbourhood, seeing the small details of community life: Reflections from a photography walking tour', Critical Social Policy, 32(1): 31–50.

Finkelstein, V. (1980) Attitudes and Disabled People: Issues for Discussion. New York: World Rehabilitation Fund Inc. Reprinted, London: RADAR, Monograph no. 5, International Exchange of Information in Rehabilitation.

Fish, J. (2012) Social Work and Lesbian, Gay, Bisexual and Trans People: Making a Difference. Bristol: Policy Press.

Fleming, J. (2000) 'Action research for the development of children's services in Ukraine', in H. Kemshall and R. Littlechild (eds) User Involvement and Participation in Social Care: Research Informing Practice. London: Jessica Kingsley.

Fleming, J. (2004) 'The beginnings of a social action group', Groupwork, 14(2): 24–42.

Fleming, J. (2005) 'Foster carers undertake research into birth family contact: using the social action research approach', in L. Lowes and I. Hulatt (eds) The Involvement of Service Users in Health and Social Care Research. London: Routledge.

Fleming, J. (2009) 'Social action' in A. Gitterman and R. Salmon (eds) Encyclopedia of Social Work with Groups. London: Routledge.

Fleming, J. (2010) SupportNet Evaluation Report, Leicester: Centre for Social Action, De Montfort University, available at: http://www.dmu.ac.uk/Images/Support%20Net%20Evaluation%20report%20-%20%20final_tcm6-71088.pdf.

Fleming, J. (2012a) 'Moving to the inside: employing young people as researchers', in J. Fleming and T. Boeck, Involving Children and Young People in Health and Social Care Research. London: Routledge.

Fleming, J. (2012b) 'Service user involvement: what it is and what it could be', in S. Carr and P. Beresford, Social Care, Service Users and User Involvement: Building on Research. London: Jessica Kingsley.

Fleming, J. (forthcoming) 'Young people's participation: where next?' Children and Society. DOI:10.1111/j.1099-0860.2012.00442.x.

Fleming, J. and Arches, J. (2007) '"Building our own monument": a social action group revisited', Practice, 19(1): 33–45.

Fleming, J. and Boeck, T. (2005) 'Can social capital be a framework for participative evaluation of community health work?' in D. Taylor and S. Balloch (eds) The Politics of Evaluation: Policy Implementation and Practice. Bristol: Policy Press.

Fleming, J., Goodman-Chong, H. and Skinner, A. (2009) 'Experiences of peer evaluation of the Leicester Teenage Pregnancy Prevention Strategy', Children and Society, 23(4): 279–290.

Fleming, J., Hine, J., Skinner, A. and Boeck, T. (2007) 'Young Researchers Network: Project Specifications', unpublished report prepared for National Youth Agency by Centre for Social Action.

Fleming, J. and Hudson, N. (2009) 'Young people and research: participation in practice', in J. Wood and J. Hine (eds) Work with Young People: Theory and Policy for Practice. London: Sage.

Fleming, J. and Luczynski, Z. (1999) 'Men United: Fathers' Voices', Groupwork , 11(2): 21–38.

Fleming, J. and Skinner, A. (2007) Influence Through Participation: A Critical Review of Structures for Youth Participation. London: Local Government Improvement and Development Agency (I&DeA), available at: http://www.dmu.ac.uk/Images/Influence%20through%20participation.%20A%20critical%20review%20of%20structures%20for%20youth%20engagement%20-%20Sept%2007_tcm6-33557.pdf.

Fleming, J. and Ward, D. (1992) For the Children to Be Alright Their Mothers Need to Be Alright: An Alternative to Removing the Child: The Radford Shared Care Project. Nottingham: Centre for Social Action, University of Nottingham.

Fleming, J. and Ward, D. (1996) 'The ethics of community health needs assessment: searching for a participant centred approach', in M. Parker (ed.) Ethics and Community, Preston: Centre for Professional Ethics, University of Central Lancashire.

Fleming, J. and Ward, D. (2004) 'Methodology and practical application of the social action research model', in F. Maggs-Rapport (ed.) New Qualitative Research Methodologies in Health and Social Care: Putting Ideas into Practice. London: Routledge.

Fleming, J. and Ward, D. (forthcoming) 'Facilitation and groupwork tasks in self-directed groupwork', Groupwork.

Fleming, J., Ward, D. and Yates, S. (2010) How To: Use a Consortium Working Approach. London: National Children's Bureau.

Fleming, J. and Wattley, R. (1998) 'One who teaches from experience: social action and the development of anti-racist research and practice', in M. Lavalette, L. Penketh, and C. Jones (eds) Anti-Racism and Social Welfare. Aldershot: Ashgate.

Flower, J. (1983) 'Creating a forum', Community Care, 21 April.

Fook, J. (2002) Social Work: Critical Theory and Practice. London: Sage.

Foucault, M. (1978) The History of Sexuality: An Introduction, Volume 1. New York: Pantheon.

Foucault, M. (1980) Power, Knowledge: Selected Interviews and Other Writings. New York: Pantheon.

Freire, P. (1972) Pedagogy of the Oppressed. Harmondsworth: Penguin.

Galinsky, M. and Schopler, J. (1985) 'Patterns of entry and exit in open-ended groups', Social Work with Groups, 8: 67–80.

Geake, R., Huston, C. and Members of Action Hall (2011) 'The Disability Action Hall tell stories, take action, change lives', in E. Whitmore, M. Wilson and A. Calhoun, Activism That Works. Winnipeg: Fernwood Publishing.

Giddens, A. (1986) The Constitution of Society. Cambridge: Polity Press.

Gitterman, A. and Shulman, L. (eds) (2005) Mutual Aid Groups, Vulnerable and Resilient Populations, and the Life Cycle. New York: Columbia University Press.

Glynn, M., Branfield, F., Beresford, P., Bewley, C., Croft, S., Fleming, J. and Postle, K. (2011) Making a Change: A Guide to Running Successful and Accessible Training. London: Shaping Our Lives.

Goldstein, B.P. (2008) 'Black perspectives', in M. Davies (ed.) Companion to Social Work. Oxford: Blackwell.

Gould, N. (1999) 'Qualitative practice evaluation', in I. Shaw and J. Lishman (eds) Evaluation and Social Work Practice. London: Sage.

Graham, M. (2007) Black Issues in Social Work and Social Care. Bristol: Policy Press.

Gray, I., Parker, J. and Timmins, T. (2008) 'Leading communities of practice in social work: groupwork or management?' Groupwork, 18 (2): 26–40.

Gray, M. (2011) 'Back to basics: a critique of the strengths perspective in social work', Families in Society: The Journal of Contemporary Social Services, 92(1): 5–11.

Habermas, J. (1990) Moral Consciousness and Communicative Action. Cambridge: Polity Press.

Hadley, J. (1987) 'Communicator, campaigner and carer', Community Care, 29 January, pp. 20–21.

Hall, S. (2011) 'The march of the neoliberals', The Guardian, 12 September 20, available at: http://www.guardian.co.uk/politics/2011/sep/12/march-of-the-neoliberals (accessed 27 November 2011).

Handley, K., Horn, S., Kaipuke, R., Maden, B., Maden, E., Stuckey, B., Munford, R. and Sander, J. (2009) The Spinafex Effect: Developing a Theory of Change for Communities, Wellington, NZ: Families Commission/komihana a whanau.

Hanisch, C. ([1969] 2006) The personal is political', available at: http://www.carolh'anisch.org/CHwritings/PIP.html (accessed 30 October 2011).

Harris, J. (2012) 'The desperate search for jobs in Warrington: shifting blame on to the jobless under the guise of positive thinking is not only demeaning but sinister', The Guardian, 7 February, available at: http://www.guardian.co.uk/commentisfree/2012/feb/07/desperate-search-jobs-warrington?INTCMP=SRCH.

Harrison, M. (1982) 'Organisational issues', in D. Ward (ed.) Give 'Em a Break: Social Action by Young People at Risk and in Trouble. Leicester: National Youth Bureau.

Harvey, L. (1990) Critical Social Research. London: Unwin Hyman.

Health Council of Canada (2011) 'How engaged are Canadians in their primary care? Results from the 2010 Commonwealth Fund International Health Policy Survey', Canadian Health Care Matters, Bulletin 5. Toronto: Health Council of Canada.

Healy, K. (2000) Social Work Practices: Contemporary Perspectives on Change. London: Sage.

Henderson, P. and Thomas, D. (1980) Skills in Neighbourhood Work. London: Allen and Unwin.

Henderson, P. and Thomas, D. (eds) (1981) Readings in Community Work. London: Allen and Unwin.

Henry, M. (1988) 'Revisiting open groups', Groupwork, 1(3): 215–228.

Hodge, S. (2005) 'Participation, discourse and power: a case study in service user involvement', Critical Social Policy, 25: 164–179.

hooks, b. (1984) Feminist Practice: From Margin to Centre. Boston, MA: South End Press.

Hope, A. and Timmel, S. (1999) Training for Transformation: A Handbook for Community Workers (Book 1). Rugby: Practical Action Publishing.

Houston, S. (2009) 'Communication, Recognition and Social Work: Aligning the Ethical Theories of Habermas and Honneth', British Journal of Social Work, 39(7), pp1274-1290.

Huffington Post (2011) 'Tax the poor: forget Occupy Wall Street, Conservatives have a different idea', available at: http://www.huffingtonpost.com/2011/10/30/tax-the-poor-conservative-plan-occupy-wall-street_n_1064685.html?ir=Canada (accessed 30 October 2011).

Hurst, R. (2005) 'Disabled People's International: Europe and the social model of disability', in C. Barnes and G. Mercer (eds) The Social Model of Disability: Europe and the Majority World. Leeds: The Disability Press.

Johnson, P. and Wilson, M. (eds) (2011) 'Groupwork student writing', special edition of Groupwork, 21(2).

Jones, O. (2011) Chavs: The Demonization of the Working Class. London: Verso.

Jones, S. (2009) Critical Learning for Social Work Students. Exeter: Learning Matters.

Jordan, B. and Parton, N. (eds) (1983) The Political Dimensions of Social Work. Oxford: Basil Blackwell.

Kindred, M. and Kindred, M. (2011) Once Upon a Group: A Guide to Running and Participating in Successful Groups (2nd edition). London: Jessica Kingsley Publishers.

Knight, C. (2007) 'The re-emergence of the importance of the "relationship" within community and criminal justice practice', British Journal of Community Justice, 5(3): 1–4.

Kreeger, L. (ed.) (1975) The Large Group. London: Constable.

Kunzru, H. (2011) 'This is where we live now', The Guardian, 13 August, p. 38.

Kurland, R. and Salmon, R. (1993) 'Groupwork versus casework in a group', Groupwork, 6(1): 5–16.

Lawson, C. (2011) Personal correspondence with Fleming.

Leboeuf, L. (1994) Approche Structurelle en Travail Social et Conscientisation. Quebec: Collectif québécois de conscientisation.

Ledwith, M. (2011) Community Development: A Critical Approach. Bristol: Policy Press.

Lees, R. and Smith, G. (1975) Action-Research in Community Development. London: Routledge & Kegan Paul.

Lewis, E. and Guttierrez, L. (2003) 'Intersections of gender, race and ethnicity in groupwork', in M. Cohen and A. Mullender, Gender and Groupwork. London: Routledge.

Littlechild, B. and Smith, R. (2012) A Handbook for Inter-professional Practice in the Human Services: Learning to Work Together. London: Pearson.

Lizzio, A. and Wilson, K. (2001) 'Facilitating group beginnings II: from basic to working engagement', Groupwork, 13(1): 31–56.

Lukes, S. (2005) Power: A Radical View. Basingstoke: Palgrave Macmillan.

Maluccio, A. and Marlow, W. (1975) 'The Case for the Contract,' in B. Compton and B. Galaway (eds) Social Work Processes. Homewood, IL: The Dorsey Press.

Maruna, S. and Farrall, S. (2004) 'Desistance from crime: a theoretical reformulation', Kölner Zeitschrift für Soziologie und Sozialpsychologie, 43: 171–194.

McCarthy, D. (2011) 'Classing early intervention: social class, occupational moralities and criminalisation', Critical Social Policy, 31(4): 495–516.

McDonnell, J. (2011) 'Reimagining the role of art in the relationship between democracy and education', Educational Philosophy and Theory. Article first published online: 2/11/2011, DOI:10.1111/j.1469-5812.2011.00802.x.

McGregor, J. (2011) 'A long way back', The Guardian Culture, 30 April 2011, available at: http://www.guardian.co.uk/film/2011/apr/30/return-irish-exiles-fim-jon-mcgregor.

McHarg, J. and Kay, E. (2008) 'The anatomy of a new dental curriculum', British Dental Journal, 204: 635–638.

McNeill, F. (2006) 'A desistance paradigm for offender management', Criminology and Criminal Justice, 6(1): 39–62.

McNeill, F. (2007) 'Desistance', in R. Canton and D. Hancock (eds) Dictionary of Probation and Offender Management. Cullompton: Willan.

McNeill, F., Batchelor, S., Burnett, R. and Knox, J. (2005) 21st Century Social Work: Reducing Re-offending: Key Practice Skills. Edinburgh: Scottish Executive.

Ministry of Justice (2010) Breaking the Cycle: Effective Punishment, Rehabilitation and Sentencing of Offenders, Cmd 7972. London: HMSO.

Ministry of Justice (2011) National Standards for the Management of Offenders. London: Ministry of Justice.

Mitchell, G. (1989) 'Empowerment and opportunity', Social Work Today, 16 March, p. 14.

Moreau, M. (1979) 'A structural approach to social work practice', Canadian Journal of Social Work Education, 5(1): 78–94.

Moreau, M. (1990) 'Empowerment through advocacy and consciousness-raising: implications of a structural approach to social work', Journal of Sociology and Social Welfare, 17: 53–67.

Moore, S. (2011) 'Put the shutters up on the shops, but not in our minds. Don't lock these kids out', The Guardian, 13 August 2011, p. 35.

Morris, J. (2011) Rethinking Disability Policy. York: Joseph Rowntree Foundation.

Mouffe, C. (2005) On the Political. London: Routledge.

Mullaly, B. (1997) Structural Social Work. Toronto: Oxford University Press.

Mullaly, B. (2007) The New Structural Social Work. Toronto: Oxford University Press.

Mullaly, B. (2010) Challenging Oppression and Confronting Privilege, Don Mills, ON: Oxford University Press.

Mullender, A., Hague, G., Imam, U., Kelly, L., Malos, E. and Regan, L. (2002) Children's Perspectives on Domestic Violence. London: Sage.

Mullender, A. and Ward, D. (1985) 'Towards an alternative model of social groupwork', British Journal of Social Work, 15: 155–172.

Mullender, A. and Ward, D. (1988) 'What is practice-led research into group-work?' in P. Wedge (ed.) Social Work: A Third Look at Research into Practice: Proceedings of the Third Annual JUC/BASW Conference, London, September, 1987. Birmingham: BASW.

Mullender, A. and Ward, D. (1991) Self-directed Groupwork: Users Take Action for Empowerment. London: Whiting and Birch.

Mullender, A. and Ward, D. (1993) 'The role of the consultant in selfdirected groupwork', Social Work with Groups (USA), 16(4): 57–80.

Munford, R. and Walsh-Tapiata, W. (2001) Strategies for Change: Community Development in Aotearoa/New Zealand. Palmerston North, NZ: School of Social Policy and Social Work.

Munn-Giddings, C. and McVicar, A. (2007) 'Self-help groups as mutual support: what do carers value?' Health and Social Care in the Community, 15(1): 26–34.

Munro, E. (2011) The Munro Review of Child Protection: Final Report. A Child-Centred System. London: Department for Education.

Muston, R. and Weinstein, J. (1988) 'Race and groupwork: some experiences in practice and training', Groupwork, 1(1): 30–40.

Napikoski, L. (2011) Feminist Consciousness-Raising Groups: Collective Action through Discussion. available at: http://womenshistory.about.com/od/feminism/a/consciousness_raising_groups.htm (accessed 29 October 2011).

NatCen Social Research (2012) Social Attitudes in an Age of Austerity, available at: http://www.bsa-29.natcen.ac.uk/read-the-report/key-findings/introduction.aspx (accessed 8 January 2013).

National Youth Bureau (1981) Enfranchisement: Young People and the Law - An Information Pack for Youth Workers. Leicester: NYB.

NCIL UK (2011) Campaigning for the Rights and Equality of Disabled People, available at: National Centre for Independent Living website http://www.ncil.org.uk (accessed 26 November 2011).

Nelson, G., Lord, J. and Ochocka, J. (2001) Shifting the Paradigm in Community Mental Health: Towards Empowerment and Community. Toronto: University of Toronto Press.

New Economics Foundation (2010) The Role of Local Government in Promoting Wellbeing. London: Local Government Improvement and Development.

Nicholls, J., O'Hara, W., Trotman, A., Roberts, J. and Shaban, S. N., Young People from the Link Unit, Minihane, S., David, G., and Mac-Callum, S. (1985) A Celebration of Differences: A Book by Physically Handicapped People. Bristol: Broadsides (Co-op) Ltd.

Northen, H. and Kurland, R. (2001) Social Work with Groups. New York: Columbia University Press.

Nottingham Patients Councils Support Group (1989) Information Pack. Nottingham: NPCSG.

Oakley, A. (1999) 'People's ways of knowing: gender and methodology', in S. Hood, B. Mayal and S. Oliver (eds) Critical Issues in Social Research: Power and Prejudice. Buckingham: Open University Press.

Oliver, M. (1983) Social Work with Disabled People. London: Macmillan.

Oliver, M. (1990) The Politics of Disablement. Basingstoke: Macmillan.

Oliver, M. (1992) 'Changing the social relations of research production', Disability, Handicap and Society, 7(2): 101–114.

Oliver, M. and Barnes, C. (2012) The New Politics of Disablement. Basingstoke: Palgrave Macmillan.

Onyx, J. and Bullen, P. (2000) 'Measuring social capital in five communities in NSW', Journal of Applied Behavior Science, 36(1): 23–42.

Ordre Professionel des Travailleurs Sociaux du Québec (1993) Code de déontologie en travail social. Montreal: OPTSQ.

O'Reilly, D. (2011) 'The grit in the oyster: professionalism, managerialism and leaderism as discourses of UK public services modernization', Organization Studies, 32(8): 1079–1101.

Orme, J. (2009) 'Feminist social work,' in R. Adams, L. Dominelli and M. Payne, Critical Practice in Social Work (2nd edition). Basingstoke: Palgrave Macmillan.

Ortega-Alcazar, I. and Dyck, I. (2012) 'Migrant narratives of health and well-being: challenging "othering" processes through photo-elicitation interviews', Critical Social Policy, 32(1): 106–125.

Papell, C. and Rothman, B. (1966) 'Social group work models: possession and heritage', Journal of Education for Social Work, 8(1): 66–77.

Payne, M. (2005) Modern Social Work Theory. Basingstoke: Palgrave Macmillan.

Pearson, G. (1983) Hooligan: A History of Respectable Fears. London: Macmillan.

Pease, B. (2002) 'Rethinking empowerment: a postmodern reappraisal for emancipatory practice', British Journal of Social Work, 32(2): 135–147.

Pease, B. (2003) 'Critical reflections on profeminist practice in men's groups', in M. Cohen and A. Mullender, Gender and Groupwork. London: Routledge.

Phillips, J. (2001) Groupwork in Social Care: Planning and Setting Up Groups. London: Jessica Kingsley.

Preston-Shoot, M. (1989) 'Using contracts in groupwork', Groupwork, 2(1): 36–47.

Preston-Shoot, M. (2007) Effective Groupwork. Basingstoke: Palgrave Macmillan.

Practical Participation www.practicalparticipation.co.uk/whatschanged (accessed 14 February 2013).

Pullen Sansfaçon, A. (2007) 'Statutory social work, the voluntary sector and social action settings: a comparison of ethics', unpublished PhD thesis, De Montfort University, Leicester.

Pullen Sansfaçon, A. (2010) 'Virtue ethics for social work: a new pedagogy for practical reasoning', Social Work Education, 29(4): 402–415.

Pullen Sansfaçon, A. (2011) 'Ethics and conduct in self-directed groupwork: some lessons for the development of a more ethical social work practice', Ethics and Social Welfare, 5(4): 361–379.

Pullen Sansfaçon, A. and Cowden, S. (2012) The Ethical Foundations of Social Work. London: Pearson.

Pullen Sansfaçon, A. and Ward, D. (2012) 'Making inter-professional working work: introducing a groupwork perspective', British Journal of Social Work. doi:10.109/bjsw/bes194

Pullen Sansfaçon, A., Ward, D., Dumais-Michaud, A-A., Robichaud, M-J. and Clegg, A. (2014, forthcoming) 'Working with parents of gender independent children: using social action as an emancipatory research framework', Journal of Progressive Human Services.

Putnam, R. (2002). Democracies in Flux: The Evolution of Social Capital in Contemporary Society. Oxford: Oxford University Press.

Ragg, N. (1977) People Not Cases. London: Routledge & Kegan Paul.

Rancière, J. (2007) The Future of the Image. London: Verso.

Rex, S. (2010). Offender Engagement Programme. Cambridge: National Offender Management Service (East of England).

Richards, N. (2011) Using Participatory Visual Methods. Manchester: Morgan Centre for the Study of Relationships and Personal Life, University of Manchester, available at: http://www.socialsciences.manchester.ac.uk/morgancentre/realities/toolkits/diary/.

Rose, C. (2005) How to Win Campaigns. London: Earthscan.

Rubyfruit Women available at: http://www.leicesterlgbtcentre.org/groups/support-and-social/rubyfruit-women (accessed 8 January 2013).

Ryan, W. (1971) Blaming the Victim. London: Orbach and Chambers.

Sabo-Flores, K. (2008) Youth Participatory Evaluation Strategies for Engaging Young People. San Francisco, CA: Jossey-Bass.

Sakamoto, I. (2009) 'Anti-oppressive practice', in A. Gitterman and R. Salmon, Encyclopedia of Social Work with Groups. New York: Routledge.

Saleebey, D. (2006) The Strengths Perspective in Social Work Practice. Boston, MA: Pearson/Allyn and Bacon.

Schnapp, J. and Tiews, M. (2006) Crowds. Stanford, CA: Stanford University Press.

Schwartz, W. (1971) 'On the use of groups in social work practice', in W. Schwartz and S. Zalba, The Practice of Group Work. New York: Columbia University Press.

SCIE (Social Care Institute for Excellence) (2004) Learning Organisations: A Self Assessment Resource Pack. London: Social Care Institute for Excellence.

Seebohm, P., Munn-Giddings, C. and Brewer, P. (2010) 'What's in a name? A discussion paper on the labels and location of self-organising community groups, with particular reference to mental health and Black groups', Mental Health and Social Exclusion, 14 (3): 23–29.

Sennett, R. (1970/ 2008) The Uses of Disorder: Personal Identity and City Life. New Haven, CT: Yale University Press.

Sennett, R. (2006) The Culture of New Capitalism. New Haven, CT: Yale University Press,

Sennett, R. (2011) 'A creditable Left', available at: http://www.agenceglobal. com/article.asp?id=2600 29/09/11.

Sisneros, J., Stakeman, C., Joyner, M. and Schmitz, C. (2008) Critical Multi-cultural Social Work. Chicago: Lyceum Books.

Smith, M. (1980) Creators Not Consumers. Leicester: National Association of Youth Clubs.

Smith, R. (2008) Social Work and Power. Basingstoke: Palgrave Macmillan.

Smolar, P. (2012) 'Moldova searches for unity', The Guardian Weekly, 13 January 2012, p. 28.

Steinberg, D. (2004) The Mutual-Aid Approach to Working with Groups: Helping People Help One Another. Binghampton, NY: The Haworth Press.

Steinberg, D. (2009) 'Mutual aid model', in A. Gitterman and R. Salmon (eds) Encyclopedia of Social Work with Groups. New York: Routledge.

Stock Whitaker, D. (2001) Using Groups to Help People. Hove: Brunner-Routledge.

Taylor, A. and Kemp, T. (undated) The Transaction Pack. London: Apex Trust.

Taylor, J., Williams, V., Johnson R., Hiscutt, I. and Brennan, M. (2007) We Are Not Stupid. London: Shaping Our Lives and People First Lambeth.

Tew, J. (2006) 'Understanding power and powerlessness: towards a framework for emancipatory practice in social work', Journal of Social Work, 6(1): 33–51.

The College of Social Work (2012) Domains within the PCF. London: The College of Social Work.

Thiara, R.K., Hague, G., Ellis, B., Bashall, R. and Mullender, A. (2012) Disabled Women and Domestic Violence: Responding to the Experiences of Survivors. London: Jessica Kingsley Publishers.

Thompson, N. (2002) 'Social movements and social justice and social work', British Journal of Social Work, 32(6): 711–722.

Timms, N. (1983) Social Work Values: An Enquiry. London: Routledge & Kegan Paul.

Todd, M. and Taylor, G. (eds) (2004) Democracy and Participation: Popular Protest and New Social Movements. London: Merlin.

Toseland, W. and Rivas, F. (2005). An Introduction to Group Work Practice (5th edition). Montreal: Pearson/Allyn and Bacon.

Toynbee, P. (2011) 'How sad to live in a society that won't invest in its young', The Guardian, 19 August 2011, available at: http://www.guardian.co.uk/commentisfree/2011/aug/19/sad-society-young-riots?INTCMP=SRCH (accessed 28 October 2011).

Trevithick, P. (2005) 'The knowledge base of groupwork and its importance within social work', Groupwork, 15(2): 80–107.

Trivedi, P. (2008) 'Black service-user involvement – rhetoric or reality?' in S. Fernando and F. Keating (eds) Mental Health in a Multi-ethnic Society: A Multidisciplinary Handbook. London: Routledge.

Union of the Physically Impaired Against Segregation (1976) Fundamental Principles of Disability. London: UPIAS and the Disability Alliance.

University of Wollongong (2006) What Do You Know and How Do You Know it: Socratic Dialogue II, available at: http://gandalwaven.typepad.com/intheroom/2006/11/one_of_the_diff.html (accessed 25 September 2011).

Vodde, R. and Gallant, J. (2002) 'Bridging the gap between micro and macro practice: large-scale change and a unified model of narrative-deconstructive practice', Journal of Social Work Education, 38(3): 439–458.

Ward, D. (1979) 'Working with young people: the way forward', Probation Journal, 26(1): 2–8.

Ward, D. (ed.) (1982) Give 'Em a Break: Social Action by Young People at Risk and in Trouble. Leicester: National Youth Bureau.

Ward, D. (1992) 'Through the looking glass: practiceled research into groupwork', paper presented to the 14th Annual Symposium for the Advancement of Social Work with Groups, Atlanta USA, October.

Ward D. (2000) 'Totem not token: groupwork as a vehicle for user participation', in H. Kemshall and R. Littlechild (eds) User Involvement and Participation in Social Care: Research Informing Practice. London: Jessica Kingsley.

Ward, D. (2008a) 'What works in probation offender management: evidence for a new direction?' British Journal of Social Work, 38(2): 395–405.

Ward, D. (2009) 'Groupwork', in R. Adams, L. Dominelli and M. Payne (eds) Critical Practice in Social Work (2nd edition). London: Palgrave Macmillan.

Ward D. and Fleming J. (1999) 'Research as empowerment: the social action approach', in W. Shera and L. Wells (eds) Empowerment Practice in Social Work: Developing Richer Conceptual Foundations. Toronto: Canadian Scholars Press.

Ward, D. and Mullender, A. (1991) 'Facilitation in selfdirected groupwork', Groupwork, 4(2): 141–151.

Ward, P. (2008) ' "It's not just what you do: it's the way that you do it": groupwork and the dental career journey', Groupwork, 18(2): 81–100.

Wenger, E. (1998) Communities of Practice: Learning, Meaning and Identity. Cambridge: Cambridge University Press.

Weyers, M. (2001) The Theory and Practice of Community Work: A South African Perspective. Potchefstrom, South Africa: Keurkopie.

White, S., Fook, J. and Gardner, F. (2006) Critical Reflection in Health and Social Care. Maidenhead: Open University Press.

Williams, P. and Shoultz, B. (1982) We Can Speak for Ourselves: Self-Advocacy by Mentally Handicapped People. London: Souvenir.

Williams, Z. (2012) 'The Saturday interview: a life on the left. Stuart Hall ....', The Guardian, 11 February, pp. 39–41.

Wilson, J. (1995) How to Work with Self-Help Groups. London: Arena.

Wood, C. (2011a) Tailor Made: Personalisation Must Work for Those Who Need It Most. London: Demos.

Wood, C. (2011b) 'Personal budgets alone do not democratise care', The Guardian on line, Joe Public Blog, available at: http://www.guardian.co.uk/society/joepublic/2011/oct/19/personal-budgets-dont-democratise-care (accessed 21 October 2011).

Wood, Z. (2012) 'We're not all in it together – you have only to look at the Christmas shopping', The Guardian, 14 January, p. 41.

Woodcraft Folk (2010) Leading for the Future. London: Woodcraft Folk, available at: http://www.woodcraft.org.uk/resources/leading-future.

Wright Mills, C. (1970) The Sociological Imagination. Harmondsworth Penguin.

Young Minds (2011) Talking about Talking Therapies, March, available at: http://cypiapt.posterous.com.

Zastrow, C. (2009) Social Work with Groups: A Comprehensive Workbook. Belmont, CA: Brooks Cole.

Zuniga, R. (2011) 'On sharing pertinent uncertainties', personal communication to Ward in preparation for a staff/post-graduate student seminar on Self-directed Groupwork held at McGill University, Montreal, Canada, 2 November.

Index